COUNTING DOWN
THE ROLLING STONES

Counting Down

Counting Down is a unique series of titles designed to select the best songs or musical works from major performance artists and composers in an age of de-sign-your-own playlists. Contributors offer readers the reasons why some works stand out from others. It is the ideal companion for music lovers.

Titles in the Series

Counting Down Bob Dylan: His 100 Finest Songs by Jim Beviglia, 2013
Counting Down Bruce Springsteen: His 100 Finest Songs by Jim Beviglia, 2014
Counting Down The Rolling Stones: Their 100 Finest Songs by Jim Beviglia, 2016

COUNTING DOWN
THE ROLLING STONES

Their 100 Finest Songs

Jim Beviglia

ROWMAN & LITTLEFIELD
Lanham • Boulder • New York • Toronto • Plymouth, UK

Published by Rowman & Littlefield
4501 Forbes Boulevard, Suite 200, Lanham, Maryland 20706
www.rowman.com

10 Thornbury Road, Plymouth PL6 7PP, United Kingdom

Copyright © 2016 by Jim Beviglia

British Library Cataloguing in Publication Information Available

Library of Congress Cataloging-in-Publication Data

Beviglia, Jim, author.
Counting down the Rolling Stones : their 100 finest songs / by Jim Beviglia.
pages cm. — (Counting down)
Includes bibliographical references and index.
ISBN 978-1-4422-5446-6 (hardback : alk. paper) — ISBN 978-1-4422-5447-3 (ebook) 1. Rolling
Stones—Criticism and interpretation. 2. Rolling Stones Songs. 3. Rock music—History and criti-
cism. I. Title.
ML421.R64B48 2015
782.42166092'2—dc23
2015019983

♾️™ The paper used in this publication meets the minimum requirements of
American National Standard for Information Sciences Permanence of Paper for
Printed Library Materials, ANSI/NISO Z39.48-1992.

Printed in the United States of America

To everyone in my hometown of Old Forge, PA:
"Let's drink to the salt of the earth."

CONTENTS

ACKNOWLEDGMENTS

The gratitude with which I am filled at having the opportunity to write this third book in the Counting Down series is matched perhaps only by the worry I feel as I write these acknowledgments, knowing that I could never possibly thank everyone who has made this possible. But I'll give it a try anyway.

First of all, I'd like to thank The Rolling Stones themselves for all of the wonderful music that I've humbly attempted to describe and detail in these pages. Unlike my first two subjects, Bob Dylan and Bruce Springsteen, I hadn't written extensively on The Stones before I started writing the book. As familiar as I thought I was with their music from being practically a lifelong fan, the research for this book unearthed numerous surprises and musical gems that I hadn't previously discovered. My appreciation for them has only deepened as a result, and it's very cool to be able to add to the reams of excellent literature available on their careers and lives.

I've included in the bibliography the books that helped me most in my research. But I would be remiss if I didn't mention the website Time Is on Our Side (timeisonourside.com), an excellent destination for those seeking information on The Stones and their songs. Run by a gentleman named Ian McPherson, this site unfailingly pushed me in the right direction in terms of quotes about the songs from the band themselves. Even now that the book is finished, I find myself heading back time and again to the site.

Once again I am hugely indebted to Bennett Graff, my editor at Rowman & Littlefield, who took a chance on me a few years back with the first of these books. His choices in editing my prose are consistently insightful and clarifying, and his encouragement in every step of the process for each book never fails to buoy my confidence. The entire staff at Rowman is outstanding at their jobs and at putting up with an author with a million stupid questions.

American Songwriter continues to give me wonderful opportunities to write about the songs and artists I love. Editor in chief Caine O'Rear assigns me the best stuff, and, considering his musical knowledge, it's an honor every time he praises my work. The readers of my *Countdown Kid* blog were with me before I was published and have stuck with me even though my posts can be few and far between when I'm in the midst of these books. What a blessing their support has been.

For my book on Bruce Springsteen, I decided to seek help with publicity. Trish Stevens and Ascot Media Group filled that role better than I ever could have imagined, providing me with a heaping helping of contacts that led to great press for the book in all forms of media. Along those lines, I'd like to thank those people to whom I spoke about the book, all of whom were exceedingly kind and put my work out there to the public at large. On a local level, Frankie Warren blew the horn for my book louder than anybody. We've become good buddies since, which has been one of the happiest byproducts of this whole experience.

Needless to say, it's impossible to mention all of the people in my life who have contributed to my overall happiness and content, without whom these books probably would never have materialized. But I must thank my two big brothers and lifelong protectors, Bob and Rich; my loving sisters-in-law, Kara and Stacie; and my nieces, Gina, Mia, Liza, and Ava, all growing up way too fast but deeply cherished by their Uncle Jim. Endless gratitude is due to my mom, Diane. She taught me lessons on self-sacrifice that I still have a hard time following, because I, like most human beings, lack her strength and courage.

I am blessed to have a daughter who gets cooler every day and could cover an infinite sea with the tiniest part of her heart. Daniele, nobody loves you more than your dad.

Finally, in the time between my last set of acknowledgments and this one, my girlfriend of almost ten years became my wife. Superlatives fall far short of describing her, the impact she's had on my life, or the depth of my love for her. So I'll just say that my three favorite words in the English language are "my wife, Marie" and leave it at that.

INTRODUCTION

To do a book like this, you have to have the right subject. In other words, not every artist is going to be worthy enough to warrant an in-depth look at his or her top one hundred songs. First of all, some artists just haven't been around long enough to compile a hundred songs that are good enough to scrutinize. Then there are those artists who have been around forever but whose work just doesn't have the consistent levels of quality that would make you want to dive deep into their catalogs.

My previous two subjects, Bob Dylan and Bruce Springsteen, cleared these bars pretty easily, and, when it became apparent that I was going to get the opportunity to do a third, The Rolling Stones were an easy choice. After all, how many other bands have been recording for more than fifty years? And, of those bands who have even approached that milestone, have there been any that have reached the levels of popularity, impact, and artistic brilliance that The Stones have maintained?

Speaking of Springsteen, an anecdote he once gave probably comes as close to describing the appeal of The Rolling Stones better than I possibly could. He was talking about growing up as a music fan and the bands to whom he was drawn as a kid growing up in New Jersey. He related how The Beatles, as he saw them, were like this unattainable ideal, so perfect in the way they looked, sang, and played. There wasn't even an inkling on his part that he could possibly be like them. As much as he loved their music, he couldn't ever hope to emulate it.

When he saw The Rolling Stones, however, he said something to the effect of "I can do that." They looked like they had crawled in from off the streets, played raucously, and sang with a sneer. This was something to which he could aspire. This was attainable.

Of course, the trick is that The Stones only made it seem that way, even as they wrote and performed music deeper, richer, and realer than just about every one of their peers. They developed a kind of innate chemistry that made their records far more than the sum of their parts. And, as time passed, they reflected the various eras that their career spanned without ever stepping up and overtly trying to be spokesmen, as others did; after all, any such move would have smacked too much of responsibility and tarnished their irreverent image.

The Stones have been the unofficial face of rock and roll for a long time now, and even as that face has wrinkled, the band still delivers the goods. That's what makes them such a natural subject for a project like this.

Before we get started, some ground rules. As in my previous books, these rankings are based on nothing other than my assessment of the songs' quality levels. I did not consider chart position, cultural impact, or other critical assessments connected to the songs in any way. It's a subjective process, of course, but I try to remove any significance the songs might have to my own life from consideration as well, so I'm trying to be objectively subjective, if that makes sense.

Only officially released recordings were considered; no bootlegs available on the street or on the Web but not given an official release by the band were included. And, as with my previous books, no cover songs have been considered. That's a big loss with The Stones, who have done some smoking homages to their blues and R & B forebears over the years, but those are the rules, folks. All songs that made the countdown were songs written, at least in part, by one or multiple members of the band.

One other note: The Stones presented a bit of a problem in terms of the release information that is included in parentheses right after each entry. First of all, their US and UK albums often featured different song rosters in the 1960s, so I tried to mention whichever country's version of the album contains a particular song when that song only appears on the album in only one of the two countries. In addition, The Stones often released nonalbum singles that would eventually appear on various compilation albums only but were not on any studio album in any country. In these instances, I tried to go with the first compilation on which the songs appeared. Please note that in these cases, the year that is listed usually pertains to the year the compilation was released and not the year the song was released as a single if the two differ.

Unlike my previous two subjects, this is the first time I've written about the entire catalog of The Stones. As a result, I feel like I've learned a lot in the writing of this book, not just about the band but about the music scene they often dominated and the times in which they performed as well. I've also had a blast digging deep into one of rock and roll's most majestic song catalogs. I can only hope that you readers, whether you're new to the band or know them inside and out, come away feeling similarly informed and entertained when you've turned this book's final page.

THE COUNTDOWN

100. "One Hit (to the Body)" (from *Dirty Work*, 1986)

We begin our journey, somewhat ironically, at perhaps the low point in the recording career of The Rolling Stones. From the album cover to the music contained therein to the relationships of the band as they recorded the thing, 1986's *Dirty Work* was a giant mess in every possible manner.

At the time, it received pretty favorable reviews from some reputable magazines and critics, as the band embraced the sounds of that time period with seeming fearlessness. Yet closer inspection reveals a bunch of guys not so much boldly going in a modern direction but rather trying to hop aboard a bandwagon not quite worthy of them in the first place. The mid-1980s, a time when the decade's more synthetic production tics ran amok, tripped up a lot of rock's heritage artists, with The Stones being perhaps the foremost example.

Of course, none of that would have mattered had The Stones produced the songs to compensate for any indecisiveness in the recording and mixing stages. With Mick Jagger pretty much a nonfactor for large portions of the recording process as he concentrated on his solo album *She's the Boss*, those songs simply weren't available on *Dirty Work*, as evidenced by the fact that guitarist Ronnie Wood received four partial songwriting credits on the album, which is four more than he usually received. In what seems like a misguided attempt to hide the lack of material, Jagger screamed out most of the songs in a voice that borders on grating.

The blame can pretty much be spread around here, and it all adds up to what many consider the weakest album in the band's canon and one whose bad vibes came as close as anything to breaking the band up once and for all. Yet even as they bottomed out, The Stones still had at least one knockout song in them on the album (actually two, counting "Harlem Shuffle," which was a cover and therefore not included in this list). "One Hit (to the Body)" manages to (mostly) sidestep the production issues that dog the rest of the album and come on with the force and menace that's emblematic of the band at their hardest-rocking best.

Wood's work stands out here, particularly in the memorable opening moments as his tense acoustic work dovetails with Charlie Watts's nervous cymbals to balance out the crushing electric chords. That leads nicely into the main groove, which stays nimble enough, even with all the crunching guitar work threatening to bludgeon it.

It's also the finest vocal effort on the album from Jagger, one that pulls back from the hectoring stuff he was doing in other songs on *Dirty Work* and manages to combine brute-force singing with some genuine connection to the lyrics. The song uses a fighting metaphor to depict the violent force with which a memorable woman jars the narrator every time she comes in and out of his life.

While that's not the most novel idea for a song (even within The Stones catalog, it had been done before), there is just enough quirkiness in the lines to get it past. Jagger sings, "You unzipped the dark," suggesting that this woman's sexual prowess is enough to metaphysically seduce even the night itself. She eventually becomes an addiction that the narrator is either unable or unwilling to shake: "I can't clean you out of my veins."

Jagger gets some help from a chorus of backing vocalists that include soul legend Bobby Womack and future Mrs. Springsteen Patti Scialfa. And, since guest stars were the order of the day during the *Dirty Work* sessions, Jimmy Page's appearance on lead guitar on the break is apropos. His wild squalling solo is the kind of showy centerpiece that The Stones hadn't really employed since the days of Mick Taylor, but it works well in the context of this song, which is over the top in an enjoyable way as a whole.

The song ends with Jagger intoning over and over, "So help me God." The case had been made well enough by the music and the lyrics by that point that the narrator really didn't need to swear on it for us to believe him, but it's still one of those charismatic, spontaneous things Jagger tends to do during a song that adds a bit of value.

In the song's video, directed by 1980s video maven Russell Mulcahy, Jagger and Keith Richards are seen doing mock battle while performing. There wasn't a lot of method acting that needed to be done, since they were pretty much at each other's throats then, leading to the epic (for them) three-year hiatus before The Stones reunited with *Steel Wheels* in 1989. "One Hit (to the Body)" probably isn't good enough to make up for all of the damage that *Dirty Work* did, but it's still a high point in a low period.

99. "Torn and Frayed" (from *Exile on Main St.*, 1972)

The good thing about a double album is that it allows you the space for just about any kind of stylistic detour you might want to take. *Exile on Main St.* left enough room for The Stones to include "Torn and Frayed," a wistful bit of shuffling country rock that wouldn't have sounded out of place on an Allman Brothers record.

After Keith Richards's contemplative acoustic intro, the rest of the band kicks in all at once to accompany Mick Jagger and Richards harmonizing on the line "Hey, let him follow you down." That moment immediately sets a sympathetic tone, imploring the listener to be accepting and forgiving of the person about to be described. This tone of good-natured abiding and understanding is sustained throughout the entirety of the track.

But who is it exactly that we're supposed to allow into our lives? Jagger paints a portrait, heavy with telling details, of a kind of lovable rake who can't get out of his own way long enough to solve his problems. "Just a deadbeat right off the street / Bound to follow you down" is how Jagger initially describes him, suggesting that this poor soul can't help but end up in the gutters and ditches of life, which is why it's all the more important that he has some company to soften the blow.

Once Jagger puts him in the midst of the rock-and-roll life, with its "barrooms and smelly bordellos / And dressing rooms filled with parasites," it becomes clear that he's drawing on his own experience for this character sketch. While he specifically mentions the guitar player, the whole band is described as being nervous and unsure onstage. It wasn't the first time Jagger would make such references; on 1968's "Jigsaw Puzzle" he gave a blow-by-blow rundown of each individual band member's peccadilloes and problems. Such a presentation is at odds with the image of The Stones as cocksure stage performers, and there's certainly no way to prove that Jagger wasn't describing another band in either case. But the characterizations are still quite unexpected and striking.

In the chorus, Jagger sings, "His coat is torn and frayed / It's seen much better days." The tattered clothing and the character are one and the same here, each now a poor substitute for their former incarnation. But the chorus then goes on to show how this sad sack of a character can make his mark even in his shambolic state: "Just as long as the guitar plays / Let it steal your heart away."

The knee-jerk assumption here is that Jagger was writing about Richards, but that's maybe too easy a leap to make. For one, Richards wasn't the only guitar player in the band. Mick Taylor, who actually plays bass on this track, could be more accurately described as filling the heart-stealing guitar player role while he was in the band, and even though he was a relative newcomer, he was already deep into the band's lifestyle of debauch by the time of *Exile*, so Jagger could have been depicting him here.

Maybe it's an amalgamation of the two guitarists with a little Brian Jones thrown in for good measure, or maybe Jagger was just describing any one of a hundred similar guitar players in bands at the time. What's ultimately important is that note of sympathy that rings out in the song that insists that this guy, as bad off as he seems, is deserving of our care and consideration if for no other reason than the way he can move us when he plays.

As if to prove the point, Al Perkins, an associate of Richards's buddy and country-rock forefather Gram Parsons, came aboard on steel guitar for the recording and provides a winning combination of feistiness and pathos with his playing in the middle section. "Torn and Frayed" as a whole is one of those just-shy-of-disheveled band performances that can be found all over *Exile*, where charm and emotion win out over intricacy and tightness.

In the song's final instrumental section, Charlie Watts imbues a little more pep and zing into his snares and the rest of the band hustles alongside of him to keep pace. It's just the right way to send out "Torn and Frayed," since we can picture the protagonist frantically catching the bus to his next tour stop, ready to steal some hearts while begging for some mercy for his own.

98. "Time Waits for No One" (from *It's Only Rock 'n Roll*, 1974)

The wisdom of the title phrase is undeniable, even if The Rolling Stones' career has flown directly in the face of it. Mick Jagger may have felt the pull of time when "Time Waits for No One" was released in 1974 and he turned thirty; but here we are forty years later, and the Stones are still selling oodles of tickets everywhere they go. Maybe Time gives some folks a break now and then; maybe The Stones are so entertaining that he just can't help himself.

Tucked subtly into the end of side 1 amid the bevy of relatively straightforward rockers that comprise 1974's *It's Only Rock 'n Roll*, "Time Waits for No One" finds the band in a philosophical, contemplative mood. There are a lot of Stones songs that brim with cleverness and intelligence, but rarely do they wear their eagerness to engage the minds of the listeners on their sleeves like this one does.

It's not like Jagger's concerns are anything new. The phrase "time and tide waits for no man" predates modern English. The lines "Drink in your summer / Gather your corn" calls to mind Robert Herrick's seventeenth-century exhortation to "Gather ye rosebuds, while ye may." And the overall "seize the day" vibe is one that the Roman poet Horace first promulgated in 23 BC.

Jagger seems to nod to these traditional sources by using some of his most formal language ("No favors has he.") It's as if his narrator doesn't want to disrespect Time personified, presented here as a ruthless, unforgiving force, taunting the humans who try to elude his grasp: "Here he comes chopping and reaping / Hear him laugh at their cheating."

And while some of Jagger's lines get a bit clunky (the forced simile "Hours are like diamonds / Don't let 'em waste" comes to mind), the overall self-awareness he demonstrates is affecting. He could have easily omitted himself from the list of those whom Time has in his sights, but that would have robbed the song of some of its resonance. As such, the stirringly direct chorus, sung in aching harmonies by Jagger and Keith Richards, reminds us that no one's escaping: "Time waits for no one / And it won't wait for me."

The music is also far more restrained and insinuating than the blunt-force approach found on much of *It's Only Rock 'n Roll*. Charlie Watts's ticking-clock beat gives way to a querulous Keith Richards riff. Subtle synthesizers, which were a relatively new instrument for the band, tug at the edges of Jagger's narrative, while guest Ray Cooper adds interesting percussion touches around Watts's persistent main beat.

The instrumental showcase on "Time Waits for No One" undoubtedly belongs to guitarist Mick Taylor, who takes over in the coda with an extended solo that revs up the Latin influences that had been audible but backgrounded in the earlier parts of the song. The playing is undoubtedly lovely and virtuosic, but there's not too much in that long closing part that stands out so much as to justify its existence. The song could have faded out after the final chorus and been just as fine.

In that way, it's reminiscent of "Can't You Hear Me Knocking?" from a few years previous, which features another Taylor extravaganza that practically split the song down the middle into two distinct parts. The transition here is a bit smoother, but there's still the feeling of excess that surrounds the closing section. Taylor's contributions during his time with the band were integral, and his stint coincided with the best music the group ever made. It's just that these one-man freak-outs somewhat contradicted The Stones' core identity.

Taylor thought enough of what he added to the song that he felt he should have received a songwriting credit. His lack of said credit was one of the reasons he cited for leaving the band after the album was completed. So in an odd way, "Time Waits for No One" was both his swan song and his final straw with the band.

That's the funny thing about The Stones. Despite all of Jagger's protestations to the contrary in "Time Waits For No One," they really have been able to cheat the clocks and the calendars in ways that most musicians and celebrities in general could only dream of doing. They've seemingly beaten time and tide; it's just the personal squabbles that trip them up now and again.

97. "Anybody Seen My Baby?" (from *Bridges to Babylon*, 1997)

There is a common conundrum that befalls even the finest of bands or artists within the rock or pop idiom. If they've had success with a certain style in the past, they can continue to mine that style as the years go by and run the risk of being criticized for their conservatism and reluctance to branch out into new musical arenas. If they try something different, they become fair game for those who say they're only trying to be trendy and, in some cases, they might end up stumbling all the way down the new avenue they've chosen.

It's certainly an issue The Rolling Stones have faced more than most in their career, simply because that career has been so long. From their first recordings in the mid-1960s through their amazing four-album run that started with *Beggars Banquet* in 1968 and ended with *Exile on Main St.* in 1972, they progressed with slick steadiness (with the one big stumble on *Their Satanic Majesties Request*) from a blues-based band to one that could handle just about all the styles that, when wedged together like pieces of a pie, comprise rock and roll.

Yet as music changed all around them in subsequent years, their efforts to stay modern by incorporating the sound of the moment were often a bumpy ride, one that included stellar highs (*Some Girls*, which skillfully worked disco and punk into the band's mix) and unfortunate lows (the one-two 1980s punch, or lack thereof, of *Undercover* and *Dirty Work*).

The latter-era Stones, a time period that begins with 1989's *Steel Wheels*, have settled on a kind of compromise in terms of their dalliances with modernity and stylistic variety. The large majority of each of the four studio albums released in that span are made up of the typical combination of thundering rockers and soulful ballads, but each also contains a couple or so tracks that can be considered experimental, at least relative to the band's norm.

On *Bridges to Babylon*, the band made perhaps their boldest stabs at modern (at least for 1997) music, even if the majority of the core quartet had to be dragged there reluctantly by Mick Jagger. Jagger brought in a bunch of different producers for the album, most notably The Dust Brothers, who made their bones on groundbreaking albums by The Beastie Boys and Beck with sample-heavy recordings that tended to combine unorthodox elements into bold sonic stews.

In the end, only three of the Dust Brothers' productions made it onto the finished album, with traditional sounds ultimately winning the day when the band employed the knob-twirling of Don Was to make the majority of the record. Of those three recordings, "Anybody Seen My Baby?" stands out as an example of a song that updates the band's sound and still sounds suitably Stonesy.

With a prowling bass, courtesy of studio pro Jamie Muhoberac, and Charlie Watts putting his spin on the sound of a funky drummer, the rhythmic sultriness of the song grabs you immediately. Some incongruous squeaks and squawks also slip into the proceedings, adding a bit of aural icing on an already rich cake. Even though Keith Richards is listed as playing on the track, the fact that West Coast session legend Waddy Wachtel is also listed on electric guitar lends credence to the view that this song is primarily Jagger's baby. (*Bridges to Babylon* was an album that was almost approached as two solo albums by Mick and Keith, each in charge of a passel of basic tracks onto which the others band members would eventually add their parts.)

Jagger's conversational lyrics about an elusive girl are fine enough on the page, but he imbues them with a kind of sexy sadness when he emotes them. In the verses, his rhythmic patter almost has a rap feel to it, which then makes the melodic run-up to the bridge stand out even more.

The chorus is a good one, so good, in fact, that it's been utilized in a pair of hit songs. Richards tells the story in his autobiography, *Life*, that his daughter Angela was listening along to the song's playback and started singing the lyrics to k.d. lang's "Constant Craving" over the top of it. That's when he realized that the band had essentially plagiarized a song they hadn't really heard before and made the proactive decision to award songwriting credits to lang and her cowriter, Ben Mink.

There is another song that's consciously included on "Anybody Seen My Baby?": Biz Markie's "A One Two," which is sampled in the brief instrumental break prior to the return of the refrain. Some Stones traditionalists likely blanched at this technique, while hip-hop fans might have wondered who those old fogeys thought they were anyway. Such is the peril of the band who tries something a little out of their comfort zone, but the evidence on this track proves that The Stones' efforts to change things up a bit give gusto to what otherwise could have been a relatively minor track. As a matter of fact, though the emotional aftertaste of the narrator may be bittersweet, "Anybody Seen My Baby?" turns out to be a breath of fresh air.

96. "Respectable" (from *Some Girls*, 1978)

As punk rock raged all around them in 1978, The Rolling Stones decided to respond. What they ended up playing on several songs on that year's *Some Girls* couldn't really be called punk in the purest sense; tracks like "When the Whip Comes Down," "Lies," and "Respectable" are aggressive and fast but lack the kind of tossed-off, anarchically brutal fury of

The Sex Pistols or The Ramones. Anyway, The Stones were too good as players to have sounded in any way amateurish or DIY in the true punk ethos.

Nonetheless, it can't be doubted that The Stones definitely revved up the engines for those aforementioned songs. "Respectable" is the best of that trio. ("When the Whip Comes Down" is solid as well, while "Lies" is grating.) Mick Jagger described the song in the liner notes to the 1993 compilation *Jump Back: The Best of The Rolling Stones* as "a punk meets Chuck Berry number."[1]

Suffice it to say that the Berry influence carries the bulk of the load. If "Respectable" is punk, you would have to consider The Beatles' version of Berry's "Rock and Roll Music" punk as well. The forward thrust of the two songs is pretty similar, even if the updated recording and production techniques give The Stones' cut a bit more snap and sizzle. Truth be told, The Stones get closer to a punk attitude on some of their tawdrier blues cuts, like "Stray Cat Blues" or "Ventilator Blues," than they do here.

The lyrics even go so far as to bemoan the fact that The Stones aren't the cultural pariahs they once were. The first lines say it all: "Well now we're respected in society / We don't worry about the things we used to be." The old adage that says that if you stick around long enough, you become the very thing against which you once rebelled clearly had some resonance with Jagger, who did the majority of the writing on the song.

In the second verse, Jagger changes his focus from "we" to "you" and takes some potshots at a girl who has also acquired the trappings of respectability despite behaving like a societal scourge. "You're a rag trade girl, you're the queen of porn," he sneers. "You're the easiest lay on the White House lawn."

Considering that he then follows up that verse with repeated, animated refrains of "Get out of my life / Go take my wife, don't come back," it's natural to assume that Bianca Jagger, who had filed for divorce from Mick just a month prior to *Some Girls'* release in June of 1978, was the target of this vitriol. In an interview with *Rolling Stone* at the time of the album's release, Mick denied that the song was a broadside at Bianca. "My wife's a very honest person," he said, "and the song's not about her."[2]

But the passing of time (and perhaps the fact that financial terms of the divorce had long been settled) apparently changed Jagger's recollection about his song. "The lyric contains no fantastically deep message, but I think it might have had something to do with Bianca," he eventually admitted in the *Jump Back* liner notes.[3]

In any case, the lyrics ultimately take a backseat to the energy of the music. The churning rhythm section of Bill Wyman and Charlie Watts doesn't allow things to spin out of control, even at the rapid pace, while the three guitarists (Jagger joined Keith Richards and Ron Wood) sprint wildly all over the place. Richards and Wood each take solos and nail the frenetic spirit.

So maybe it wasn't quite punk, even if punk helped prod the song into its final form. Just because they were becoming "respectable," The Rolling Stones weren't about to slow down.

95. "Out of Time" (from *Aftermath*, 1966)

The Stones have always been a tough band to cover, because so much of their magic comes from the chemistry they have as players and not necessarily from the strength of their songs as words and music on a page. That's not to say that they're not expert songwriters, because the Jagger/Richards duo have been proving for almost fifty years that they are. But the inimitable spice and personality that they lend to their own material tends to make other versions seem superfluous and second-rate.

Yet "Out of Time," which first appeared on the 1966 UK edition of the album *Aftermath*, has been a source of several outstanding cover versions, maybe because it's a bit of an oddity among Stones songs. If you didn't know the song and were introduced to it simply by hearing the instrumental tracks without Mick Jagger's unmistakable vocals on top, you'd probably think it was a Motown number, thanks to its combination of rhythmic light feet and melodic richness.

As such, it's been ripe for cover versions almost from the get-go. Just a few months after The Stones released it, British artist Chris Farlowe used a demo provided by Jagger as the basis for a string- and horn-laden take. It shot to No. 1 on the British charts thanks to Farlowe's Tom Jones–like crooning, becoming one of the most successful Jagger/Richards songs ever recorded by another artist. Around that same time, The Bee Gees took a shot at it, taking the chorus harmonies to the places that only the Brothers Gibb could ever quite reach.

The late Del Shannon did a rollicking version on his 1982 album, *Drop Down and Get Me*, backed by Tom Petty and The Heartbreakers.

Even punk-rock legends The Ramones took on the song, giving it a righteously rocking take that practically reinvents the track. All of these versions are excellently done, and none of them sound too much like The Stones' original, which is quirky and catchy all at once.

The distinguishing characteristic of the version found on *Aftermath* is the marimbas part played by Brian Jones. Jones was a master at adding just the right unexpected touch to Stones songs from that era. Unlike the sly coolness he coaxed out of the instrument on the much more famous "Under My Thumb," the marimbas he adds here are playfully melodic and set a light tone for what, lyrically, is a somewhat nasty song.

The Motown vibe is expertly sustained by Bill Wyman's limber bass line and Charlie Watts's peppery drums. Ian Stewart adds some chunky organ fills while Keith Richards picks away at an acoustic guitar during the verses, adding wistful counterpoint to Jagger's vocals. It's a recording that shouldn't work with all those seemingly clashing elements at play. But when it all comes together on the surging refrains, it's difficult to resist.

Jagger's lyrics have a precision and conciseness about them that betrays the fact that "Out of Time" was meant to be performed by other artists in an effort to court the pop charts (and pump up those royalties in the process), but his trademark sassiness, directed here at a wayward girl who wants to return to the narrator's life, is undiminished. Indeed, some of the lines are cutting in ways that Bob Dylan, master of the caustic putdown track in that same era, would have appreciated.

"You're obsolete, my baby," Jagger sings, almost tauntingly. His vocal tenor is one thing that sets the song apart from its cover versions. While those other artists pulled back a bit on the reins and projected a kind of reluctant sympathy toward the girl, Jagger seems almost gleeful for the comeuppance she is receiving. That kind of edge feels more in line with the band's sensibilities than the unusual music.

On the 1975 cash-grab album *Metamorphosis*, put together by the band's estranged manager Allen Klein out of outtakes and leftovers, a version of "Out of Time" is included that features Jagger's vocals on top of the original demo that was utilized by Farlowe. Even with the strings trying to soften the blow, it's still an odd push and pull between the lush music and Jagger's bile. No matter how many times it was covered or reworked, "Out of Time" earns respect as an outlier in the band's catalog that still carries the bite and sting of their more typical work.

94. "Sister Morphine" (from *Sticky Fingers*, 1971)

There may not be a more harrowing song in the career of The Rolling Stones than "Sister Morphine." Recorded in 1969 but not released by the band on an album until 1971's *Sticky Fingers*, the song is intended to tell the story of a victim of a car accident whose final moments are filled with desire for painkilling drugs. Context usually dictates how these things are heard, however, so most fans likely think of it as the firsthand reportage of guys with serious drug problems dealing with the fact that the medication intended to help them kick said problems can be equally addictive.

"Sister Morphine" has always been a source of consternation considering its composition. Mick Jagger's late 1960s squeeze, Marianne Faithfull, released an obscure version featuring most of The Stones as her backing band that sank without a trace. Faithfull always claimed authorship for the song's lyrics and eventually coaxed a cocredit out of the band years after the fact in the 1990s. For his part, Jagger has disputed this and claims that Marianne only helped with some of the lyrics.

In any case, those lyrics are certainly eerily vivid in their depiction of the narrator's nightmare in a hospital bed. The patient's sense of disorientation and confusion leads to grotesque hallucinations: "Why does the doctor have no face?" Still he pleads with Sister Morphine, begging her to come and ease his pain in the way that only she knows. "Please, Sister Morphine, turn my nightmare into dreams," Jagger sings, playing the part so well that you can practically hear the cold sweat encasing his shaking body.

The way the narrator clearly understands that his death is imminent only adds to the spookiness. "Oh can't you see I'm fading fast?" he asks. "And that this shot may be my last." Not even the arrival of Cousin Cocaine to double the efforts of Sister Morphine can stay the inevitable. In the final lines, the narrator offers the gory details of his own death: "Cause you know and I know in the morning I'll be dead / Yeah and you can sit around, yeah and you can watch all the clean white sheets turn red."

Needless to say, the song isn't exactly a pick-me-up. Yet the music, while not betraying the foul mood, has enough dynamism to help make the thing eminently listenable. Keith Richards's plaintive acoustic guitar sounds as if it's already attending the funeral. Meanwhile, rock and blues ace Ry Cooder guest stars on bottleneck slide and pretty much steals the show. The song was recorded at a time when Brian Jones had effectively checked out of the band (he was fired in June of 1969 and was dead a month later) and before Mick Taylor joined, so Cooder's appearance was born of necessity. It turned out to be the element the song needed most, a jolt of instrumental brilliance to what could have been an unbearably miserable affair.

In a bit of sad irony, Faithfull claims the song became a self-fulfilling prophecy of a sort for her, as she went from not using drugs at the time it was composed to nearly becoming a drug casualty just a few years later. Faithfull thankfully avoided that fate and continued her music career down the road to much critical acclaim, even recording another version of "Sister Morphine." But her story is emblematic of something that crops up again and again in the story of The Stones, which is how so many of those who came into their orbit often tumbled inelegantly (and sometimes tragically) out of it as if it were simply too much for them to handle, while The Stones themselves (with the sad exception of Brian Jones) seemed to endure it all and come out none the worse for wear.

While the debate might never be settled concerning who deserves the most credit for "Sister Morphine," the recording on *Sticky Fingers*, surreal as it may be, delivers a you-are-there view that seems like it couldn't possibly have been fabricated. Listening to the song, one believes that the narrator is actually going through this hell and that it's not simply the figment of a fevered imagination. It's that authenticity, with a big assist from Cooder, that makes the song somehow both riveting and revolting all at once.

93. "Star Star" (from *Goats Head Soup*, 1973)

"That's real, and if girls can do that, I can certainly write about it because it's what I see. I'm not saying all women are star f***ers, but I see an awful lot of them, and so I write a song called that. I mean, people show themselves up by their own behavior, and just to describe it doesn't mean you're anti-feminist."[4]

That was Mick Jagger defending himself to *Rolling Stone* in 1978 against allegations that his song "Star Star" was demeaning and degrading to women. When the song was released five years previous to that interview on *Goats Head Soup*, it was castigated by all kinds of women's groups and social critics and banned from airplay on the BBC.

All of the outrage was pretty predictable to even the most casual observer, which only helped The Stones out in terms of gaining publicity for their record. The cynics would probably even suggest that it was a calculated move by the band, one that drummed up press for an album that didn't approach the lofty standards they had set in their previous four LPs, all of which could be deemed masterpieces.

If you're one to be outraged over such things, "Star Star" certainly gives you plenty of ammunition. The title can't hide the fact that the chorus is made up of a profane appellation for groupies chanted gleefully by the band over and over again. In the verses, Jagger addresses a girl who has an overflowing bag of tricks for sexual use that includes fruit, Polaroids, and "tasty foam." Throw in the celebrity-baiting shout-outs to Steve McQueen, Ali McGraw, and John Wayne (Jagger would add Jimmy Page to that list in concert), and you've got a full house of controversy ready to be dredged up by those looking for a fight.

Jagger's defense quoted previously is reasonable enough, although the guy's not naïve. He had to know that certain parties were going to take extreme offense to the song, so protesting about the protests seems a bit unnecessary. The furious reaction was one that was pretty much preordained the minute he decided to include the song as the closer to *Goats Head Soup*, so this was a case of him and the band pretty much asking for it.

All of that leaves out the relevant matter of the song's merits. Had Jagger just come up with a piece of shoddy work peppered with blatant provocations, it wouldn't be sitting here on this list. ("Some Girls," for example, is similarly ire-raising, but it's also a lazy effort.) Luckily, "Star Star" has enough pep and catchiness that you're likely to find yourself singing along to that refrain, as long as you're not too offended by it.

The music is basically a Chuck Berry homage right down to the "Johnny B. Goode"–flavored intro by Keith Richards, albeit with a slightly slower pace so that Jagger can really savor each bite of the lyrics. The rhythm choogles along nicely thanks to the locked-in duo of Bill Wyman and Charlie Watts as well as Ian Stewart's rollicking piano licks.

And, like it or not, Jagger presents his case quite well. "All those beat-up friends of mine got to get you in their books," he sings. Those friends are all "lead guitars and movie stars," the only types in which this girl has any interest. He's willing to pursue her from Los Angeles to New York, his desire outweighing any objections to her behavior.

That's an important point to make about "Star Star." Yes, Jagger is certainly taking some cheap shots at the groupies on the scene. But based on the way the narrator reacts here, following her all over and practically begging for another night with her, it's clear that she holds the upper hand in the relationship. That's not quite the way you would expect the power dynamic to be in a rock star–groupie coupling, but that's the way it plays out here.

Will that subtlety ever be enough to appease the feminists who might object to the song's treatment of women or the moral police who might disdain the song's rampant profanity? It hasn't to this point, so there's no reason to believe it will now. But "Star Star" passes the test as good music, even if it fails the test, for some, in terms of decency and good taste.

92. "Flip the Switch" (from *Bridges to Babylon*, 1997)

Having Charlie Watts as your drummer immediately gives you a leg up on the rock-and-roll competition. Having Charlie Watts and Jim Keltner each drumming on a track is an embarrassment of riches. The rest of the band could pretty much grunt and snort, and the resulting song would still have its merits.

Luckily, the rest of The Rolling Stones were also at the top of their games for "Flip the Switch," the rip-snorting opening track on 1997's *Bridges to Babylon*. Combining the two drummers' percussive mastery with an energetic song about embracing the darkness was a can't-miss, giving the band a late-era track that wouldn't have seemed a bit out of place on their late 1960s, early 1970s classics.

Keltner's appearance was par for the course for an album that welcomed all kinds of friends and newcomers into the recording studio. As iconic as they are, The Stones have never hesitated to use outsiders on their records. With Mick Jagger and Keith Richards having such powerful personalities, there's never been a concern about the band's identity being diluted by guest performers, so the policy has always been the more the merrier, as long as it means the track will be better off for the company.

So Keltner, legend of session work for luminaries (including Bob Dylan, the solo Beatles and countless other artists), and Watts set the rapid pace, one that Jagger and Richards would go on to claim was the fastest in the band's history in terms of beats per minute, outdoing even the frenzied "Rip This Joint" from *Exile on Main St*. That may be technically true, but the older song still seems faster, because it's just this short of completely out of control, which is a big part of its charm. (Plus Jagger sings it like his hair is on fire.) "Flip the Switch" always keeps its wits about it, even as the scenery hurtles furiously by, with Keltner and Watts a big part of the reason why.

Even at top speed, the track is pretty loose limbed, in part because an acoustic bass is employed, played by Jeff Sarli. Richards also tears across the beat with his electric guitar, giving the song a grinding edge that suits it well.

The lyrics would skew morbid if the music would allow them to do so. But when backed by the vibrant playing all around them, Mick Jagger's opening lines ("A scrap of flesh and a heap of bones / One deep sigh and a desperate moan / Three black eyes and a busted nose") sound practically celebratory. In that way, the song could be considered a second cousin of "Jumpin' Jack Flash," which also seemed to revel in terrifying imagery, due to its unstoppable music.

As the song rushes on, Jagger starts to dare his tormentors to bring on their worst. "I'm not going to burn in Hell," he sneers. "I've cased the joint, and I know it well." He promises that he's ready for his descent, having acquired a shaving kit, a toothbrush, and mouthwash for the journey. Just because you're damned doesn't mean you shouldn't look and smell your best. That's a Jagger-ish sentiment if ever there was one.

By the end of the song, with the narrator having courted lethal injection, the title phrase seems to take on a double meaning. While it could refer to the on-switch that will bring about this guy's ultimate demise, his defiant attitude suggests that it could be the trigger for his rebirth. Death will only start him up, to paraphrase another Stones firecracker.

It's refreshing that at that point in their career, when The Stones had been rendered somewhat harmless simply by the fact that they had existed so long and hadn't brought about the fall of Western civilization, they could still rip into a blood-and-guts number like this one and make it sound so thoroughly convincing. In a way, there's also a disheartening element to the song, because in an age where albums are no longer pored over by anything but diehard fans and album tracks are often forgotten for that reason, a song like "Flip the Switch" can become not just underrated but unconsidered, an even worse fate.

That's why it's wholly inaccurate when folks who don't know better write off the music The Stones have released in the last twenty-five years. "Flip the Switch" might as well be aimed right at those folks, because even on a song about the horrors of death, Jagger and his buddies provide evidence that they can still come to vigorous life in a heartbeat.

91. "Who's Been Sleeping Here?" (from *Between the Buttons*, 1967)

Between the Buttons, released in 1967, can't help but be an overlooked album. *Aftermath*, the 1966 album that preceded it in The Rolling Stones timeline, was the group's first full-length album to utilize exclusively original material, and it was a triumph. *Their Satanic Majesties Request*, released later in the same year as *Between the Buttons*, was somewhat of a mess but has achieved notoriety over the years in a train-wreck kind of way. Sitting in between those two albums without any major hits on it (on the UK version, anyway; the US version included the monster singles "Let's Spend the Night Together" and "Ruby Tuesday" to beef it up considerably), it's somewhat of a lost album for the band.

Some of the blame for the album's lack of reputation can be laid on producer Andrew Loog Oldham's heavy-handed production style. As Bill Wyman recounted in his candid 2002 autobiography, *Rolling with The Stones*, "Andrew's influence was on the wane and this was his production swan song with us. He still had dreams of being an English Phil Spector, if only by cranking up the reverb to 11. Production subtlety was not Andrew's bag."[5]

Still, Oldham can't be entirely blamed, since the quality of the songs was not quite up to the level of *Aftermath*. Even The Beatles had slowed to an album per year by 1967, but The Stones churned out the aforementioned three albums in a twenty-month stretch in 1966 and 1967. The songwriting engine of Mick Jagger and Keith Richards was somewhat mired between churning out poppier numbers and going deeper into the roots-based music that was always their strong point. They wouldn't quite work out the balance until the 1968 masterpiece *Beggars Banquet*.

If you dig deep into *Between the Buttons* though, you'll unearth some nifty little gems. "Who's Been Sleeping Here?" is one of the best of those, an elegant piece of romantic paranoia that has held up well. This was about the time that Bob Dylan's influence started to infiltrate the songwriting of just about every rock artist you can name. The Jagger/ Richards combination was no different.

On later albums, The Stones would make their pinches of Dylanesque wordplay fit a bit more seamlessly into their sound on songs like "Sympathy for the Devil" and "Jigsaw Puzzle." "Who's Been Sleeping Here?" is an homage to *Blonde On Blonde*–era Dylan, right down to the music. Brian Jones punctuates Jagger's utterances with high-pitched harmonica fills, Keith Richards weaves his acoustic and electric guitars around the lyrics while Bill Wyman's bass trips delicately through, and Jack Nitzsche adds the flurrying piano runs, playing the role Paul Griffin played on Dylan's songs.

All of that combined leads to something that's a bit more weightless than The Stones' usual thunder, but they execute the entire pastiche quite well. (And, it must be noted, Oldham's production is unobtrusive in this one.) The big departure from what Dylan had laid down comes in Mick Jagger's vocals, which try to stay deadpan cool in the verses, like Bob, but keep getting fired up with palpable tinges of disgust and spite in the refrains.

Jagger uses the trappings of a fairy tale in the lyrics as a way of subverting expectations. No happily ever after is possible once the heroine has been unfaithful. He both mentions Goldilocks in the lyrics and alludes to her with the title. In addition, he calls on a whole cast of characters, both from nursery rhymes (the butcher, the baker, etc.) and from his fevered imagination ("the noseless old newsboy") to inform him of the identity of the cheater.

That identity isn't really of import to him though. What he's really looking for is the confirmation of his suspicions about the girl in the song. "Who's been eating / Eating off my plate?" he asks incredulously. "There must be somewhere / Somewhere you can stop," he sings, hinting that her wanton disregard for his loyalty is rampaging out of control.

Maybe that's why the narrator feels justified at the end of the song to take some cheap shots at his former lover. He runs down a list of possibilities for the unidentified bed-sharer, starting with the benign (Mummy, Daddy, Uncle, and Aunt) and progressing to the risqué: "Was it your boyfriend, your girlfriend? / Who's been sleeping here?"

Considering The Stones had pushed the envelope in that year's big single, "Let's Spend the Night Together," simply by suggesting that a couple do just what the title implores, a sneaky reference to a lesbian tryst pretty much rips that envelope in half. The relative anonymity of "Who's Been Sleeping Here?" probably protected it from intense scrutiny. But, based on its quality, the song really shouldn't be anonymous at all, even amid The Stones' imposing catalog of hits and sleepers.

90. "Hand of Fate" (from *Black and Blue*, 1976)

Black and Blue has to go down as one of the strangest Rolling Stones albums, due to the circumstances under which it was recorded. With Mick Taylor having left the band following the making of *It's Only Rock 'n Roll* in 1974, The Stones spent the latter part of that year and the early portion of 1975 recording in Europe with a series of different guitarists with a dual purpose: to put together a new album and to find a new band member to replace Taylor.

As one might expect, the results on the album were a tad disjointed, although that can also be attributed to the fact that Mick Jagger and Keith Richards had written songs in a variety of different genres, including soul ballads, funk, and even reggae. Yet even as the styles vary, the quality is consistently solid, so you can put this one in the underrated category when discussing Stones full-lengths.

For all the stylistic diversity, however, "Hand of Fate" manages to hew as close to a classic Stones sound as any song on the album. Wayne Perkins, one of the trio of guitarists whose work would find its way onto the finished LP, does the honors on this song and contributes a pair of sparkling solos to a gritty tale of murder and its insidious consequences.

Murder songs are an integral part of the blues tradition, as songs like "Stagger Lee" and "Delia" plumbed dark corners of the human soul and mercilessly demonstrated how easily passion and violence can intertwine. Rock artists would add full-band musical heft to songs like this, whether interpreting older material, like Jimi Hendrix on "Hey Joe" or The Band on "Long Black Veil," or writing their own, like Bob Marley on "I Shot the Sheriff." (One of Perkins's pre-Stones gigs, fittingly enough, was on sessions with Marley and The Wailers.)

The difficult part about writing a song like this is finding the balance between including the story's details and highlighting the inner life of the characters involved. Mick Jagger, who worked out the lyrics in tandem with Keith Richards for "Hand of Fate," talked about just this conundrum with *Rolling Stone* in 1976. "It's very hard, actually—unless you're really good—to get any kind of narrative into a song of four and a half minutes," he said. "It's so complicated: 'And then he . . .' If it got as complicated as it could have been, it would really have got boring. And the thing is to not say a lot."[6]

"Hand of Fate" manages to tiptoe that line between exposition and emotion quite deftly. Jagger and Richards keep the story beats to a minimum as the narrator efficiently tells his tale of how his love once belonged to another man, leading to a gunfight that the narrator wins, barely ("He shot me once, but I shot him twice").

Jagger does indulge in some clichés that set the song more in the Old West than in a Southern Gothic area. There are mentions of barrooms and a "one-horse town," and there's even a corrupt judge. Card-game metaphors also keep popping up throughout, giving the song title a double meaning as both the justice-wielding instrument of a personified Fate and as a reference to what card players might call a "bad beat" in the game of life.

The narrator might try to justify his actions to his listening audience ("I had to save her life" the harmonies insist in the catchy bridge), but he knows there will be no reasoning with his pursuers. "Hand of Fate" thus plays out like an extended chase scene, with the driving music acting as the catalyst. Charlie Watts's snares are tough and relentless, even double-timing toward the end of the song to mimic the enemies closing in on this doomed soul. "I'm on the run. I hear the hounds," Jagger sings, and it's easy to make the leap that those hounds are not only the dogs chasing his trail but also the hounds of hell.

Wayne Perkins, of course, didn't get the job; Ronnie Wood, who was featured on the cover of *Black and Blue* once it was finally released in 1976, even though he only played guitar on three songs, won out; some say for his guitar ability, some say for his cohesiveness with Richards, and some say because he was British. In any case, Perkins left a lasting impression during his dalliance with The Stones thanks to his work on "Hand of Fate," a story as old as the hills that gets a thrilling retelling here.

89. "Rip This Joint" (from *Exile on Main St.*, 1972)

Man, that must have been some session at Keith Richards's Villa Nellcôte the night that "Rip That Joint" was cut. However, they managed to accomplish it, or perhaps it's better to say, with whatever extracurricular help they utilized to accomplish it, all the players involved conjured a heaping helping of extra energy to lay down this wildest of *Exile on Main St.* tracks.

Calling "Rip This Joint" organized chaos is a bit of a generous description. It's more like disorganized individual strains of chaos that have all agreed to a common purpose, even if they don't agree on how they're going to achieve it. As it burns through its two-and-a-half-minute running time, it bowls over everything and everyone in its path until you, the listener, have no choice but to submit to its unruly, uncouth, and yet undeniable charms.

It begins with Keith Richards's frenzied electric guitar riff before what seems like every passerby at Richards's mansion grabs an instrument and jumps into a frantic groove. Bill Plummer guest stars on the standup bass, giving the song a jump-blues feel that predates even Little Richard, the song's most obvious rock influence.

About midway through the song, the invaluable Bobby Keys tears into a juicy saxophone solo that clears the air ever so slightly before it thickens once again with the dense thrust of the band. That producer Jimmy Miller manages to get something vibrant out of what could have been a messy sonic olio is just another piece of evidence that the fact that his time as the band's producer coincided with its greatest stretch of music can't be taken as mere coincidence.

The vocal harmonies of Mick Jagger and Richards are almost comically raucous, but they get the job done. Through it all, only Charlie Watts manages to keep his composure and timing, even as he revs the beat well up into the red. It may be somewhat overshadowed by Jagger's wild screams, but Watts's playing just might be the most crucial component in the song, the tether that keeps the thing from crashing and burning beyond all coherence.

Speaking of coherence, you might not realize that Jagger is singing actual English words in the song and not spouting utter gibberish. In a way, "Rip This Joint" is a lot like "Louie Louie," the immortal garage-rock classic by The Kingsmen. Since fans can't hear the words enunciated clearly on these two songs, they project onto the lyrics the most sinister or salacious things their imaginations can create.

In the case of "Rip This Joint," there are a few points when the lyrics do get a tad ribald. In the chorus, "Rip this joint" is followed up by the phrase "Roll this joint," and there aren't too many ways you can interpret those three words. (If only censors had thought to edit that line in the same way they did on Tom Petty's "You Don't Know How It Feels" by rendering the word "joint" backward; that could only have added to the wild and woolly vibe of The Stones' track.) The mention of Dick and Pat, which just happened to be the names of the president and First Lady at the time, in "old DC" holding on to illegal stuff for the narrator isn't so much subversive as blatantly anarchic. And the "butter queen" who joins Jagger in Texas was a reference to a groupie who used the dairy product in ways that can delicately be described as imaginative.

Yet even with these snickering asides dotting the lyrics, Jagger is basically rehashing his tour schedule along with the various triumphs and tribulations that accompany each stop. Maybe you could make a case that some of the locations hold deeper meaning as hotbeds of the music that Mick and the boys were so good at appropriating, but you could just as easily claim that the cities were chosen for their suitability to the rhyme and meter more than anything else. Either way, this is clearly a case of words that are not so important for what they mean as for how they are sung, which, in this case, is hilariously manic.

Even though there's nothing else quite like it on the record, the song somehow makes perfect sense in the midst of its brethren on *Exile on Main St.* Profundity and import are all well and good, but sometimes you're just "fit to pop." On those occasions, a song like "Rip This Joint" is the only thing that will do.

88. "Sad Sad Sad" (from *Steel Wheels*, 1988)

Diminished expectations greeted The Rolling Stones on their return from a recording absence of over three years with *Steel Wheels* in 1989. The public acrimony between Mick Jagger and Keith Richards during that hiatus was flat-out ugly. Their previous two albums were generally considered among the weakest of the band's career. And there, looming as it had been probably since the mid-1970s, was the question of whether these old guys had anything left in the tank.

How refreshing it must have been then when fans who picked up their *Steel Wheels* cassettes or CDs (or LPs, for the true diehards) put the thing on and were greeted by "Sad Sad Sad." Was it a groundbreaking track? By no means. But it set the tone as the opening track for an album that was a reassuring return to form. And it stands on its own merit as one of the most upbeat rockers about unmitigated sadness that you'll ever hear.

The first thing that you hear on the recording is a familiar jolt of open G-tuned electric guitar, but that's actually Mick Jagger playing it and not Keith Richards. Charlie Watts soon kicks the proceedings into gear with his typical combination of snap and timing, bringing us into a rough-and-tumble groove. Richards adds a wonderfully off-kilter solo that scrapes across the proceedings just enough to dirty up the crystalline production.

That production, courtesy of The Glimmer Twins (Jagger and Keith Richards) and Chris Kimsey, does suffer from the sterility of sound that was common in that era (although it's a far cry less dated than what was perpetrated on *Dirty Work*, The Stones' previous album, so at least there was an improvement). There's also not enough space for the horns to really get involved in the action, representing a bit of a wasted opportunity.

Still, there's a lot more that went right here than went wrong. *Steel Wheels* as a whole has more of an open-hearted, positive vibe than most Stones albums. It's not a color that you might think the band would wear well, seeing as how it's not exactly in line with the bad-boy image they once cultivated almost effortlessly. Yet the warmth that this album surprisingly and effectively exudes is one of the best things to recommend it, and "Sad Sad Sad," despite the title, is emblematic of this trait.

It's a song where Jagger plays the voice of logic to a female who seems to be losing her mind for no good reason other than it's something to do. Taking life advice from a Rolling Stone might not be the most obvious choice for improvement, but when you hear his argument, complete with crazed metaphors about being flung into orbit and elephants in the bedroom and grace notes like the use of the word "sleaze" as a verb, it makes perverted sense.

In the bridge, Jagger seems ready to embrace whatever hard times fate has to throw at him, practically getting off on it: "I get a cold chill / I get a cool thrill." He then goes on to challenge his paramour to show the same kind of disdain for adversity rather than succumbing to it: "Are you ready for the gilded cage? / Are you ready for the tears of rage? / Come on, baby, don't let them drown you out."

Maybe the lyrics here aren't the easiest thing to parse, but, backed by the rocking goodwill of the music, they come off like a no-BS blast of self-help arriving in the nick of time. In the same manner, the chorus, as direct as it gets, refuses to allow into the ballpark the possibility that a recovery won't happen: "Sad, sad, sad / But you're going to be fine." Jagger and backing vocalist Bernard Fowler belt out those words with the indelicacy of a concert shout.

It's possible to hear in the song The Glimmer Twins speaking to each other about all the bickering that had gone on in the previous years (although "Mixed Emotions," the first single from *Steel Wheels*, seems to be much more explicitly in that vein). Yet the advice of "Sad Sad Sad" works on the larger audience in part because The Stones are the ones delivering the message.

Who, after all, is better equipped to opine on the merits of persistence and perseverance than Jagger and Richards? Especially considering the uncertainty that surrounded the band circa *Steel Wheels*, "Sad Sad Sad" provided the kind of positive vibes that their fans desperately needed to hear from them.

87. "Tops" (from *Tattoo You*, 1981)

If you're looking for an unsung hero in Rolling Stones history, look no further than Chris Kimsey. The band needed songs for an album so that they could tour in 1981, but the relationships between the band members, particularly Mick Jagger and Keith Richards, were frayed, which meant that nobody had the desire to head into the studio.

It was Kimsey, a longtime associate of the band, who came up with the idea of sifting through their unreleased material from the 1970s and seeing if there was anything usable. What he found were outtakes, half songs, and bits and bobs of music that had gobs of potential if they could be given a little tender loving care. Mick Jagger did most of the rest, working out melodies and lyrics where they needed to be inserted. *Tattoo You* was the end result, and it was widely hailed as another classic album from a band that had more than a few of those in their rear view.

Another stroke of inspiration surrounding the album was the idea to divide it into a rock-and-roll side and a ballad side. This allowed The Stones to show off distinct sides of their personality. They're bold, brash, and snotty on the first side, tender, sultry, and soulful on the second. It's hard to imagine that the band could have done much better with a finished product featuring fresh material, even if they had been firing on all cylinders. Sometimes leftovers just taste a little better.

"Tops" is one of those second-side slow ones, a quirky yet engaging piece of music backing a nifty bit of role-playing by Jagger. His career as an actor never quite took off like many thought it would after a couple striking early performances during The Stones' late 1960s, early 1970s heyday (although he's had a bit more success producing films), but Jagger clearly understood the machinations of Hollywood, particularly pertaining to would-be starlets and the men in power who prey on their naiveté and ambition, to get this story right.

There's a clever dichotomy going on between the disingenuous patter the sleazy movie mogul pitches to the young girl and the anguished way that Jagger delivers these lines, usually in multitracked harmony with himself. It's almost as if he's trying to communicate to the female character just how badly it will all turn out if she falls for the shtick. "Don't let the world pass you by," beseeches the impresario on the make, but we the audience can tell from Jagger's vocal that her world might actually be ruined if she takes his advice. He punctuates his lines with falsetto cries of "Hey baby," nailing the unctuous tone of this predatory character.

Musically, the song backs off the electric guitars a bit, with the exception of the moody opening and Mick Taylor's soaring solo at song's end. (Even though Taylor had long since departed The Stones, he played on this track when the bare bones of it were laid down in 1972 during the sessions for *Goats Head Soup*, another example of the bizarre nature of the *Tattoo You* project.) Instead, it's carried on the light feet of Nicky Hopkins's tripping piano and Charlie Watts's strolling beat.

The music keeps veering back and forth between the playfulness of the verses and refrains and the intensity of the connecting sections. In that way, it mirrors the push and pull between the golden promises that the guy keeps making and the stark reality of what he most likely will deliver.

While tales of the casting couch are nothing new in Hollywood, they are relatively unusual as subjects for rock and roll. That Jagger dipped his own toe in the movie-making pool helped to give this song a ring of authenticity that other bands might not have been able to pull off. And it made for a nice change of pace, one that might have felt out of place on other albums but fits in well with the anything-goes aesthetic of *Tattoo You*.

In the closing moments, the producer gets desperate and applies a bit more pressure to the girl, saying, "You better take your chance now, baby

/ Or be sorry for the rest of your sweet loving life." His smoothness starts to crumble, and his true colors start to show. One hopes that it's because the girl can see through his empty promises, but it's impossible to be certain. No matter whether the end result of "Tops" is a comeuppance or a cautionary tale, it's a song, like so many others on the album that featured it, that was eminently worthy of being rescued from the scrap heap.

86. "Midnight Rambler" (from *Let It Bleed*, 1970)

Let's start right off the bat by saying that moral objections to the subject matter of "Midnight Rambler" are beside the point for the purpose of our discussion here. If you believe that The Rolling Stones went too far by unapologetically depicting a serial murderer and rapist in song without doling out some sort of punishment to him or at least showing their disdain for his actions, you're likely not going to care about said song's artistic merits. If, on the other hand, you think that art is meant to reflect true life, even the darkest aspects of it, you're more likely to give the song a pass and judge it based on those aforementioned merits.

That leads to another point about "Midnight Rambler" or any other song that sports such polarizing subject matter. The song shouldn't get extra points simply for being daring or provocative or controversial. While the fact that The Stones refused to play things safe and took a giant chance with the song should be applauded, it doesn't mean the song gets an automatic pass to greatness.

With that out of the way, "Midnight Rambler" can be properly judged as a piece of music. It turns out to be one whose ambition and execution more than compensates for the fact that the topic is sort of an end in itself, a well-told boogeyman story that doesn't communicate any deeper meaning about human nature and its propensity for violence.

This is an example of a song where Mick Jagger and Keith Richards really worked in tandem to compose it and arrange it, as Jagger recounted in *According to The Rolling Stones* in 2003. "Keith and I went to Italy, and Keith had this idea for 'Midnight Rambler', so we just started changing the tempos within the tune," he said. "Melodically, it remains the same thing, it's just a lot of tempo changes. We worked on it with acoustic guitar and harmonica, just jammed it, went through the tempo changes and had it all organized by the time we had to record it for *Let It Bleed*."[7]

Jagger, on vocals and harmonica, and Richards, on both electric and slide guitar, do most of the work on the finished recording as well. Richards's slide and Jagger's harmonica snake their way around the main riff throughout the song, even as the tempo shifts wildly. Give credit to the rhythm section of Bill Wyman and Charlie Watts for keeping with the tricky changes of pace.

Richards has referred to the song in many interviews as a "blues opera," and the ingenious music communicates the themes more efficiently than the lyrics. The tempo changes, starting with a comfortable mid-tempo trot, then a rapid sprint in the "Don't do that" middle section, then a slow crawl with climactic crashes, and finally another race to the finish, mimic both the rhythms of sex and the creeping, murderous moves of a killer. In that way, they make salient points about the nether region where sex and violence intersect, a region that this reprobate killer inhabits in terrifying fashion.

Since the lyrics seem to be mostly improvised, they can be excused for being somewhat inconsistent. At times, Jagger seems to want to distance himself from the violence ("Well, honey, it's no rock-and-roll show"). Yet there are other times when he seems to sympathize with the plight of the Rambler ("He's sighing down the wind so sadly"). Nor does the fact that he shifts between the first person and the third person perspective throughout the song make it any easier to determine where his allegiances lay.

Whatever the case may be, Jagger hints that no one should consider themselves safe from this kind of monster. The "marble hall" down which the Rambler crawls symbolizes opulence, while the "plate glass windows" and "steel plate door" that he threatens to destroy seem to offer no security. That the tendrils of violence can reach anywhere they want seems to be the one overarching point that "Midnight Rambler" deigns to make.

It's a cathartic blues workout in any event, one that has provided fodder for many memorable live performances by The Stones. In its studio version, "Midnight Rambler" doesn't even fade out; it just crashes back out the window from whence it came, and it's gone. Enjoy it thus as you would a horror-movie villain who can always come back for a bloody sequel when you least expect it. Just don't go looking for answers to any bigger questions raised by the song, for they're as elusive as the Rambler himself.

85. "Almost Hear You Sigh" (from *Steel Wheels*, 1989)

It's become a pastime of sorts among music critics and even some Stones fans to simply write off their work post–*Tattoo You*. That's an overly simplistic view that overlooks a truckload of excellent music that has emanated from the band in that period.

While it can't be doubted that the band hasn't produced a classic album in that span or at least one on par with their very best, those albums are by no means clunkers. (*Dirty Work* is probably the only one that fits into that lowly category.) They just suffer from consistency issues. Many individual songs from those LPs rise from the pack and can rank with the group's best, as this list will demonstrate as we get closer to the top.

In particular, the four albums the band has released since the 1989 rapprochement between Mick Jagger and Keith Richards succeed on their own terms because they no longer seem to be trying to compete either with the band's legacy or with the whippersnapper modern rock and pop bands all around them. Those albums are just four guys (and many assorted guests) making the music that comes naturally to them, music that the fans who grew up with them can easily understand and appreciate.

And for all the jokes about the ages of the band members and their insistence on playing a young man's game, these later albums often project an autumnal vibe, especially on ballads such as "Almost Hear You Sigh." In interviews and on stage, the band members may still inhabit their roles as eternal rapscallions and ne'er-do-wells, but songs like this one show wells of sorrow and heartbreak that can only be accumulated over a long period of time by, to put it bluntly, men of a certain age.

"Almost Hear You Sigh" was born out of Keith Richards's sessions for his *Talk Is Cheap* album. Even though that project was one of those that helped fuel the enmity between the two Stones leaders, Richards dipped into the sessions for this outtake and handed it over to Jagger for a lyrical buffing. Steve Jordan, drummer on Richards's solo album, was granted a songwriting credit for helping craft the original track.

Maybe the origins of the song are the reason it sounds somewhat atypical of the band's output, copping as it does a brooding, urban rhythm-and-blues vibe. The groove effortlessly conjures images of people hustling about crowded city streets in cold, driving rain, the anguished narrator walking amid them with his mind in torment and his heart in a vice. Jagger plays this role to the hilt, keeping a composed shell at times and uncorking raw feelings in others.

Richards may have handed over his song to Jagger to sing, but he's still very much in control of the emotional tenor. He and Ronnie Wood don't do anything showy with their electric guitars other than sustain the aforementioned groove and add in a stray, pained lick now and again. It's when Richards takes over with a solo on classical acoustic guitar that he grabs the spotlight and holds it with streaks of notes that are the aural equivalent of the streaming tears the protagonist can't hold back any longer.

The lyrics are a fine example of craftsmanship by Jagger, taking Richards's basic idea and fleshing it out to make it truly sound like the tale of a love in vain. Just as he restrains his vocal performance until the latter portion of the song, Jagger also holds back some of the deeper wounds in the lyrics initially, subtly setting the scene before eventually bringing down the hammer.

When the bridge arrives, he can hold back no longer. "Did it mean nothing?" Jagger asks, the first of a series of questions to which he probably doesn't want to hear the actual answer. Note how he unwinds out of a tortured delivery back to a more sedate reading of the lines "And have you set me free? / Or will I wake up in the morning / And find out it's been a bad dream?" Again, the experience he evinces in the performance is in perfect keeping with the subject matter of the song.

"Almost Hear You Sigh" has nice little touches all over the place, like the cooing backing vocals and Charlie Watts's no-nonsense drumming. But it's the whole that really impresses here. The band doesn't demand your attention so much as insinuate their way into your soul by utilizing their innate skills and their learned craft. And, who would have thought, by acting their age.

84. "Let It Loose" (from *Exile on Main St.*, 1972)

Exile on Main St. is generally regarded as the record where The Rolling Stones took the time to indulge in every genre of music that informs what we know as rock and roll. "Let It Loose" feels like it hits every one of those genres in the space of one song.

It's the longest song on the double album, but at no point does it feel overdone or excessive. There is a seemingly endless cast that performed on the song in addition to The Stones themselves (minus Mick Taylor, who sat it out), and yet everyone fills an integral role. "Let It Loose" sprawls, sighs, and surges, the product of musicians at the peaks of their powers doing just what the title implores.

Mick Jagger stated in a 2010 interview with *Uncut* magazine that the song came mostly from Keith Richards, even the lyrics.[8] Indeed, the words do seem to tumble forth in short phrases that don't always connect in linear fashion but always sustain the emotional narrative, a style that's emblematic of Richards's way of writing.

"Let It Loose" at times seems to be advice from one friend to another and at others seems to be a first-person lament, but the gist of the message never changes. Romance ain't worth the heartache, the lyrics consistently insist. Yet no one ever seems to listen to that sagacious counsel, which is why the "bedroom blues" need to be sung.   .

Even if the lyrics bounce all over the place, Jagger manages to pull them together with a performance that absolutely empties the tank. Maybe he felt inspired to rise to the occasion when surrounded by the amazing bigender, biracial chorus of backing vocalists. He simply pours everything he has into his vocals, setting a standard that even the classic soul belters who influenced him would have been pleased to match.

The music is a slow build. With Richards's watery guitar effect (achieved by playing it through an organ amplifier) leading off, the track starts off somewhere in the haze of a lingering dream. The piano of Nicky Hopkins soon brings a little clarity, which is bad news for the narrator, because that clarity only intensifies his blues. (It should be noted that some sources list Dr. John, the New Orleans rock legend who is definitely part of the backing chorus, as the piano player on the track, either on his own or in addition to Hopkins's work. The chaotic nature of the *Exile* sessions breeds many discrepancies like this one.)

As the song progresses and Jagger puts more and more weight behind his exhortations, the backing chorus becomes more involved, often seconding those words or performing in a kind of call-and-response with the lead singer. Even though the subject matter isn't exactly religious, the track still oozes gospel feeling, and the backing singers are a big reason for that. The way that they sing it, the refrain of "Let it loose, let it all come down" might just signal the protagonist's path to redemption instead of his road to ruin.

Once the horns, courtesy of Bobby Keys on saxophone and Jim Price on trumpet, join the party, the song is pushed in a soulful direction. Through it all, Charlie Watts is there with powerful fills that transition the track seamlessly and inventively from one section to another. Every instrumental part here is played with touch and feeling.

Jagger is the constant running through it all, bellowing and whooping with seemingly limitless energy. "I ain't in love, I ain't in luck," he wails, the horns trying their best to prop him up. Maybe Jagger, as he has claimed, didn't quite understand what was going on in "Let It Loose," but, thanks to his efforts, it makes perfect sense to the listener.

The song is in no hurry to leave the stage even after Jagger has told his sorry tale. Bar after sumptuous bar of music passes, each one more potent than the last, everyone playing to the hilt, and it's impossible not to get swept away in the catharsis of those closing moments. A little bit of everything sometimes turns a song into a sloppy mess. You might be able to argue that the all-encompassing "Let It Loose" is messy as well, but it's a glorious mess all the way.

83. "Can't You Hear Me Knocking" (from *Sticky Fingers*, 1971)

When considering "Can't You Hear Me Knocking" and its status in The Rolling Stones' catalog, it might be best to split it into two. There is the scuzzy, grimy, blistering first part of the song, and then there's the extended jam that comprises the second half. Whatever connection there might have been intended between the two parts really gets lost in the shuffle, so much so that if you hit the pause button just before that long run-out begins, you can pretend that *Sticky Fingers* is actually eleven songs long instead of ten.

Some folks may be able to groove to that second part of the song. Certainly, it's very much of the time, when bands like Santana spiraled off into extended jams in an attempt to show off their instrumental proficiencies and blow their audiences' collective minds, approaching rock music as jazz musicians might, trying to unlock hidden levels of meaning through improvisational flights of fancy.

With Mick Taylor on board, The Stones had the kind of player who was suited for these kinds of flights, and it's undeniable that his soloing at song's end is furious and impassioned. Nor can it be denied that Bobby

Keys's long saxophone showcase that precedes Taylor's soloing on the track effectively conjures urban paranoia.

Yet there still remains the question whether or not the song's stretched-out dénouement actually embellishes in any way the product that was established in the first part of the song, and that's where things get a bit dicey. There's just not much in that long run-out that really separates it from what was being done as well or even better by other jam proponents at the time. Nor is it ever really clear whether this is the kind of thing that Stones fans were looking for from their band anyway.

In interviews after the fact, several of the players, including guitarists Taylor and Keith Richards, claimed that the jam was an impulsive, one-take thing that occurred on the spur of the moment without any forethought. That would fail to explain why guest players on the track like Keys or conga player Rocky Dixon aren't heard until that jam begins. Were they just sitting around with their instruments in the studio waiting for a jam to break out, and, lo and behold, "Can't You Hear Me Knocking" provided their chance?

More likely than not, the jam, if not the specifics of it but the fact that it would actually take place, was planned out in some shape or form beforehand. That choice certainly made "Can't You Hear Me Knocking" a prime showcase for those involved, but it doesn't really do too much for the overall coherence or meaning of the song.

With all of that said, the first part of the song is so explosively gritty that it easily overcomes any qualms about that jam session. Richards kicks things off with one of his dirtiest riffs, practically serrating the speakers. That compels Charlie Watts to fire up an unforgiving beat, which then spurs Bill Wyman to come hopping into the gaps with mischievous swagger. Before Mick Jagger even says a word, this thing is on fire.

Lyrically, the song comes on like the kind of vivid nonsense that filled up other rocking groovers of the era, like The Band's "Chest Fever" or The Beatles' "Come Together." Yet Jagger slowly and cleverly weaves a tale out of these word associations. While the title might suggest a romantic suitor pleading for the object of his affections to let him in the door, this seems more like the plaint of a junkie trying to score, using every method in his arsenal to make it happen.

After describing the person on the inside in terms ("cocaine eyes," "speed-freak jive") that imply that he or she is more than able to fulfill his request, he attempts to get in using his wastrel charm. "Hear me ringing big bell toll / Hear me singing soft and low," Jagger sings with Richards chipping in with coyote harmonies. He then gets desperate: "I've been beggin' on my knees / I've been kicking, help me please."

When that doesn't work, he switches over to a more sinister vibe. But the way he phrases these threats sound as if they're directed at a much bigger audience than his would-be supplier. "I'm all around your street now," Jagger promises. "I'm all around your town." Suddenly it seems that not even the most humble burg is safe from a wee-hours knock on the window or door from characters just as desperate and dangerous as this one.

All through this narrative, the music intensifies along with Jagger's howling mania, the fuse burning down much too fast for the staid world to react in time. That it eventually explodes into a somewhat clichéd jam session makes "Can't You Hear Me Knocking" a tale of two songs: one full of menace and might and one that overstays its welcome.

82. "Crazy Mama" (from *Black and Blue*, 1976)

"That's a Rolling Stones track, right?" is how Mick Jagger described "Crazy Mama" to *Rolling Stone* interviewer Chet Flippo in his blow-by-blow account of the songs on 1976's *Black and Blue*.[9] It would seem like a pretty self-explanatory statement, but, on further examination, it's revealing in how it pinpoints what sets the song apart from some of its cohorts on the album.

Most Stones fans remember *Black and Blue* as the album where the band auditioned guitarists to replace Mick Taylor, eventually settling on Ron Wood. But what also sets the album apart a bit is that it's one of the first in which the band deviates from its formula of mashing up rock, country, and blues, one they'd been utilizing since the late 1960s. That formula had grown a bit stale on *Goats Head Soup* and *It's Only Rock 'n Roll*, the albums that preceded *Black and Blue*, so it was a refreshing bit of self-examination for the band to realize this and try some different avenues the next time out of the box.

Hence, *Black and Blue* contained reggae ("Cherry Oh Baby"), funk ("Hot Stuff"), after-hours jazz ("Melody") and whatever you want to call the potent stew that is "Hey Negrita." At the end of all that musical wandering sits "Crazy Mama" as the final track, and what Jagger was getting at in that quoted statement was how the song is a kind of capitulation to the classic Rolling Stones sound, albeit one that's entirely committed and refreshingly energetic, proving that the old formula could still be mined for exciting results.

Perhaps one of the main reasons the band sounds so much like its classic self here is that none of the newcomer guitarists are on the track, with the exception of Wood, who handles some of the guitar duties. Otherwise Keith Richards carries most of the load on lead guitar and bass, while Jagger joins in on some rhythm guitar. Some of the guitar weaving that Richards and Wood would later perfect is evident here, albeit within a bluesy context as opposed to the more streamlined modern rock they would churn out on subsequent albums.

"Crazy Mama" turns out to be a descendant of "Honky Tonk Women," rolling along at the same loping pace and featuring the same contrast between Jagger's drawled vocals in the verses and the homey harmonies in the refrains. (There's even some cowbell here, provided by Ollie Brown.) On first listen, you might assume that there are some female backing vocalists helping out on the track, but, in actuality, the chorus consists of Wood, Richards, and Billy Preston, with Preston providing the high notes that cause the confusion.

With The Stones locked into Charlie Watts's tough rhythm, Jagger barks out a series of warnings to the titular character, a kind of caricatured Southern girl whose actions have the narrator's blood boiling, and not in a good way. Instead of wilting from her craziness, he promises to "take it all head on." Some might feel uneasy with his threats of violence (each chorus promises her comeuppance in the form of his bullet), but the whole setup of "Crazy Mama" is overdone to almost cartoonish proportions, rendering it more harmless than the lyrics might suggest. It's probably not even wise to try to wedge it into the bluesy tradition of violence between lovers, because this one feels like more of a one-off lark than any kind of traditional homage.

What carries it is the pure catchiness of it all, the way those refrains pop out and grab you and the overall locked-in feel of the thing. If it seems like the band has done this kind of song a thousand times before— that's true—and yet the whole enterprise feels fresh.

Ironically, this kind of classic Rolling Stones track would fall by the wayside in years to come. The rock songs on the band's forthcoming releases, with Wood firmly established in the band, were generally played fast and loud, sacrificing some of the nuance and sway of songs like "Crazy Mama" in favor of tempo and thunder.

So it is that history has proven "Crazy Mama" to be both a winning throwback to the band's classic era and a kind of last hurrah of a certain sound. It succeeds no matter the context as an example of swaggering, timeless rock and roll.

81. "Who's Driving Your Plane?" (from *No Stone Unturned*, 1973)

Casual Rolling Stones fans perusing this humble little book might be at a loss when they reach this page, since they may not have ever heard of either this song or the album that contains it. "Who's Driving Your Plane?" is a bit of an obscurity, because it was originally a B-side for a nonalbum single, a phenomenon that seems odd now but wasn't all that rare in the 1960s.

The hierarchy of releasing music was far different then than it is now. In 1966, the year that "Who's Driving Your Plane?" was released as the B-side to "Have You Seen Your Mother, Baby, Standing in the Shadow?," the single was still very much the dominant mode of delivering music to the public. A few bands (led by, who else, The Beatles, who released the double whammy of *Rubber Soul* and *Revolver* in 1965 and 1966) were exploring the possibilities of the album as an art form, but, for the most part, recording a hit single was still the surest way to popularity and success in that time period.

As a result, many of these singles were never even released on a studio album. Among the list of monster Stones hits not included on one of their UK studio albums are "(I Can't Get No) Satisfaction," "Get Off of My Cloud," "Jumpin' Jack Flash," "Honky Tonk Women," and many others. Compilations such as *Through the Past, Darkly* or *Hot Rocks* became essential, the best way for fans to eventually collect all these hits in one place.

Yet the B-sides didn't enjoy the same fate. Whereas The Beatles eventually wrapped up all of their extraneous songs in a neat bow with the *Past Masters* albums, The Stones' B-sides were jettisoned off to all manner of strange collections, in part due to the varying levels of control the band had over their music as a result of record company and management squabbles. "Who's Driving Your Plane?" first showed up in album form on 1973's *No Stone Unturned*, a full seven years after its initial release. (The Stones' *Singles* box sets that started showing up in the 2000s rectified these problems somewhat by releasing the singles and their B-sides in chronological order, albeit in bulky, pricy collections.)

In a lot of cases, these B-sides were little more than afterthoughts, so losing them to the mists of time isn't that big of a deal. Yet "Who's Driving Your Plane?" is anything but a throwaway. It's actually far more effective than the single it backed; "Have You Seen Your Mother, Baby, Standing in the Shadow?" is a bizarre, overproduced mess that sounds like The Stones on Broadway.

Andrew Loog Oldham's production on "Who's Driving Your Plane?" is also a bit strange, yet it's effective in counterintuitive fashion. On what's ostensibly a relatively straightforward twelve-bar, Chicago-style blues, all the instruments are blended into a single mass of sound, which makes this track more powerful in a bludgeoning kind of way than it otherwise might have been. He also ladles reverb on Mick Jagger's vocal, again not what you might expect from a blues track and yet somehow apropos here, considering the surreal drift and modern sting of Jagger's lyrics.

This is another song where Jagger seems to have been influenced by some of Bob Dylan's more biting compositions. In fact, you could look at "Who's Driving Your Plane?" and its portrait/sarcastic putdown of a would-be social climber as the flipside of Dylan's "Ballad of a Thin Man." (By the way, Dylan's song concerns a certain "Mr. Jones," which some folks say was a reference to Brian Jones himself.)

When Dylan played the blues, at least back in the 1960s, he did so with the help of crack studio musicians that brought professional polish, even elegance, but little recklessness; Dylan handled that with his vocals. Where The Stones have the advantage is how their chemistry, buoyed by years of experience playing together and by an innate bond that's audible even on this somewhat forgotten track, allows them to go a bit off the rails and still hold the core together. So Jagger can play a bit with the language and the production can flirt with psychedelia, and the song still sounds authentic.

Maybe Jagger and company dismissed "Who's Driving Your Plane?" to B-side status because they saw it as just another blues in a long line of them that they could seemingly turn out in their sleep. But 1966 was a heady time, and some of that headiness somehow attached to this song, making it a blues that keeps turning out new pleasures each time you listen. For those of you unfamiliar with this track, it's worth the effort to seek it out.

80. "The Spider and the Fly" (from *Out of Our Heads*, US version, 1965)

In Great Britain, it was released as the B-side to "(I Can't Get No) Satisfaction," one of the most monumental singles in rock history, so it's understandable that "The Spider and the Fly" has been somewhat overshadowed in Rolling Stones lore. Yet it holds up well today, both as an early indication that the band could slow down their blues to great effect and as an honest representation of life on the road as hot-blooded rock stars attempting to resist temptation and stay faithful to the girls back home.

In a 1995 interview with *Rolling Stone*, Mick Jagger spoke about how "The Spider and the Fly" surprised him a bit when reflecting on it some thirty years after it was recorded. "I wasn't really that mad about it, but when you listen to it on record, it still holds up quite interestingly as a blues song," he said. "It's a Jimmy Reed blues with British pop-group words, which is an interesting combination: a song somewhat stuck in a time warp."[10]

Jimmy Reed was an electric blues pioneer from Chicago, whose laid-back rhythms on classics such as "Bright Lights Big City" are clearly mimicked here by The Stones. By slowing things down and allowing the song to breathe a little bit, each of the individual elements stands out a bit more, whether it's Keith Richards's economical lead licks, Jagger's harmonica punctuation, or the slice-of-life narrative that sinks surprisingly deep.

The title is borrowed from the children's fable of the same name, wherein a thrifty spider eventually cons a tentative fly into its lair and sudden death by plying the fly with flowery words about its beauty. It's meant to teach children the dangers of believing in idle flattery.

The Stones' retelling flips the perspective a bit. We aren't meant to concern ourselves too much with the plight of the fly, who in this case is an unsuspecting female who falls for the sexual advances of the narrator. Her fate after she jumps into the spider's web is unimportant, at least as far as the song goes.

Instead, we're privy to the inner workings of the spider/singer, who seems to want to lure the girl not because he's sinister but because he's bored and maybe a little bit depressed. Yet he's torn between his urges and his desire to stay faithful, a conundrum that he sums up with just a single line: "Don't want to be alone, but I love my girl at home."

Her words of warning keep ringing in his ear, sounding rather nagging when you get right down to it: "My, my, my, don't tell lies / Keep fidelity in your head." The last warning implies that it's the spider who'll end up getting felled should he disregard this advice: "Jump right ahead, and you're dead."

Temptation and boredom are a wicked combination, however, and, sure enough, this spider finds himself within easy reach of some potential prey: "Sitting, drinking, superficially thinking / About the rinsed-out blonde on my right." Here it's the fly who does the flattering: "She said she liked the way I held the microphone." This last bit of information removes any last barrier from the narrator and Jagger himself, the singer seemingly daring his audience to read the song as autobiographical.

His final decision: "I said, 'My, my' like a spider to a fly / 'Jump right ahead in my web.'" At that point, Jagger goes into one final harmonica solo that's undeniably jubilant. It's as if the choice the narrator made to spurn the advice of his girl at home and succumb to his desire has finally freed him.

That's why Jagger's comment about the song containing "British pop-group words" isn't entirely accurate. Even though the Jagger/Richards songwriting partnership was only in its nascent stages, they were already writing songs with the kind of honesty and candor that few of their peers were attempting. Consider how coyly John Lennon plays the one-night stand in The Beatles' "Norwegian Wood (This Bird Has Flown)," also released in 1965. That seems chaste next to The Stones' frankness.

In 1995, The Stones trotted out "The Spider and the Fly" on their acclaimed album *Stripped*, which mined songs from the back catalog and reimagined them in acoustic arrangements. On "The Spider and the Fly," Jagger takes the phrase "she looked about thirty" and switches it to "she looked about fifty," a playful concession to the passing years. Yet this song manages to stay in that "time warp," as Jagger called it, no matter when it's played, thanks to its clever combination of the traditional and the modern.

79. "Tell Me" (from *The Rolling Stones*, 1964)

If you look at the songwriting credits on The Rolling Stones' 1964 self-titled debut album in the Untied Kingdom, you'll notice songs from a hodgepodge of blues artists, a track by Chuck Berry, and another by the Motown team of Holland/Dozier/Holland. There are also a couple songs credited to Nanker Phelge or just Phelge, which was a pseudonym utilized by the group for compositions by members of the band. (That winking name would be phased out by the second half of the decade.)

There is just one song credited to the now-famous team of Jagger/ Richards. Considering that this was a band known for their blues credibility and raucous behavior, "Tell Me," the lone song from Mick and Keith, surprises a bit by being an earnest pop-soul ballad filled with tenderness and heart-on-sleeve emotions. The pair was defying expectations even at their earliest stages.

Mick Jagger spoke about the song's ability to buck the tide in a 1995 interview with *Rolling Stone*. "But it's very different from doing those R&B covers and Marvin Gaye covers and all that," he said. "It's a very pop song, as opposed to all the blues songs and the Motown covers, which everyone did at the time."[11]

The famous story that Andrew Loog Oldham, the group's manager, locked Jagger and Keith Richards in a room until they emerged with an original song is often mentioned in reference to the "The Last Time," the first Jagger/Richards-penned UK single and a No. 1 hit across the pond. Jagger and Richards have gone on record to say that story has more than a touch of urban legend to it, and, anyway, "Tell Me" predates "The Last Time" and shows the pair already delivering an excellent effort that pierced the American Top 40 (it was not released as a single in England).

The kernel of truth that can be found in the Oldham story is that either the group or their management had the wherewithal to realize that covers of old blues and soul records would only satisfy their audience for so long. In order to achieve the kind of worldwide superstardom that The Beatles had already pulled off by 1964, original material would have to be a big part of the equation. That the pair came out of the box with something as solid as "Tell Me" certainly anticipated the songwriting success that was in both their near and distant futures.

What comes across from listening to "Tell Me" is the soundness of the songcraft. Jagger and Richards may have been infatuated with the blues and other black music, but they also clearly had their ears tuned to pop radio and understood the nuances that made certain songs hits. The dynamic they achieve between the quiet, lurking verses and the stomping choruses is hard to resist when executed correctly, especially on a ballad.

Richards's twelve-string acoustic guitar sets a luscious table right off the bat, allowing Jagger to enter with his tale of woe. It's the kind of story that's been told in song a million times before, one where a guy pleads with his girl to forgive his past misdeeds and return so he can make it all right. Yet when Jagger tears into the chorus with Richards moaning and groaning behind him, it all seems fresh.

While the words are pretty basic for much of the way, Jagger does flash some dexterity in the final verse. "I hear the knock on my door that never comes," he sings. "I hear the telephone that hasn't rung." Depicting the narrator as imagining the sounds of his lover's possible return to him goes a long way to expressing just how tormented he actually is.

Even if "Tell Me" takes the form of a basic pop ballad, that doesn't mean The Stones abandoned their foremost influences to record it. The singing in the chorus is full of anguished soulfulness, while the basic story could easily be squeezed into a twelve-bar blues with a little adjustment. It's a sign that The Stones could cater their sound to their audience without betraying their true musical selves.

"Tell Me" finds this band of rogues and rascals getting in touch with their feelings and displaying them for the world to hear in memorable fashion. Maybe this first songwriting effort from the pens of Mick Jagger and Keith Richards isn't quite emblematic of their images as bad boys and blues purists, but it is certainly representative of the quality of the work they would turn out throughout their career.

78. "Dear Doctor" from (*Beggars Banquet*, 1968)

It's safe to say that "Dear Doctor" is the first capital "C" country song to appear on a Rolling Stones record. There were other songs on previous releases that flirted with country, albeit with the bedrock of the blues securely underpinning everything. This track off *Beggars Banquet* goes all-in, both lyrically and musically, and reveals in the process yet another genre of music that The Stones could deftly handle with their personality intact.

Jagger explained in *According to The Rolling Stones* how the progression to country music was a natural one for the band. "You just let certain parts of you out when you wanted to," he said. "When we first started out we wanted to be a blues band and then we became more pop-oriented—because we wanted to get popular and be played on the radio—and then we started to become more of an eclectic band."[12]

Gram Parsons, the patron saint of alt-country, is often credited with introducing The Stones to country music, but he didn't meet Keith Richards until 1968, the same year this song was recorded, so the timeline makes it pretty unlikely for him to have had much impact on "Dear Doctor." In actuality, Jagger and Richards were longtime fans of the genre, with Mick in particular tapping into the lighter side of the music. "There's a sense of humor in country music anyway, a way of looking at life in a humorous kind of way," he said, "and I think we were just acknowledging that element of the music."[13]

In later years, Jagger would tiptoe the line between planting his tongue in his cheek in his country songs and sticking his foot in his mouth; see "Far Away Eyes" for an example of a song that seems to insult the genre more than pay homage to it. On "Dear Doctor," the band gets it just right, and the fun is undeniable, even in the midst of a song about the seemingly limitless torment of a would-be groom.

Employing back-porch instruments like tack piano and stand-up bass, the band finds just the right kind of homey energy to fit the subject matter. Much credit goes to Brian Jones, whose harmonica wends its way through the narrative and hits all the highs and lows on cue. Dave Mason guests on acoustic guitar with Richards, while Nicky Hopkins's piano chugs alongside of Bill Wyman's bass to keep the story moving. *Beggars Banquet* was the first Stones album produced by Jimmy Miller, and his expertise can be felt here in the way that the song seems comfortably off the cuff without getting listless.

Jagger's countrified accent is probably overdone, but Richards keeps chiming in with high lonesome harmonies to pull him back on track. The narrator in the song is about to be married to a "bow-legged sow" and can't stand the thought of it. Even as his mother props him up with bourbon and gets him ready for his close-up, he keeps entreating the nearby doctor for some ghoulish medical attention: "There's a pain where there once was a heart / It's sleeping, it's beating—can't you please tear it out / And preserve it right there in that jar?"

As he stands sweating in his monkey suit, he enjoys a last-minute reprieve out of the blue. Jagger switches over to a hilarious falsetto mewl to read the contents of a letter from the bride-to-be saying that she is running off to Virginia with Cousin Lou. We leave him stepping down from the figurative ledge, wiping his brow in relief, and preparing to relocate his heart and move on with his life.

Is there a bit of parody targeting some of the extremes of country songwriting hidden in the nooks and crannies of Jagger's story? More than likely. Yet it's affectionate enough here that we can give him a pass, especially since it allows us to indulge in all the other pleasures the song has to give. It's hard to say what country audiences must have thought about "Dear Doctor" at the time, if they even gave it a thought at all, but time has proven the musical backing to be inspired, even if the tale is a little wacky.

Country songs would soon become regular features on future Stones albums, often played for laughs but always containing an honest hint of melancholy, that kind of laughing-through-the-tears mentality that the genre does better than any other. "Dear Doctor" was a test run that passes charmingly, one of the first examples of the band stretching out beyond the blues and pop and displaying the versatility that might just be the most underrated reason for their success.

77. "The Last Time" (from *Out of Our Heads*, US version, 1965)

It wasn't the first Jagger/Richards composition. You could even argue that it wasn't a Jagger/Richards composition at all really, or at best a partial one. But the importance of "The Last Time" in the songwriting progress of the two leaders of The Rolling Stones can't be denied, nor can the direct, visceral power of the song itself be ignored.

As Keith Richards spoke about in *According to The Rolling Stones*, it wasn't the act of writing hit songs that proved daunting to the two men but rather the act of writing a song worthy of the band in which they played. "We were going to lay it on our own guys," he said. "It was not like fooling somebody in Tin Pan Alley and letting them add a nice arrangement—we had to lay this song to The Stones."[14]

This was not a song that would be buried away as an album cut in an era when albums were subordinate to singles. "The Last Time" would be a British single, the first to come from the songwriting pens of Jagger/

Richards. That fact, plus what Richards mentioned about the intimidation factor of writing for The Stones, may be the reason why the two men clearly borrowed from a gospel song by The Staples Singers titled "This May Be the Last Time." Although the musical backing of the two songs are vastly different, the part of "The Last Time" chorus where Mick Jagger and Richards sing in harmony ("May be the last time, I don't know") is a direct sound-alike to The Staples Singers' original.

This kind of appropriation of older material is, of course, a common practice in the pop/rock music game. It's not like The Stones have tried to hide it, as Richards has often mentioned The Staples Singers' influence, saying that it was a record with which he and Jagger were familiar. It sounds like the band used the older song as a jumping-off point more than anything else, so the claims of theft that have been hung on the band through the years don't really hold up. (If so, James Brown, whose "Maybe the Last Time" came out at around the same time, would also have to be held accountable.)

What's important about "The Last Time" is that it establishes The Stones' persona and attitude. They could have scored with a florid pop song, but that would have damaged their reputation as the bad-boy antidote to the good-boy Beatles. (Florid pop songs were in their future, of course, but not before their status as rock superstars had been established, giving them carte blanche to write and perform whatever they wanted.) Instead, they scored with a song that feels unforgiving and merciless. The Beatles' first singles were all about love and bringing two people together; The Stones first original UK smash was all about a guy threatening to leave.

Brian Jones plays that memorable, countrified guitar riff that keeps coming back around again in unrelenting fashion. Charlie Watts's beat gallops along while Richards adds in the rhythm guitar. Even when he plays in the instrumental break, Richards doesn't so much solo as he does chunk out yet another series of riffs. The band may have been invading the pop charts, but it was doing so with a sound that concentrated more on rhythmic dynamism than melodic ingenuity.

Jagger nails the part of a boyfriend who seems completely unbothered by leaving. If anything, he practically taunts his girlfriend, insinuating that she's to blame for any pain his departure might cause. "Cause I'll be gone a long, long time," he yelps. To add insult to injury, he takes a not-so-subtle shot at her past when he wonders why she can't give him what he wants: "You don't try very hard to please me / With what you know, it should be easy."

There's nothing too fancy in the approach, which actually works in the song's favor, because anything extraneous might have diluted its power. With Jagger chanting, "No, no more," as the song heads to the fade-out, the band has established that they are a force with which to be reckoned and won't be played as fools by anyone.

As Richards said, "'The Last Time' was a kind of bridge into thinking about writing for The Stones. It gave us a level of confidence; a pathway of how to do it." It may have been a bridge to bigger and better things for The Stones, but "The Last Time" is strong enough that many lesser writers and performers would consider it a destination.

76. "Let It Bleed" (from *Let It Bleed*, 1969)

Ending side 1 of the 1969 album with which it shared its name, "Let It Bleed" is a genially ragged number that projected a kinder, gentler Rolling Stones image without skimping on the debauchery for which the group had become notorious. Its message of togetherness is targeted squarely at those folks on the margins of society who often are bypassed by love and mercy.

Maybe The Stones saw in the hard-luck deviants and junkies their own reflections, what might have become of them had not rock and roll intervened. There is a case to be made as well that some of the band members ran in pretty much the same company as the folks detailed in the song. In any case, the band throws their arms around them all on this big-hearted track with loose morals.

The song was recorded in the brief time after the departure of Brian Jones and the hiring of Mick Taylor, so Keith Richards pulls double-duty on acoustic and electric slide guitar. (It should be noted that some sources list Ry Cooder as the slide guitar player on the track.) Most important to the overall sound is the playing of longtime Stones cohort Ian Stewart. His piano tumbles alongside the rhythm, providing welcome color and more than a little bit of wiggle to the proceedings.

"Let It Bleed" deploys that strolling, swaggering tempo that the band had perfected around this time. It seems to take its time and still manages to keep you moving with a little spring in your step. It's also a song that demonstrates how the band could take all of their disparate influences, filter them through their own skills and experience, and come out with a sound that defied easy inclusion in any specific genre of music. There's country, blues, folk, and even some boogie-woogie in there, but it all comes out sounding inimitably like The Stones.

In this era, Jagger was fond of dropping his protagonists in the midst of almost surreally seedy situations and seeing how the guys would hold up. Hence the bizarre verse about the "steel guitar engagement" that ends with the narrator in the company of a tea-drinking, knife-wielding (or maybe needle-wielding) femme fatale and a "jaded, faded junky nurse." "Oh, what pleasant company," he exclaims at the end of the verse before the chorus comes around to prop him back up for his next adventure.

There's more than enough overt sex and drug references in this single song to fill an Aerosmith album. The woman offering her breasts, cocaine, and a "space in her parking lot" is just the tip of the iceberg. Don't forget the refrains, where Jagger calls out to everyone in the vicinity to let them know that he's available for leaning, bleeding, feeding, dreaming, creaming, and coming.

All of the innuendo might draw snickers, but Jagger's point comes through loud and clear: that there is a need for all human beings, even those lost in squalor or vice, to connect with someone else, even if only for a moment to ease the pain. The sex and drugs may be temporary solutions, but the helping hand of a friend means a lot more.

Much has been made of the song's title, since the phrase "Let It Bleed" doesn't actually appear in the song. There are certainly drug connotations attached to the phrase. It's also noteworthy that, around the time "Let It Bleed" was recorded in 1969, The Beatles were in the midst of recording their own album, *Let It Be*, which would go on the shelf until 1970 due to the band's internal squabbling. Some see the similarities in the titles as The Stones winking acknowledgment of the difference in outlooks between the two bands.

Most likely the phrase is just another kind-hearted, if morbid, offer to match all of the other ones found throughout the song. In the midst of the unrest at the end of the 1960s, many people were suffering and looking for some sort of lifeline. With "Let It Bleed," The Rolling Stones improbably and credibly provided a place for the figuratively wounded, no matter their lots in life, to turn.

75. "Out of Tears" (from *Voodoo Lounge*, 1994)

Considering that they're the perpetual torch-bearers for rock and roll in all its raucous glory, it's sometimes easy to overlook The Rolling Stones' facility with the slower stuff. Ever since the days of "As Tears Go By" and "Ruby Tuesday," The Stones have shown a fetching willingness to change tactics and play it soft and tender instead of fast and rough every now and again.

In the last twenty-five years, the sporadic album releases by the band have demonstrated that they haven't lost their touch on the weepers one bit. If anything, the slow songs are often the best things on the later albums, if only because the rockers often drift into autopilot Stones mode and can tend to become almost indistinguishable from each other. The slow songs each seem to have their own distinct personality.

Look no further than "Out of Tears," an affecting love-gone-wrong song from 1994's *Voodoo Lounge*, as an example of the band pulling back the reins and producing a downright lovely piece of melancholia. The piano, played with feeling by Chuck Leavell, is the driving force here instead of the guitar. That instrumental switcheroo seems to free the band up to both a different kind of melodic approach and a more vulnerable and heartfelt lyric than is the norm.

Mick Jagger composed "Out of Tears" as the band was putting together the material for *Voodoo Lounge*. He also takes center stage with a vocal performance that's relatively unshowy compared to most of his vocals, which is the right move for this song. Had he really laid it on thick, the song's built-in sorrow might have been overplayed. As it is, his vocals combine with the piano and strings for just the right amount of heart-tugging.

Jagger writes the song from the point of view of a man who is already resigned to the fact that his love is about to leave him. There are no details given about how this happened or who's to blame, which makes it somehow more painful to hear. Instead, the verses describe his numbness to the whole scenario; his very first line is "I can't feel, feel a thing."

He enters a kind of meditative state as a defense mechanism against the torment he's likely to suffer. Seemingly unable to function on even the most basic level, all he can do is suck in the contrasting pangs of love and pain with each breath. The reason, as the chorus makes plain, is that he has finally been drained of overt emotional responses: "I won't cry when you say goodbye / I'm out of tears."

Ronnie Wood steps in for a well-measured solo on slide during the instrumental break. Meanwhile, Keith Richards lurks around the edges of the narrative with telling guitar fills. The strings are also done just right, enough to sting a little bit but not so much that they overwhelm. Overall, it's a nice production by Don Was and The Glimmer Twins.

The narrator bravely steps out of his comatose state in the run-up to the refrain, showing the kind of resilience that lets us believe that he just might make it to the other side of this breakup. "And I just can't pour my heart out to another living thing," Jagger sings. "I'm a whisper, I'm a shadow, and I'm standing up to sing." Those lines allow us to hear the chorus somewhat differently. Instead of him being cried out, it makes it seem like he's choosing to put the tears away for the sake of moving on.

What pushes across a song like "Out of Tears" is the believability factor, the sense that the song isn't just a put-on for the sake of filling out an album, the feeling that all the players are heart-deep in the material. The Stones do an excellent job with it, keeping things on the subtle side, suggesting instead of exclaiming, letting the emotions arise naturally in the performance instead of forcing them. By doing it that way, the same kind of emotional response tends to sneak up on the listener in turn, making for a surprisingly affecting experience.

Such is the magic you can work when you're a band the caliber of The Rolling Stones. Some might say that time and experience helps them on a song like "Out of Tears," but their balladic bona fides have been in little doubt pretty much since the get-go.

74. "Before They Make Me Run" (from *Some Girls*, 1978)

Of course it's impossible to sum up a human being in a single song, let alone a being as endearingly complex as Keith Richards. Yet if an alien landed tomorrow and forced you to play a single song to define The Rolling Stones' lovable rake of a guitarist, "Before They Make Me Run" would be the obvious choice, and there's probably not a runner-up that could make a case.

Recorded at a time when Richards had a drug arrest and the possibility of life in prison hanging over his head, putting his future and that of his band in serious doubt, "Before They Make Me Run" waxes defiant with its music, even as the lyrics dare to show the pains and fears behind the bravado. That Richards escaped that arrest with minor consequences helped to put this song in a brighter context, whereas a different, direr outcome might have rendered it much less harmless than it now seems to be.

It's interesting how the song, sung by Richards and likely written mostly by him with some help with the lyrics from Mick Jagger, is the one on 1978's *Some Girls*, an album notable for its nods to punk pace and disco rhythms, that seems the most like a throwback to an earlier Stones sound. If not for the fact that Charlie Watts's snapping drums are far more prominent in the mix to keep up with the style in the beat-obsessed late 1970s, you could easily imagine this song fitting in somewhere on *Exile on Main St.* It has the same looseness bordering on chaos to it, with the guitars coming in all angles and at unexpected times and Richards's vocal phrasing sounding like he was singing the words only when he could remember them all.

It's as if Richards refused to bow to the whims of taste and popularity with the song, preferring to stick in the rock-and-roll wheelhouse he knew best. In 1977, he said, "I don't think that Bowie or Johnny Rotten or all the Zeppelins are anywhere in the future let alone the present." While it's comical to think how the artists that he lumps together in that quote couldn't be more different from each other, his point seems to be that his band's music, having stood the test of time, is therefore timeless.

It's also somewhat amusing to think that Richards also shrugged off for years the possibility that the song was consciously autobiographical when discussing "Before They Make Me Run" in interviews. In his 2010 book, *Life*, he finally fessed up, saying, "That song, which I sang on that record, was a cry from the heart."[15] Since Richards sings it in typical devil-may-care fashion, it's easy to miss the hurt that's palpable in the lyrics.

"Only a crowd can make you feel so alone," he sings in the very first couplet, a line that incisively cuts into the lonely life of the performer. That's where self-medication enters the picture: "Booze and pills and powders, you've got to choose your medicine." But the consequences of those choices are unavoidable: "Well it's another goodbye to another good friend." Many cite the 1973 death of Richards's buddy Gram Parsons as the influence for this line, but farewells are the price that a restless soul like the narrator has to pay almost on a daily basis.

This song wouldn't truly capture Richards's persona though if it was just a lot of moaning and groaning about life on the road. His black humor emerges in the second verse when he practically dares death to come after him: "I'm going to find my way to heaven 'cause I did my time in hell-oh year / I wasn't looking too good but I was feeling real well." Referencing the public's perception of him as a living skeleton is his way of saying that the joke's on everybody else but not on him.

In the chorus he justifies his refusal to stop, to quit, to allow his problems to engulf him in misery. "After all is said and done," he sings, "I've got to move while it's still fun / Well let me walk before they make me run." In the later refrains, Ronnie Wood and Jagger chip in some harmonies, his fellow bounders helping him on the getaway.

Richards on lead vocal was still a relatively rare occasion in The Stones catalog when "Before They Make Me Run" was released in 1978, but it started a tradition of the guitarist taking center stage on at least one song per Stones album after that. The band probably realized what an invaluable and charismatic perspective he provided. That perspective hasn't changed too much since that song, perhaps because it wouldn't be like Richards to change, but also because that song said so much about the man and said it so well.

73. "Heart of Stone" (from *Out of Our Heads*, UK version, 1965)

By the time the third album by The Rolling Stones released in their native Great Britain rolled around, their songwriting skills were starting to show signs of sharpening. While there were still only three songs credited to Mick Jagger and Keith Richards on their 1965 release *Out of Our Heads*, the consistency of that trio stands out. "Gotta Get Away" ended side 1 of the album with a relaxed vibe that was contrasted nicely by the pointed lyrics, while "I'm Free" closed out the album with a declaration of liberation that's enhanced by the psychedelic drone of the melody.

Best of all is "Heart of Stone," which finds The Stones going the ballad route once again, not too long after the success they had with "Tell Me." The difference is that "Heart of Stone" has an iciness about it that stands out from both "Tell Me" and the other fawning slow songs of the era. It showed that The Stones could change the pace without sacrificing their standby attitude of defying just about everything in their path, which, in this song's case, turns out to be the vulnerability that accompanies love.

The release schedule of Stones material was sometimes haphazard in the early days in terms of comparisons between the United States and the United Kingdom, and this song was no different. Even though "Heart of Stone" didn't come out in the United Kingdom until the release of *Out of Our Heads* in September of 1965, it received a test run as a single in the States in December of 1964. The fact that this chilly meditation on romance hit the Top 20 speaks not only to the US public's voracious appetite for the Beatles-spurred British Invasion at that time but also to the fact that The Stones execute it so well that it turns out quite catchy even if the sentiment isn't your typical radio fare. In years to come, The Stones would actually go a long way toward changing what constituted typical radio fare anyway.

The musical template for "Heart of Stone" can be found in the songs of soul balladeers like Otis Redding or Solomon Burke. The Stones employ the same kind of strolling tempo, while Jagger utilizes the technique of sticking to the minimum of words in the main verses before cramming in as much as he can in the bridge to the refrains, something that guys like Burke, Redding, or any number of belters popular in that era had made into an art form.

By recognizing those similarities, it then becomes easy to hear the moments where The Stones start to make the song into something that's uniquely their own. The jangly guitars of Keith Richards and Brian Jones scrape against the low-down bass of Bill Wyman, formulating some interesting tension in the process. Richards also explodes into a solo seemingly out of nowhere following one of the verses, as if his warbling guitar is an extension of Mick Jagger's id.

As for Jagger, the phrasing might have come from some of his soul heroes, but the vibe he projects is all his own. When he talks about the girl who is the most current object of his affection, he sings as would a child inspecting a new toy. "What's different about her? I don't really know," he muses, as if the answer isn't so much important as something that's amusing to him.

We find out that what attracts her to him is the fact that he can't seem to torture her in the same way he has all his former loves. "No matter how I try," he sings, "I just can't make her cry." His admiration for her is tempered by the fact that he's unwilling to really dig deep and see what makes her tick for fear that she might become too much of an obsession, or, even worse, someone who might be able to break his stony façade and do some damage.

The refrain is pulled off to intense effect. Richards joins Jagger in a taunting chant of "Cause she'll never break, never break, never break, never break," the music jacking up all around them to a climax. Then it drops away, leaving Jagger alone as the music drops into a minor key for the punch line: "This heart of stone."

While it's easy to hear the standoffishness and the aforementioned defiance in other parts of the song, a different dimension sneaks in on that line. Jagger sounds lonely, almost wounded. It's a brief glimpse into the consequences such a stand on romance ends up causing in a person, and it humanizes this protagonist, makes him sound like less of a cad, if only for a moment.

As a result, "Heart of Stone" briefly captures the sorrow at the heart of the great soul songs it emulates. That it does so in the midst of a pitch-black stance on romance keeps it from compromising The Stones' unforgiving personality in the process.

72. "2,000 Years from Home" (from *Their Satanic Majesties Request*, 1967)

The reputation of The Stones' much-maligned, sometimes-praised 1967 album *Their Satanic Majesties Request* will probably never achieve anything close to a consensus among critics, fans, or whoever happens to come across this fascinating mess. There will always be those contrarians who find the mysteries of the universe have been unlocked by the thing, while others will continue to scratch their leveler heads at the excess and folly of it all.

In truth, the album features a few really cool tracks, some experimental stuff that could use a lot more focus, and a low point or two. (We're looking at you, "Gomper.") The album wasn't so much a reaction to The Beatles' masterpiece *Sgt. Pepper's Lonely Hearts Club Band*, which was released earlier in 1967, as it was a reflection of The Stones' desire to innovate in a studio setting much like The Fab Four had done.

But with no George Martin to guide the experiments toward some semblance of coherence, The Stones ended up sounding adrift and strangely bored at times with the whole endeavor. If nothing else, the album made it clear to them both where their musical hearts truly beat and that they needed a solid producer; the Jimmy Miller–produced years to come would be the band's unmistakable high point.

Speaking of high points, one of the grooviest on *Request* is the extra-terrestrial odyssey "2,000 Light Years from Home." Allegedly written by Mick Jagger in the one night he spent in prison following a drug bust at Keith Richards's Redlands estate in February of 1967, the song takes a view of space exploration that's both wondrous and terrifying all at once. One could look at the schizoid nature of it as a metaphor for the highs and lows of the drug culture, which Jagger must have been contemplating within the prison walls as he penned it.

The song predates David Bowie's "Space Oddity" by a couple years but shares its eerie calm and sci-fi trappings. The musical atmosphere of "2,000 Light Years from Home" emanates in large part from Brian Jones's brilliant work on the mellotron. Swooping and diving at odd angles, only to settle in screeching holding patterns every now and again, Jones's playing emulates space travel to chilling effect. He fearlessly shows us the dark side of any attempt to slip the bonds of Earth, suggesting that there might not be any way home again.

Richards plays a somewhat minimal part in the song, but his subtle contributions are essential. After the dissonant piano intro, it's Richards's flickering guitar figure that awakens the song as it prepares for its flights of fancy. Later on, he carves out some grungy riffs that sound like a capsule crash landing and thudding out of control across the surface of some distant planet. The element of danger wouldn't quite be so tangible without those moments.

Jagger sings the song with detached, almost trancelike calm. It's rare to hear him hold the same emotional vibe throughout an entire track; that he never explodes into his trademark howls or bellows only intensifies the fright somehow. It's as if the physics of space, the same quirks that cause us to float weightless and drown out our voices, also clamp down on emotional expression.

When you add all of these ominous elements, you get aural frigidity that is far from the Day-Glo, flower-power sounds of the Summer of Love. If there was a group that may have influenced The Stones on this track, it certainly wasn't *Pepper*–era Beatles but rather Syd Barrett–era Pink Floyd. "2,000 Light Years From Home" doesn't have the same kind of disassociated wildness, but the sense that those who explore too far from reality might not like what they find, achieved through the music's weird beauty and Jagger's zombielike observations, is certainly similar to what creeps around the edges of the Floyd's early work.

By the time Jagger's far-out traveler gets the A-OK from ground control to land on Aldebaran, "safe from the green desert sand," there is no sense of relief. There's just the repeat of the refrain, which lays bare the loneliness that's implied in the rest of the song. The Rolling Stones didn't quite commit to the psychedelia of *Their Satanic Majesties Request*. On "2,000 Light Years From Home," they perhaps inadvertently give you the reason why, suggesting that the outermost regions of both the Milky Way and the human mind may be fun places to visit, but you wouldn't want to get trapped in either location.

71. "Blinded by Love" (from *Steel Wheels*, 1989)

One of the unfortunate side effects of the compact disc era has been the bloat of album releases. The CD offers more space for longer running times than vinyl, allowing artists to cram their full-lengths with material that otherwise might have stayed on the cutting room floor.

The Stones have been as guilty of this as anybody else. Their four studio albums released since 1989 have contained twelve, fifteen, thirteen, and sixteen songs. That makes about a total of sixteen songs that might not have seen the light of day back in the day. (Of course, The Stones might be able to justify this super-sizing more than most, because they've only released four albums in a span of a quarter century. So there's probably more of a demand for overstuffed records from them.)

The glass-half-full way to look at all this is that some of those songs that might otherwise have been excised in the group's golden era are those that allow the band some room to experiment with music slightly left of center from their normal repertoire. One such song is the beguiling "Blinded by Love," which comes out of nowhere on *Steel Wheels* with a historical twist on familiar subject matter and a mash-up of musical styles that shouldn't work but does and then some.

Maybe the most accurate description for "Blinded by Love" is baroque country and western. Matt Clifford's piano part sounds like it's been beamed in from Nashville or, for an older vintage, Bakersfield. Yet his harmonium puts a medieval spin on the proceedings. In a similar fashion, guest player Phil Beer adds some down-home fiddle and some gondola-worthy mandolin.

This isn't the kind of alchemy that the band pulled off on *Exile on Main St.*, when seemingly every genre of American roots music informed the songs yet blended into a seamless amalgamation that sounded in the final mix like nothing other than Stones music. On "Blinded by Love," both the country and the baroque-pop parts somehow occupy the same space, kept in line by Charlie Watts's rim shots. It shouldn't be as elegant and affecting as it turns out to be.

Since it's a somewhat strange musical arrangement that eventually pays off, it's only fitting that the lyrics veer from the norm and still manage to hit home. Mick Jagger decides to warn us about the dangers of hasty, unconsidered love by citing historical and biblical examples. So Antony and Cleopatra, Samson and Delilah, and King Edward and Mrs. Simpson are all trotted out in the lyrics to demonstrate the consequences that can befall those who ignore his advice.

Maybe it's justifiable to take a shot at Jagger for only mentioning examples of men who were brought down by their love of a particular woman, since he certainly could have found enough similar cautionary tales of women felled by their love of a man. Worrying about pleasing all constituencies is a sure path to songwriting mediocrity, however, so maybe it's better in the long run that the boys earn a few demerits on the political correctness scorecard but deliver an undiluted point of view in the process.

Since Jagger is flying back through the mists of time for his tales of romantic destruction, he adopts a formal language that's suitable to the stories he's telling. Hence you get a retelling of the Antony and Cleopatra saga replete with a boat "burnished with gold" and "royal purple" sails. He even manages to work the word "parvenu" into the lyric without sounding too foppish.

For all the vivid descriptions and antiquated language, the rise and fall of the melody, backed by the counterintuitively pretty music, carry a lot of the weight. That melody leads directly into one of the oldest Stones standbys in the book: Jagger and Richards harmonizing on the refrain. In the midst of everything else going on in a busy kind of song, those voices together bring it all back home to the emotional core.

"Blinded by Love" contains all of the offhand charm and subtle oddness of a cherished B-side. Perhaps it might have even gained more acclaim if it had indeed filled that role instead of being an album track in The Stones' latter era, when their LPs lost some of their cachet. Regardless of how it was presented, the bottom line is that it deserves space on any playlist of the group's most underrated songs.

70. "You Got the Silver" (from *Let It Bleed*, 1969)

It's a little hard to imagine, now that his voice graces at least a couple tracks per Rolling Stones album and he fronts his own critically acclaimed side-project band, but there was once a time when Keith Richards played lead guitar and sang backup and harmony but never stepped up to lead vocals. Mick Jagger carried the singing load on every track on every album for the first five years or so of the band's existence.

Many bands have this kind of time share, and it's not like Richards didn't have some impact on the microphone, since his harmonies were often crucial to the overall effect of certain songs. But they left it up to Jagger to provide diversity from track to track. While he managed this quite well, there is no doubt that having Richards's inimitable lead vocals to change the pace added a great deal to later albums, often to the point where Keith's leads were the highlights.

Part of the reason that he didn't take center stage early on was that it was rare that he wrote songs back in the 1960s without any input from Jagger. Unlike The Beatles, who would usually divvy up singing responsibilities between John Lennon, Paul McCartney, and George Harrison based on who the sole writer of a song was, Jagger and Richards tended to work in tandem most of the time, and then Jagger would do all the singing. (One notable exception to this was "Ruby Tuesday," a song composed entirely by Richards but sung by Jagger to great effect.)

Whether it was a conscious decision by the band or just the fact that Richards started to gain more confidence as a solo composer and singer, "You Got the Silver" became the first in a long line of Keith-centric songs when it appeared on *Let It Bleed* in 1969. Richards got his feet wet the previous year by duetting with Jagger on "Salt of the Earth," from *Beggars Banquet* (he also briefly sang lead on the jokey "Something Happened to Me Yesterday," from *Between the Buttons* in 1967), but "You Got the Silver" was all him all the way, the first Stones song with no contribution from Jagger. The band did record a version of the song with Mick on lead, but it was scrapped, and rightly so considering the excellent job Richards did.

Richards's voice was a much clearer instrument on "You Got the Silver" than the cigarette-affected croak it became as years passed. He also hadn't yet acquired the trademark hiccups and asides that would become a definitive part of his phrasing down the road. As a matter of fact, he modulates his performance here in much the same manner as Jagger, starting off cool and collected, or maybe cool and dejected would be more accurate, before erupting with whoops and bellows in the song's climax.

The music moves along in much the same manner. Richards handles all of the guitar work, starting off with an acoustic before bringing in electric slide parts to add a lonesome touch. Brian Jones twangs away on autoharp while Nicky Hopkins's organ work provides a soulful counterpoint to the dusty guitars. In the final verses, the rhythm section of Bill Wyman and Charlie Watts join the party for a rollicking finish.

Richards's lyrics over the years tend to stick to either semiautobiographical outlaw sagas or lovelorn treatises on romance, with the occasional bawdy song thrown in for good measure. Here he's singing about romance, in particular with a girl to whom he willingly gives everything he has even though he knows there's a chance he might get little in return. Richards was in the midst of his tempestuous relationship with Anita Pallenberg at the time, and you can certainly hear in his voice the honesty of both his devotion and frustration.

Over the next thirty-five years or so, Richards would string together a long line of vocals that somehow both honor his soused, disheveled persona and contrast it by showing the emotional reality behind the caricature. It all began with "You Got the Silver," which proved that Richards's vocal stylings were as compelling, in their own idiosyncratic way, as Jagger's and that The Stones, going forward, would have two potent points of view on the microphone.

69. "Always Suffering" (from *Bridges to Babylon*, 1997)

Here is another example of the late-period Rolling Stones releasing a song that butts up against their persona as mega-rich, globe-trotting, have-it-all superstars. Of course, an album full of songs playing up the ritzier aspects of life as a Stone wouldn't ever be very relevant to the average fan anyway, so the idea that their music should always promote decadence is a nonstarter. But it's still striking when a song as downbeat and pain-wracked as "Always Suffering" slips through the façade. And when they pull it off with as much genuineness as they do here, The Stones make you believe they're feeling the pain as well, or at least they were at one point.

"Always Suffering" comes from Mick Jagger's songwriting pen, and, as do so many of the other songs on 1997's *Bridges to Babylon*, it gets ample assistance from an all-star team of collaborators. Among the bold-faced names that can be found in the credits for this one are Blondie Chaplin, a former Beach Boy who joins the lush chorus of backing vocalists seconding Jagger's tortured emotions; Benmont Tench, a core member of Tom Petty's Heartbreakers who adds some subtle organ touches; and Jim Keltner, session drummer supreme who throws in some percussion embellishment to Charlie Watts's drumbeat and also joins on backing vocals.

The most profound contribution comes from Waddy Wachtel, whose mournful acoustic guitar sets the mood for the track. It says something about the humility of Keith Richards that, despite his stature as a guitarist in the rock world, he's fine with letting other axe-men take the spotlight on songs that bear The Stones' imprimatur. That's in keeping with the band's longtime willingness to accept any and all comers to help out on songs.

Richards does get to lay down some electric licks in an instrumental break that also includes some time front and center for Wachtel's acoustic and Ronnie Wood's pedal steel. Instead of having just one soloist on the track, the three guitarists seem to be having a conversation with each other. Wachtel's part is anguished and gutted, while Richards and Wood are more resigned, accepting of the heartbreak that the song details. It's a lovely section of a song that once again demonstrates the musical might of this band, even at their quietest and most contemplative.

Jagger's lyrics start by looking back to better times with a former lover. The song isn't about how the relationship fell apart though. It's, rather, a reflection of how gloomy the two protagonists' lives have become in contrast to their halcyon youths. Mick starts the song by trying to get back to that youthful feeling, hoping that a bit of reminiscence can revive the dormant feelings of happiness inside them.

It's common for people in the doldrums to idealize better times, and that seems to be what Jagger is doing here, describing the former actions of the couple as noble and exemplary: "While the whole world was wondering / We walked a steady line / While all our friends were wavering we kept on trying." But fate has not rewarded them in any way, their idyllic youthful summer replaced with the signifiers of the blues: rain, darkness, and a howling midnight train.

In the bridge, Jagger's vocals become noticeably more animated as he pleads for his companion to dig deep and try and locate that former glow. It's safe to say that it's not so much a rekindling of their love affair that he desires but rather a recurrence of the joy that permeated their lives when they were together.

Out of the affecting instrumental break, Jagger emerges with some of his most heartfelt and poetic pleas. "For life is but a chance / On a windswept hill," he sings, the weather once again utilized to symbolize the emotional status of the characters. "And the seeds of love are swirling above," he sings. "Let them be still." Like the answers blowin' in Dylan's wind, these seeds are right in front of their eyes, seemingly within their grasp, yet ever elusive.

"We're already lost," the chorus concludes. That's the moment when these dreams of returning to a better, brighter day dissipate, yielding the cold reality that the torment is bound to continue long beyond the present time. The Stones mine some exquisite angst on "Always Suffering," another song from the later years that presents them as beaten by the world, as opposed to the common assumption by their fans that it's the other way around.

68. "Lady Jane" (from *Aftermath*, 1968)

What a revelation *Aftermath* must have been on its release in 1966, especially to those detractors of The Rolling Stones who saw the band as uncouth, uncivilized, and, to be frank, unintelligent counterparts to The Beatles and other more palatable pop groups. The album revealed just the opposite of those aforementioned characteristics throughout, which was truly eye-opening considering every one of the fourteen songs came courtesy of the writing team of Mick Jagger and Keith Richards.

Aftermath was the fourth Stones album released in Great Britain. On the previous three, slightly more than two-thirds of the songs featured the band covering other artists. And many of those early original songs were relatively forgettable, with Jagger/Richards only truly hitting their writing stride with the release of "(I Can't Get No) Satisfaction" in May of 1965 and the subsequent string of smash singles that followed. Still, releasing one or two well-written songs every few months or so was a far cry from the complete artistic statement that is *Aftermath*.

That the band would even attempt something as far from their seeming comfort zone as "Lady Jane," the Elizabethan-era homage that is one of the album's true highlights, was excellent progress in and of itself. That they would nail the song, displaying engaging delicacy while still sneaking in some of their trademark prickliness, is downright staggering.

Anyone under the assumption that The Stones were semiskilled instrumentalists only capable of a rowdy approximation of the blues couldn't have possibly made that statement with a straight face after hearing the evidence of "Lady Jane." As he did on so many songs in the mid-1960s, Brian Jones added a part that was more than mere embellishment; Jones's Appalachian dulcimer distinguishes "Lady Jane" from the glut of other baroque-pop songs that became all the rage in that time period.

It's telling that such unique instrumentation for the most part disappeared after Jones left the band. Part of the reason for that was because The Stones entered into their rootsy period after he died, sticking to the typical guitars-bass-keys-drums approach, and it's hard to argue with the stellar results they coaxed out of the Mick Taylor–graced lineup.

Yet maybe the single most important reason for this change in musical philosophies is that no guest player would have had the same sympathetic touch on the material as Jones displayed on a wide multitude of instruments not generally considered to be rock oriented. As Mick Jagger said in *The Bittersweet Symphony*, Rob Chapman's wonderful 1999 tribute article to Jones in *Mojo* magazine, "Brian was a sensitive person and that translated into his playing."[16]

And sensitivity was just what a track like "Lady Jane" needed to balance out the subtle acidity of the lyrics. Jones received able assistance on the song from Keith Richards's precise acoustic arpeggios and Jack Nitzsche's harpsichord part, which thickens the melodramatic air in the bridge. Yes, it feels like something that might have been conjured at the court of Henry VIII, but the melody dives into sadder territory that transcends eras.

Jagger need not have sung a word and "Lady Jane" would have been mesmerizing. Yet his posh enunciation and antiquated wordplay, exaggerated though they may be, go a long way to sustaining the feel. Those looking for some kind of historical connection between the names (Jane, Anne, Marie) of the three fair maidens who have dalliances with the narrator might be after the wrong prey, since it seems like Jagger chose them more for meter and rhyme than for any kind of significance. What matters is how his hero, or antihero might be more appropriate, interacts with these women.

In the first verse, he acts the humble suitor in his pursuit of Lady Jane, promising loyalty and coming off as the subordinate in the relationship: "Your servant am I and will humbly remain." Yet his loyalty only extends as far as what she knows about his activities, since the second verse makes clear that he's been carrying on with Anne as well.

Had the song ended there, he might have maintained a stitch of nobility, since he at least breaks it off with Anne to return to Jane. Yet the final verse shows him entreating a third fair lady named Marie, hinting that the only reason that Jane is his ultimate choice is because of her "station." "Life is secure with Lady Jane," he ends—ironic, since none of the women to whom he sings can feel the same security amid his fickle desires.

Taking into account all of his actions, it becomes clear that the elegant sorrow of the music truly belongs to these three women and not to the peripatetic paramour serenading them. Their hearts are the ones stroked so tenderly by Brian Jones on "Lady Jane," and he touches all of ours in the process.

67. "Hang Fire" (from *Tattoo You*, 1981)

The Rolling Stones have always shied away from overtly political material over the course of the band's long, illustrious career. One could make the argument that one of the reasons fans flock to the band's music is because they want a release from the pressures of the times. Hence the band's avoidance of stuff that's topical is actually a good thing to those people.

There has been the odd dip into the pool of issue-driven material over the years, such as "Sweet Black Angel," a breezy lament for an imprisoned civil rights activist on *Exile on Main St.*, or "Sweet Neo Con," a strident verbal assault on then-president George W. Bush that caused a bit of controversy when it was released on *A Bigger Bang* but was quickly forgotten because it's not effective enough as a song to merit much consternation. But, for the most part, the band tends to let any social commentary be subtext lurking between the lines yet subordinate to the more pressing concern of writing and playing good rock and roll. Maybe The Stones could have been like early Dylan or later Lennon and pitched their political concerns to a wider audience, but that's not where they chose to go with their music, and it's hard to argue with the results they've produced in their career.

You can locate some topical issues without looking too hard into the lyrics of "Hang Fire," the band's Top 20 US hit off *Tattoo You*. At the time the song was being worked up in the *Some Girls* sessions a few years earlier, England was suffering through financial problems that were worsened for the indigent by a removal of many financial safety nets. Many other artists would have tackled this topic by attacking the powers that be for allowing the country to deteriorate into such a mess or for their lack of effort on behalf of those less fortunate.

Instead, Mick Jagger settles into the role of one of those struggling folks and seems to suggest that there's no beating the system. So, instead of trying to work his fingers to the bone in an effort to pick himself up out of the doldrums, he essentially concedes defeat and lies back. The phrase "Hang Fire" is British slang for doing nothing, which is the course of action that this chap decides to take, industriousness be damned.

That might have been a rather depressing look at it had not the music provided such unmitigated pep. From his opening roll to the final crash, every snare shot by Charlie Watts provides another jolt of adrenaline. The electric guitars gurgle in the background while Bill Watts plays a pogoing bass and Ian Stewart boogies along on piano. In the instrumental break, Keith Richards lets loose a cackling solo that seems to mock all the problems lurking in the background of the lyrics.

Jagger's energy as a singer never flags here, even as the character he plays favors laziness. "In the sweet old country where I come from," he begins. "Nobody ever works, nothing ever gets done / We hang fire." That bit of nostalgia in the opening line for Olde England is quickly undercut by the reality. And this guy can't even be bothered to take the easy way out: "You know, marrying money is a full-time job / I don't need the aggravation, I'm a lazy slob."

The bridge lays out the situation as plain as day: "We've got nothing to eat, we've got nowhere to work / Nothing to drink, we just lost our shirts." Yet instead of railing at the politicians or the business owners, he advises indifference: "Say what the hell."

In the final verse, Jagger's voice rising as the band chugs alongside, the narrator exhibits a disdain for sensible economic practices: "Yeah, take a thousand dollars, go and have some fun / Put it all on at a hundred to one." Some may take this last lyric as a bit of a cheap shot at the working class, and many critics have pounced on the song over the years at what they perceive as the rich and pampered Stones having some fun at the expense of those in need.

Those who hear the song in that manner might interpret Jagger's playful falsetto "doo-doo-doo" refrains as an example of The Stones laughing while England starves. Yet "Hang Fire" isn't concerned about taking the proper side of the issue. It's simply an astute character sketch set amid the backdrop of economic turmoil, one enlivened by bracingly energetic music. And by taking this catchy, black-humor-laced approach, the band indirectly brought these issues to the masses listening to pop and rock radio, which seems to be a net positive in terms of the song's redeeming social and political value

66. "Live with Me" (from *Let It Bleed*, 1969)

Notable for being the first Rolling Stones session to include both new band guitarist Mick Taylor and saxophonist Bobby Keys, who would go on to contribute to many classic tracks over the next several years as the band's special guest, "Live with Me," from 1969's *Let It Bleed*, rips out of the speakers with vengeance and abandon. The band took the grittiness of "Jumpin' Jack Flash" and amped it up a few notches here, adding some appropriate squalor in the lyrics to really sweeten the deal, or sour it if you're not the daring type.

The first thing you hear is a funky bass run. Only it's not Bill Wyman doing the honors; it's Keith Richards. Richards's bass parts always tended to be a bit more showy and attention-grabbing than Wyman, which was in keeping with the personas that both men struck in the band. Whereas Wyman was usually content to fill in gaps and lock in with Charlie Watts's drumming to provide a steady, unassuming, yet still integral presence in songs, Richards, ever the iconoclast, tended to shake things up a bit. His work on bass here is essential, especially at the end as he starts spitting out notes that goad the music into a euphoric climax. All of his work on the instrument is even more impressive when you consider he also forms one half of the twin guitar attack with Taylor.

As Taylor became more comfortable within the confines of his new band in later years, he started to display some of the lyrical playing that would become his trademark of sorts. That lyricism could be overdone at times, however, and there is a lot to be said to the more visceral tactics he uses with Richards on "Live with Me," where the stabbing guitars form almost another source of percussion, joining in with Charlie Watts's double-timing drums to make a jolting combination that never allows the song to recede from your attention.

Keys is allowed to provide what melodic touches there are with his squawking solo, although even his part is played to make a guttural impact on listeners rather than to charm them or cast a spell. The 1970s hitmaker Leon Russell joins Nicky Hopkins on piano, and this pair, like all the rest, keeps things fast and dirty. Take it all together, and it's ruthless and unforgiving, forcing the listener onto a precarious ledge from which they won't want to be talked down, for fear that the thrills might stop.

Jagger's lyrics are hilariously honest about the kind of life awaiting a woman if she accepts the offer found in the song's title. There's a passel of grimy, homely kids locked away in a nursery. The staff engages in all kinds of inappropriate activities, which seem not just to be abided by the master of the house but encouraged. And don't forget the company that this guy keeps: "My best friend he shoots water rats and / Feeds them to his geese."

It's fair to compare this debauched household with The Rolling Stones as a sort of thrown-together family of misfits. Certainly the rat-shooting best friend sounds like a dead ringer for Richards, Jagger's partner in musical crime. It would take a brave soul to be willing to enter this wild, self-destructive scenario. Yet the music and Jagger's lean delivery make it seem like this homebound traveling circus is the absolute best place in the world a person could be.

"Live with Me" is one of those songs that helped to solidify the public view of The Rolling Stones as uncontrollable monsters at large. It was as if the band was taking the image formed by the conservative press and lapped up by the non-record-buying public, an image of them as wild men with no sense of decency or decorum, and broadening it rather than attempting to change it. Taking all the insanity and beyond-the-pale behavior that one might associate with a Stones tour and placing that in the context of a household was a brilliant stroke.

Jagger's final question reveals his true motives for wanting this woman to be a part of his happy, hedonistic home: "Don't you think there's a place for you / In between the sheets?" "Live with Me" is a ribald portrait of The Rolling Stones' version of domesticity, one that's likely to scare off the timid but prove irresistible to those thrill-seeking, death-defying wild men and women who'd take the boys up on their titular offer in a heartbeat.

65. "Fool to Cry" (from *Black and Blue*, 1976)

1976's *Black and Blue* found The Rolling Stones in between guitarists, since Mick Taylor had departed and Ronnie Wood wouldn't join full time until 1978's *Some Girls*. As a result, the band used the album to audition potential replacements. One way to get around the absence of a prominent figure on guitar was to put out a ballad as the album's lead single, which is what the band did with the surprisingly successful "Fool to Cry," a Top 10 hit on both sides of the pond.

The song itself is executed beautifully by the band and a couple special guests, so it's understandable that it was a chart fixture. Some might have thought it surprising that it should come from The Stones, who usually introduced an album to the world with a raucous blend of guitars and attitude as the lead single. Still, the No. 1 smash "Angie' from 1973 had demonstrated how the band had acquired the kind of elegant songcraft that can turn a soul-searching ballad into a major hit, and "Fool to Cry" follows in that tradition.

What was most surprising about it at the time was the subject matter, which, in the first verse at least, depicts a tender, honest moment between a hurting father and the loving daughter who attempts to lift up his spirits. That the members of The Stones had children was well known, of course, but that they would sing about the topic seemed to herald a newfound era of maturity for the band. It was a color they wore well, as ballads full of insight, tenderness, and beguiling vulnerability would become a steady part of the band's repertoire for years to come. "Fool to Cry" was one of the first in this long line.

Keyboards of all different stripes are the driving musical forces on the song. Mick Jagger starts things off with a soulful, unfussy series of chords on the electric piano. He's soon joined by Nicky Hopkins, who usually played piano for the band on their more contemplative numbers, because Ian Stewart preferred the ravers. Hopkins's free-flowing, intuitive counterpoint to Jagger's basic playing helps set the musical tone, and then he doubles his duties by playing the synth strings that sky above the earthier tones beneath them.

There are guitars on the song as well, played by Keith Richards and Wayne Perkins, who eventually lost out to Wood to join the band. They intertwine in the open spaces between the keyboards, while Bill Wyman and Charlie Watts keep the rhythm spare and light.

Instruments aside, this is Jagger's show, a chance to show off his soulful, pained side. He utilizes his affecting falsetto in the choruses, which, coupled with a shift into a minor key, makes them the bluesiest parts of the song. When you imagine those words ("Daddy, you're a fool to cry") coming out of the mouth of a young girl hoping to cheer her pop up, you've got a moment that's unafraid of its sentimental trappings.

As the narrative progresses, Jagger adds some extra touches like a woman "on the poor side of town," a line that recalls the Johnny Rivers oldie, and concerned friends. All send the same message, that this guy is foolishly wasting his time on tears. We tend to get caught up in the public personas of artists way too much, and, in some cases, it's hard for them to transcend those images. The Stones, whose collective image as affectless rebels and rabble-rousers was set in stone practically the first time they took a stage, have always possessed the talent to make whatever they are performing believable. They prove it beautifully here, with Jagger playing a guy just this short of depressed and selling it with aplomb.

"Fool to Cry" isn't afraid to spread its musical wings as the running time stretches out past the usual hit-single length. There's time for an extended coda, which takes its cue from the refrains and takes a turn for the downbeat and anguished after the cool and collected verses. The guitars of Perkins and Richards get their chances for a bit more commentary on the proceedings, while the synth strings of Hopkins turn from comforting to yearning. It's a nice touch that keeps the song from skewing maybe a tad too lightweight and somehow deepens the consequences of the events described.

In that closing section, Jagger really digs deep with his performance, improvising variations of the title and making this guy's pain palpable in the process. That turn in the final moments of "Fool to Cry" leads us to believe that there are some problems that even a daughter's love can't quite alleviate, a tough realization to make during an otherwise tender ballad.

64. "She's a Rainbow" (from *Their Satanic Majesties Request*, 1967)

Maybe *Their Satanic Majesties Request* was a folly, but it's a fascinating folly, one that left us with a few indispensable additions to The Rolling Stones' catalog. Chief among these is "She's a Rainbow," in which the band indulged in the happier, groovier side of psychedelia and emerged with something that even Sgt. Pepper himself would have saluted.

Like so many of the songs on that ill-fated album, the band threw about a thousand ideas at the wall in their efforts to construct "She's a Rainbow." Luckily in this case, there were a few sublime elements in place that held down the center so well that all the frippery on the periphery could serve as pretty window dressing instead of distracting ephemera.

In Nicky Hopkins's brilliant piano part, The Stones had a musical motif to which they could always return when things got a bit hairy. The way the delicate piano work segues over and over to the lush full-band sections provides a rush each and every time this transition is made. And the melody, whether it's being limberly played by Hopkins or earnestly sung by Mick Jagger, is sturdy and pretty enough to shake off all manner of strangeness going on around it.

Jagger's lyrics all seem to emanate from the single image of a captivatingly beautiful girl running a comb through her air. All of the sights and sounds that burst forth from this moment are captured in his glowing lyrics, full of vivid imagery and evocative similes. Maybe there's a double entendre to be found in the refrain's repeat of "She comes in colors everywhere," but "She's a Rainbow" seems to be chasing something more innocent than all that. It's a simple salute to the kind of beauty that enriches everything around it. "Have you seen a lady fairer?" Jagger asks over and over, and the combined efforts of his wordplay and the engaging music seem to both answer a resounding no.

Other highlights on the track include Brian Jones's subtle work on the mellotron, which conjures both the quivering stringlike noises that sit alongside Hopkins's piano and the regal horns that festoon the choruses. As for the actual strings, which veer from stately to strange as the song progresses, they were arranged by John Paul Jones, who in just a few years' time would go on to do some major work for one of The Stones' chief rock contemporaries and competitors, a band called Led Zeppelin.

With all of these excellent qualities, "She's a Rainbow" turns out to be more than strong enough to withstand a few of those aforementioned excesses. Jagger and Keith Richards, who also adds some energetically strummed acoustic guitar, sing the backing vocals like little kids skipping through the fields. There is a false ending or two to throw off the listener, and bongos appear for no good reason. And the song, so unabashed in its glorification of loveliness, ends not with a lilting fade-out but with a sort of strange, jarring crash.

Instead of detracting, these moments that must have seemed like absolutely brilliant ideas at the time just end up adding some crazy charm to the whole thing. Hey, it was the 1960s after all, the Summer of Love no less. That the song emerged as coherent as it did is a minor miracle, as evidenced by some of the less compelling material found elsewhere on *Their Satanic Majesties Request*.

"She's a Rainbow" also flies in the face of the misconception that all the music from that era is better enjoyed with a heavy helping of mind-altering substances. No one knows exactly what The Stones were up to or were on when they put this heady concoction together, but you need only have a set of ears to enjoy the delights on hand here.

Some critics have perceived the band's total immersion into this flowery flight of fancy as a way for them to satirize the peace-and-love vibes that were dominant at the time, but that seems unlikely. There are no arched eyebrows or tongues in cheek evident in the way the band throws itself into the song; any evidence of such would have torpedoed this feathery boat in an instant. The year 1967 was an era when just about everybody was feeling the love, even a band known for its dark side. "She's a Rainbow" shows that, in small spurts anyway, The Stones could rhapsodize in Technicolor as well as in shades of gray.

63. "Doom and Gloom" (from *Grrr!*, 2012)

The greatest of the greats in music, especially those with longevity, can tend to play havoc with your notion of common sense. Common sense dictates that artists who have been at it for a long time might tend to slow down in later releases or lose some of what made them special in the first place, age getting the best of them like it does with all of us. Yet the best of the best find a way to defy expectations even into the stages of their careers when most working folks have already retired.

When The Rolling Stones dropped "Doom and Gloom" on an unsuspecting world almost without notice in October 2012, one might have expected, without hearing it, a standard rehashing of the band's former glories. Timed as the release was to coincide with the fiftieth anniversary of The Stones' origins and tacked on as one of two new songs to yet another compilation of hits (*Grrr!*), such a reaction was understandable.

Then we heard "Doom and Gloom," and we found all our doubts vanishing in a maelstrom of blood-pumping rock and roll. The song was as vital and fierce as some of the band's best tracks and sounded as relevant and animated as anything from younger artists on rock radio at the time. A half century into their existence and The Stones sounded brand new again.

The song was primarily written by Mick Jagger, who even provided the stinging riff that kicks off the track. A thumping Charlie Watts beat is the motor, so much so that the verses pretty much keep all instruments out of the picture and let Jagger spit out his rap against nothing but the backbeat. That bit of starkness allows for the guitars of Ronnie Wood, who plays lead, and Keith Richards to create even more force and impact when they butt in for their cutting commentary. Don Was's production is spotless and yet maintains the band's inherent grittiness.

Here is another set of Jagger lyrics that makes unflinching reference to current events and issues debilitating mankind but refuses to take any sides. Jagger just lays out the facts of life in 2012: war, drought, famine, income inequality, environmental degradation, and the whole parade of ills that we sadly take for granted. While he tosses in some barbs here and there at the powers that be ("Lost all the treasure in an overseas war / It just goes to show you don't get what you pay for"), he rolls out this laundry list of horrors as if it's unavoidable.

Before he gets to the real-life problems, he first tells us about a bizarre dream. On a runaway plane full of crazed passengers, Jagger takes charge, crashes the plane in a "Louisiana swamp," and fends off a "horde of zombies." "What's it all about?" he asks. "Guess it just reflects my mood." The humor disarms the listener immediately.

The narrator carries his proactive attitude into the refrains, where he refuses to wallow in the muck and mire of this everyday hell. "All I hear is doom and gloom," he sings, which is somewhat comical, because he's doing a pretty good job himself of cataloging such bleakness. But there is some hope, or at least a way to combat this cavalcade of human suffering: "And through the night your face I see / And baby take a chance—baby won't you dance with me?"

This is a classic Stonesian sentiment, one that can be traced all the way back to "Jumpin' Jack Flash." Life is pain and torment, but you don't have to let it get you down. It may seem trite when simply spoken, but when rendered by this still-smoking band with a song that's brimming with hooks and as catchy as anything they'd done in more than twenty years, it makes all the sense in the world.

"Doom and Gloom" went from surprising people with its vibrancy and stimulating power to raising expectations for more of the same from the band. If they could do this, were there more like it in the pipeline? Maybe that long-awaited best album since *Tattoo You* was actually in the works after all and not just the product of hopeful music critics force-feeding the title on unworthy releases.

Well, two years (at the time of this writing) have passed since then, and, while the band is active and touring, still no new album. "Doom and Gloom" whet our appetites, but, knowing The Stones, the full meal will probably arrive when we've long since lost hope of it ever showing up.

62. "Loving Cup" (from *Exile on Main St.*, 1972)

"Loving Cup" had a long history in various recording studios on its way to its final destination as the closing song on disc 1 of *Exile on Main St.* in 1972. The Stones during that time period tended to have material lying around in different stages of readiness for recording, so reworking that material was a way for the band to spend their studio time and not get into too much trouble (although that plan didn't always work, as the band's various scrapes with the law around then can attest).

The song was first recorded during the sessions for *Let It Bleed* in 1969 and featured the angular twin guitars of Keith Richards and Mick Taylor, along with a herky-jerky beat not unlike "Honky Tonk Women" from around that same time. In that version, Nicky Hopkins's piano part takes a back seat after the intro, and, even though the tempo is a slow grind, this take, all hard edges, is firmly planted in the rock category.

After the song made its way through France and Los Angeles for the *Exile* sessions, it emerged as something less easily defined and far more intriguing. Hopkins's playing has more of a gospel lilt to it and is more prominent throughout the song, yet another of his brilliant turns with the band on their slower stuff. The electric guitars are largely absent (Taylor sits this version out completely), replaced for the most part by some acoustic guitar from Richards. The tempo kicks up a little bit, Charlie Watts providing a constant high-hat patter when he's not unleashing inventive fills to carry the band from one bar to the next.

The biggest deviation from the older version (which can be heard in the album of *Exile* outtakes released with the reissued, remastered album in 2010) comes via a brass section consisting of Bobby Keys on saxophone and Jim Price on trumpet. The pair provides a soulful fanfare in the middle eight and then takes the song home during a coda that takes a detour through the streets of New Orleans for a joyous parade.

With all of those elements in place, the many genres of music that are found all throughout *Exile*, such as gospel, rhythm and blues, country, even a little bit of jazz with the finishing horns, are distinguishable. Producer Jimmy Miller brings it all together seamlessly. Miller was unafraid of denseness in his productions, trusting that the overall thrust of the band members, so in tune to each other and the demands of the song, would propel the song in the right emotional direction without the need for much sonic separation between the instruments. That formula is repeated to magical effect time and again on *Exile*, and "Loving Cup" is one of the foremost examples.

Jagger plays the kind-hearted country bumpkin at the heart of the song with an exaggerated drawl and winning humility. The bucolic life is the one that he has chosen, even if it means that he's muddy and dirty all the time and can't afford a working automobile. Images of pristine hillsides and redemptive sunshine accompany him on his quest to win over a girl with flowers and sweet talk. Richards is along braying harmonies at his side just about all the way through the action.

Even though he's comfortable in his country life, the narrator's true bliss lies in the arms of this girl. "Give me a little drink from your loving cup," he belts. "Just one drink and I'll fall down drunk." Her love overwhelms him, yet he's willing to be toppled time and again. It's a sentiment that's totally apropos for the character Jagger charmingly plays here while receiving a huge assist from his band's loose-limbed chemistry.

You could even say that this yokel's desire for the cup is a stand-in for The Stones' fans yearning for the band's wonderful blend of music. One listen to this song, which shifts shapes several times yet always maintains momentum right toward the heart, can certainly have a tipsy effect. Maybe there are those who prefer the earlier version, especially if they also prefer the band at its toughest and most uncompromising. But these lyrics call for the tenderness and light-hearted nature that the players all bring to the table on the take that ends up on *Exile*. That's when the "Loving Cup" truly runneth over with the brilliance of The Stones at their genre-bending best.

61. "Undercover of the Night" (from *Undercover*, 1980)

In 1983, tensions were bubbling to the surface of The Rolling Stones' camp, and songs like "Undercover of the Night" were a big part of the reason why. On the one hand, there was Keith Richards, a staunch rock and blues traditionalist who would have been perfectly happy if the band never deviated from that rich vein of music. On the other, there was Mick Jagger, who was somewhat repulsed by the thought of stagnation and tended to restlessly push forward onto musical avenues that were flashy, trendy, and often a little out of the band's comfort zone.

Considering that those two men handled The Stones' songwriting duties, it's amazing that there weren't more big flare-ups over the years. Coupled with the personal animosity that had been brewing between the pair, the 1983 album *Undercover* really set things at a boil. Released right smack dab in the heart of the MTV era and all its production-heavy, danceable, glossy excess, the album featured the band striving for modernity over classicism, and Richards wasn't too pleased about it.

As he stated in his 2010 autobiography, *Life*, he feared that Jagger's quest for cultural relevance would come at the expense of music with more staying power. "Mick was chasing musical fashion," Richards wrote. "I had a lot of problems with him trying to second-guess the audience. This is what they're into this year. Yeah, what about next year, pal? You just become one of the crowd. And anyway, that's never the way we've worked."[17]

It's a point well taken, and much of the evidence on *Undercover* bears out Richards's fears. Many songs seem like they were written production first, which leads to a lot of bang and clatter but little resonance. Yet Jagger's efforts to modernize the band while still keeping their identity intact bore strikingly memorable fruit with the album's opening track and lead single, "Undercover of the Night." This song didn't sound like The Stones pandering to a new audience. It sounded like them showing this new audience they could not only keep up with the freshest sounds but also marry these sounds within a song that lingered in the imagination long after the buzz of the first few listens wore off, something a lot of other hits of that era couldn't claim.

Needless to say, Richards had very little input on the song, leaving Jagger to do the heavy lifting. Again, we have a case here of The Stones dipping their toes into the well of politicized songwriting without truly jumping in completely. Jagger lays out his tale of oppression, corruption, and persecution in South and Central America in a few broad strokes. Inspired by the William Burroughs novel *Cities of the Red Night*, Jagger doesn't concern himself with filling in all the details or sermonizing about these current events, instead simply conjuring a vibe that's equal parts alluring exoticism and creeping menace.

He's aided in this attempt by music that's completely simpatico with the tenor of the lyrics. Underpinning the song are the hip-swiveling rhythms of Robbie Shakespeare and Sly Dunbar, the Jamaican rhythm section whose list of credits in the worlds of rock, reggae, and rhythm and blues are simply staggering. That rhythmic nimbleness is contrasted by the serrated guitars and sledgehammer drums that attack the song's core from time to time.

As a result of these clashing elements, "Undercover of the Night" never allows you to get too comfortable. Whenever you start to groove to it, those drum and guitar effects will have you dodging as if you were watching a 3-D movie and someone was throwing knives directly into the camera. Ronnie Wood throws in a squalling guitar solo that sounds as if it's running for its life amid all the musical mayhem crashing down around it.

Jagger navigates it all with a delivery of heightened intensity and falsetto cries, as if he's dancing on hot coals. In the final verse, he screams out in helplessness at the dueling sensations: "The smell of sex, the smell of suicide / All these dream things I can't keep inside."

"Undercover of the Night" thunders along in the vein of an overstimulated reverie right until the final echoing guitar blast leaves you wondering if it's going to come back to haunt you yet again later in the evening. Personal taste will probably dictate whether you agree with Jagger or Richards on the debate between whether The Stones' forays into modern sounds represent a band bravely forging ahead or one trying too hard to stay relevant. There's no doubt, however, that Jagger, delivering a track with a lot on its mind and even more up its sleeve, won this round.

60. "Black Limousine" (from *Tattoo You*, 1981)

Back in the days when vinyl albums were still the major mode of music delivery and bands sequenced their songs with consideration for the sides of an LP, *Tattoo You* was constructed with two distinct sides in mind. The first side would represent The Rolling Stones at their rocking and raucous best, while the second would be comprised of tender ballads driven by lyrics and melody.

"Black Limousine" ended up on side 1, because musically it's a bluesy romp not altogether different from what might have appeared on one of The Stones' first few albums in the 1960s, before their pop and rock sensibilities took over. Yet in terms of its lyrics, it is far more akin to the reflection and melancholy that permeates those songs on side 2.

The song was begun in the sessions for *Some Girls* in 1978, attempted again a year later in the *Emotional Rescue* sessions, and then finally completed during the excavation and completion of old unfinished material that resulted in *Tattoo You* in 1981. Mick Jagger never thought too much of the song and barely squeezed it on the album, only to be surprised at the reception to it by Stones fans.

Maybe Mick thought of it as a simple blues, or maybe he was turned off by the fact that he had to cede a piece of the songwriting pie to Ronnie Wood, making it one of those rare Stones tracks that contain something different from the Jagger/Richards stamp. As Wood remembered in *According to The Rolling Stones*, he had to battle to get his name included, even though he came up with the main lick that serves as the musical impetus for the song: "I fought until I was blue in the face to get the credit, going on and on: 'I wrote that, I wrote that.'"[18] Of course, Wood admitted also that the lick was partially nicked from an obscure guitarist named Hop Wilson, so maybe he didn't have quite the righteous leg to stand on in his quest for credit.

In any case, The Stones, as they did in the old days, do a wonderful job of imbuing what could have been a standard blues with enough grit and personality to make it shine like brand new. Jagger's squawking harmonica is unkempt yet memorable. In the instrumental break, he and Wood muscle each other for attention for the first few bars before Wood takes over with an impassioned solo.

The song is also a throwback in a way to the thick productions of the *Exile on Main St.* era, with the instruments sort of thrashing about and weaving around each other. You get a flash of Ian Stewart's rhythmic piano here, a quick blast from Bill Wyman's bass there, and so on. Rendering these elements more crisply could have made the whole thing sound sterile; instead, it comes off as edge-of-your-seat lively.

In the midst of this rowdiness, Jagger manages to express a deep sense of regret and longing for a time now past. He does this by comparing and contrasting the high times that his narrator used to share with a former lover with their lousy lots in life in the present time. He goes into a little deeper detail about how hard and far she has fallen, saying that she's among the "living dead" and that she's "wrecked out now, washed up on the beach."

It's possible to read the key lines "Well now look at your face now, baby / Look at you and look at me" as a taunt, that he's lording over her the fact that he's doing fine and she's struggling as a kind of revenge, possibly because she left him long ago. Yet it seems more accurate to hear those lines as his admission that he's right down in the basement of life with her. That would make sense in context with his idealization of the past and their status as the limousine-riding, dressed-to-the-nines hoi polloi.

There's also the way he makes reference in the first verse to their "drinking and dancing all inside our crazy dream," which seems to imply that these better days were illusory and ephemeral. When he brings dreams back into the picture in the final verse, it's his way of illustrating how things have changed: "Those dreams are gone, baby, they're locked away and never seen."

The "Black Limousine" at the heart of the song is also a hint to this notion of deteriorating fates, considering that such a vehicle can signal opulence but also conveys the dead to their final resting place. It's just another reason why this one cuts far deeper than just your average blues throwback, thanks to its multifaceted, or, to use the parlance of vinyl, two-sided excellence.

59. "Sweet Virginia" (from *Exile on Main St.*, 1972)

The Rolling Stones sound gloriously inebriated on "Sweet Virginia," one of the myriad surprises that pops up on listening to *Exile on Main St.* Never had they appeared more overtly trashed on a record, barely did they even try to hide the references to drugs and drink in the lyrics, and yet somehow they come off sounding pure, innocent even.

By 1972, the counterwave to the psychedelic era of the late 1960s had pretty much swept through rock and roll, leaving the mainstream to the singer-songwriters and other purveyors of simpler sounds. Much of that began with Bob Dylan and The Band making their secret *Basement Tapes* in Woodstock, New York, in 1967 and 1968. Although it was still just a bootleg at the time of *Exile on Main St.* in 1972, that collection had left a profound impact on those who had heard it. Even The Beatles themselves had briefly tried to scale back with *Let It Be* after becoming enamored with what Dylan and The Band had been doing.

It's difficult to link The Stones' own realization about the diminishing returns of psychedelia in rock to Big Pink. They were a band who had always been roots oriented, although they lost their way a bit with *Their Satanic Majesties Request*. Their recommitment to earthier sounds may have come at around the same time those mysterious tapes started circulating, but it seems coincidental. It's more likely that The Stones only realized what they did best by struggling on something that didn't come naturally to them, not because Dylan was guiding their way.

Still, it's easy to hear "Sweet Virginia" as a kind of debauched second cousin to the *Basement Tapes* recordings. It has that same kind of back-porch vibe, albeit swathed in the haze that floated around Keith Richards's Nellcôte villa during the sessions for *Exile*. If you had only heard the intro, with Richards's tenderly strummed acoustic guitar accompanying Mick Jagger's dreamy harmonica solo, you could easily have imagined some of The Band's gospelized harmonies kicking in once the singing began.

Instead what you do hear on "Sweet Virginia" is Mick Jagger singing in a somewhat catatonic state, slurring through the verses as if his mouth is slow to pick up his brain's signals to sing. His first words are "Wading through the waste," not exactly the most idyllic imagery in the world. What follows is a catalog of every mind-numbing substance, connoted by grimy slang terms, that one might ever care to imbibe, inhale, or intake in some manner. This is not exactly what you would expect to hear at a sing-along with Grammy and Pappy.

With the "desert in his toenail" and the "speed inside my shoe," the narrator stumbles forth to call out to the titular girl, who is given a particularly homey name. (The Band even mentioned "Old Virginny" in their song "Rockin' Chair," although they were referring to the state and not a girl.) What he implores her to do is not to hold him tight or to sit with him by the fire (à la "Loving Cup" from *Exile*) but rather to "scrape the sh** right off your shoes." While manure wouldn't totally be out of place in this song, Jagger is actually referencing one of Richards's more colorful euphemisms for low-grade heroin.

In such a folky setting, a saxophone would usually have no place, yet Bobby Keys's lively romp through the middle section somehow works in the midst of this wildness. Meanwhile, the backing vocalists seem to come in whenever they feel like it as the group runs through the refrain a few times at song's end. It's absolutely anything goes on this back porch.

And yet the song is kept from skidding completely off the rails into shoddy musical territory by the work of Richards and Mick Taylor. Richards is the steady-as-it-goes rhythmic pulse for the track, while Taylor picks around at the edges with far more thoughtful commentary than one might think necessary on a song this disheveled, thereby classing up the joint a tad.

"Sweet Virginia" seems to be both paying homage to the kind of back-to-nature recording ethos of the times and gently taking the stuffing out of it at the same time. What ultimately matters is how The Rolling Stones prove that even when they sound slightly out of their minds, they can still perform at the top of their games.

58. "Winter" (from *Goats Head Soup*, 1973)

Sometimes an artist can be his own fiercest critic. Consider this quote from Mick Jagger as he looked back at the period following The Rolling Stones' incredible run of albums that began with 1968's back-to-basics triumph *Beggars Banquet* and ended with the 1972 double-LP masterpiece *Exile on Main St.* "I sort of remember the album *Exile on Main St.* being done . . . and after that going on tour and becoming complacent, and thinking, 'It's '72. F*** it. We've done it.' We still tried after that, but I don't think the results were ever that wonderful."[19]

Now, you have to remember that there are few artists more unsentimental about their past work than Mick Jagger, so that statement has to be understood in that context. The Stones did release work on albums like *Some Girls* and *Tattoo You* and with individual songs here and there that was, if not quite at that ridiculous level that they maintained from 1968 to 1972, at least as good or better than anything that their contemporaries in the rock world could manage. So Jagger's statement, while honorable in its candor, isn't entirely accurate.

But there is something to be said for the letdown that even the greatest rock and pop performers suffer after an incredible run such as that. It happened to Dylan, The Beatles, Bowie, and just about any artist you could care to name. In The Stones' case, the nature of the work essentially changed.

That incredible four-album run featured songs that were almost uniformly revelatory. After that, the sort of in-the-pocket brilliance of that span was replaced with a professional, polished product that often engaged and excited the audience but rarely surprised them. You pretty much knew following *Exile* that Stones albums would contain a mix of adrenalized rockers and silky ballads. When they deviated from that formula, as in the early 1980s, the results were uneven and often downright clunky.

"Winter" is a good place to explore this phenomenon. As it is a ballad featuring a string section but no contribution from Keith Richards, it is often compared to "Moonlight Mile" from *Sticky Fingers*, a song that contained those same characteristics. But "Moonlight Mile" is quirky, exotic, an elusive dream of a song that captivates in every moment of its existence. "Winter," from *Goats Head Soup*, is an excellent song; otherwise it wouldn't be this well placed on this list. But its charms are more tangible, less mysterious.

Jagger's narrator in the song has no use for the coldest time of the year, constantly shaking off the bitter air and the signposts of the season as he dreams of warmer times, times where love is in season instead of burned out. He even wishes he'd been there to see Christmas blackouts in California and Stone Canyon, the pretty lights of the season extinguished, his only hope of joy in such a dismal time.

Mick Taylor delivers fills that are expertly cribbed from Curtis Mayfield. He later gets an extended solo in the long coda that dovetails nicely with Jagger's improvised complaints toward the end, which are the first time he even mentions that a broken heart might be the cause of his seasonal blues. When he complains, "Sometimes I want to, but I can't afford you, baby," it adds a little bit of humor to an otherwise somber affair.

The strings come sweeping in with authority to add a little pomp to the sorrowful circumstance. "Winter" sustains that melancholy mood in a moving manner. And that's a wonderful accomplishment by the band, one that shouldn't be sullied in any way because it lacks the innovation or headiness of some of the group's dizziest high points.

Goats Head Soup can be viewed as the album where brilliance stopped coming so easy to The Stones. Idiosyncratic yet brilliant songs and off-kilter yet potent recordings of those songs no longer rolled off The Glimmer Twins' assembly line with the push of a button. Perhaps the most telling part of Jagger's above quote is where he says, "We still tried after that." On the previous albums, there seemed to be no trying at all, it all just happened.

Yet the band pressed on, relying on craft, talent, skills, and experience to get the job done. More often than not, the results were top notch. "Winter" shows that they could churn out the slow stuff with touch and heart to spare. Mick need not have been so critical, even if he had a bit of a point.

57. "Sittin' on a Fence" (from *Flowers*, 1967)

One of the characteristics of the finest artists in rock is that such artists often, throughout their histories, shelve songs for which other lesser mortals would trade their entire catalogs. The Stones were guilty of this on occasion, particularly with the musically lovely yet lyrically biting "Sittin' on a Fence."

The tour documentary *Charlie Is My Darling* shows the genesis of the song, as Keith Richards plays snippets of it on acoustic guitar in a hotel room while Mick Jagger offers his suggestions for the lyrics. The song was recorded during the sessions for *Aftermath* at the end of 1965, but the band held it back. Funny decision that, since the song would have fit seamlessly on that album of originals, which demonstrated the emerging songwriting prowess of Jagger/Richards.

Perhaps they shelved it because they knew they were going to offer it to others, in this case the obscure duo Twice As Much, who were also clients of Stones manager Andrew Loog Oldham and turned the song into a Top 40 UK hit as their debut single in 1966. The Stones version wouldn't emerge until the American cash-grab compilation *Flowers* in 1967 as one of two unreleased songs on the disc. It wouldn't appear on a UK album until 1969's *Through the Past, Darkly (Big Hits Vol. Two)*.

That's a lot of indifference toward such an outstanding effort, but songs can indeed fall through the cracks when you've got a bunch of great ones in the pipeline. "Sittin' on a Fence" emanated from that fascinating time in the band's career when, influenced by some of the modern sounds swirling around them in that wonderful time for music, they were starting to try on other genres and styles besides their standby blues. Even as they embraced prettier sounds and ornate arrangements, the acidity of their worldview often persisted in the lyrics, providing the ideal contrast.

"Sittin' on a Fence" is driven musically by a flittering Spanish guitar lead part. Alas, credits from that era differ depending on the source, so it's hard to praise the performer without knowing exactly who it is. It seems most likely that it's Brian Jones playing the Spanish guitar while Richards backs him up on acoustic rhythm. That would leave session wizard Jack Nitzsche on the harpsichord that appears out of nowhere on the final verse, a surprising element that nonetheless charms. Whoever deserves the praise, copious amounts of it should be delivered to them, because the interplay is mesmerizing.

Yet Jagger isn't about to match the beauty in the music with pillowy sentiments. He kicks off the first verse by admitting that he might not be the most reliable narrator: "Since I was young, I've been very hard to please / And I don't know wrong from right." That doesn't stop him from making a dig at womankind for the "sick things" they do to men. It seems like a cheap shot until he expands on his argument in subsequent verses. (All right, it's still a cheap shot even then, but at least there's more context for it by then.)

Jagger's real enemy in the song is marriage, or at least the kind of marriage that occurs because it's deemed the proper course of action by society and not because the couple really loves each other. "All my friends at school grew up and settled down," he sings. "And they mortgaged up their lives." Their reason for settling: boredom ("They just get married 'cause there's nothing else to do").

The narrator chooses to stay away from all that noise. The phrase "sittin' on a fence" usually connotes a kind of ambivalence or unwillingness to choose sides on an issue. Years later on "Mixed Emotions," Jagger would sing to a wavering companion, "Get off the fence now, it's creasin' your butt." But on this older track, it seems to suggest a refusal to jump into anything that's going to define the narrator or tie him down. The fence here represents that zone where all manner of societal expectations are shunned in favor of the freedom of nonconformity.

Considering it has no percussion outside some tambourine and possesses that oddly late introduction of the harpsichord, there's a possibility that The Stones' version of "Sittin' on a Fence" was merely a demo to be completed later, only they never got around to it. No matter though, because it's quite fine the way it is, a tasty blend of the tender and the tart.

56. "Memo from Turner" (from the *Performance* soundtrack, 1970)

This one may be a bit of a cheat to include on a countdown of The Rolling Stones' finest songs since it was initially released as the first ever solo recording by Mick Jagger, who performed the song in a bizarre sequence in the equally bizarre 1970 film *Performance*. Luckily there are enough connections to The Stones that it's not that much of a stretch to list it here.

Of the three versions of "Memo from Turner" in circulation, two were recorded in 1968 sometime around the time of the *Beggars Banquet* sessions. While it's debatable exactly who played with whom, the consensus is that some members of Traffic, including Steve Winwood, were involved, along with Al Kooper on guitar. One of these early takes was shelved but clearly served as a blueprint for the eventual single, while the other, a loose, sped-up, jammy take, eventually surfaced on *Metamorphosis*, a 1975 collection of outtakes that the band never wanted to see the light of day in the first place.

In 1970, Jagger either recorded a new version or sent an earlier vocal along to a top-notch lineup of session pros. Among those who were likely involved with this take, which would become the single and is the finest version of the song, included legendary piano man Randy Newman and Elvis Presley cohort Jerry Scheff on bass. What is not debatable is that Ry Cooder provides the signature slide guitar on the single, giving the track some true grit and just a touch of sadness that helps to ground Jagger's somewhat surreal lyrics.

In addition, the song is credited to the songwriting partnership of Mick Jagger and Keith Richards, even if Richards probably had nothing to do with its creation and only got the credit because of the contractual agreement between Jagger and him. Regardless of all of these confusing facts, there have probably been other songs considered to be a part of The Stones' catalog that have received even less input from the core members than "Memo from Turner," so it passes muster.

Besides, it needs to be a part of the band's recorded history because it's just a fabulous track. Say what you want about Jagger's sometimes actorly approach to his singing, but it's impossible to deny that he plays his role here with gusto and relish, easily piercing the façades of the supposedly respectable men he's addressing until they're figuratively stripped bare at the end of the song. (In the movie, they're literally stripped bare, but that's a whole other story.)

There's a little bit of "Sympathy for the Devil" in the lyrics in the way Jagger combines a polite form of address to his companions with barely contained menace in his words. The song also takes a cue from Bob Dylan's "Ballad of a Thin Man" with how it exposes the seedy underbellies of white-collar businessmen, men whom the chaste world believes to be pillars of society.

Instead Jagger reveals them to be deviants and murderers, men whose wealth and power cloak the lascivious urges and impulses that emanate from their true selves. Jagger seems to suggest that a comeuppance is coming for these men in time. There's some class warfare going on here as well as a generational battle and even some conflict between differing sexual preferences, and in every case, the narrator implies with glee, these "gentlemen" are doomed to be on the losing end.

"How forgetful I'm becoming," Jagger sings, yet the joke is that the narrator remembers everything these guys have done and he's somehow been there to see it all. He prefers his own kind of self-destruction to theirs: "You'll still be in the circus when I'm laughing / Laughing in my grave." And his final in-your-face rejoinder to these guys, "that you all work for me," seems to symbolize a shot across the bow of staid society and the secrets it can't quite keep. Even if it takes a little blackmail to get it done, the revolution will take place.

Mick Jagger wouldn't be credited again as the artist on a single until 1984 when he collaborated with the Jacksons on the overblown "State of Shock." If you believe that "Memo from Turner" belongs to him, you can say he started his solo career with a bang. Since the ethos, attitude, and sound of the record are heavily indebted to The Stones, you can just as easily put it in their scorecard. Either way, this is a track that needs to be recognized, which puts it in line with the message of the song's eloquently imposing protagonist.

55. "All about You" (from *Emotional Rescue*, 1980)

It's a somewhat accurate statement to say that the quality of Rolling Stones albums often falls when the level of discord between the band's two leaders at the time of recording rises. In other words, when Mick Jagger and Keith Richards aren't getting along, the work tends to suffer. That maxim doesn't quite hold for 1980's *Emotional Rescue*, which is somewhat underrated, getting the job done at a time when Jagger and Richards were clearly at odds.

While there might not be an abundance of classics on the album, it also doesn't have any clunkers, with the possible exception of the grating "Where the Boys Go." There's a really nice diversity of music throughout the disc, with stops for playful reggae, discofied funk, island balladry, danceable pop, and peppy rock.

The final track, "All about You," is pure soul, courtesy of Keith Richards. Jagger sits the track out, which is probably a good thing since the pointed complaints of the song seem to be aimed squarely at him. Richards had emerged from his late 1970s drug issues to find Jagger in complete control of the band. When Keith tried to reassert himself, friction inevitably ensued.

So while Richards at different times has claimed that this album-closer was about his tempestuous affair with Anita Pallenberg, which had finally run its course around the time *Emotional Rescue* was in production, or, we kid you not, a particularly flatulent Dalmatian, the preponderance of evidence suggests it's a dig at his fellow Glimmer Twin. In his autobiography, Richards partially confessed as much: "There's never one thing that a song's about, but in this case if it was about anything, it was probably more about Mick," he wrote. "There were certain barbs aimed that way. It was at that time I was deeply hurt."[20]

That sense of hurt is palpable throughout "All about You," and it's what makes it such a compelling track. Richards pours his all into the song, singing and playing not just guitar but also bass and piano on the finished recording. Charlie Watts does a subtle but brilliant job of drumming, providing a stuttering pace but also knowing when to lie back and let the wonderfully arranged harmonious voices of Richards and Ronnie Wood do the talking. Old Stones buddy Bobby Keys provides the drowsy saxophone parts that accentuates the after-hours vibe of the track.

Richards's vocals can be a taste that some folks never quite acquire, especially if they're into such technicalities as power or the ability to actually hit notes. Those who know better will tell you that the emotional transparency of Keith's singing is what makes it so special, and never has he sounded as nakedly vulnerable as he does here. Even when he's taking potshots at the person he's addressing, he can't quite laugh away the sting.

"Well if you call this a life," he begins. "Why must I spend mine with you?" It's a legitimate question, one of several that he asks, even though you get the feeling that the answers might only cause him more pain. At times he gets somewhat nasty in his assessment of the person in question, calling him (we'll go with the masculine from here on out since we're assuming it's Jagger) a jerk and a dog. But it feels more like the narrator is lashing out due to his own frustration rather than because these are his genuine feelings.

What he really wants is some sense of reciprocation of feelings from his former friend, but none are forthcoming. "Well I may miss you / But missing me just isn't you," he sings, a sneakily trenchant assessment. Even with all the resentment and hurt he feels, he can't imagine being away from this person: "Who'll tell me those lies / And let me think they're true?" The punch lines of the chorus serve a twin purpose, both revealing the identity of the accused and nailing him for his egoism. "And they weren't about me, they weren't about her," Richards sings, his voice touchingly cracking before he gets the support from the backing vocals for the kicker: "They were all about you."

The final line is an admission of dependency on the part of the narrator: "How come I'm still in love with you?" This song began a late-period Stones tradition of Richards getting in the last word on an album with a downhearted ballad. In this case, that final word just happens to come at the expense of Jagger, who's somehow more of a presence on this song in absentia than on some of the ones he sings on *Emotional Rescue*. Richards proves on "All about You" that there is a way for The Stones to get around the musical malaise that often sets in when his relationship with Jagger frays. He just writes about what that fraying does to him and comes up with a wonderful weeper.

54. "Play with Fire" (from *Out of Our Heads*, US version, 1965)

Those who might be unfamiliar with the story of The Rolling Stones and are perusing their early album credits might be wondering who this Nanker Phelge fellow is and what relationship he had developed with the band that he wrote so many of their early songs. Well, old Nanker happens to be a pseudonym that The Stones used when the song in question was composed by the band as a whole.

Most of the early songs that received this credit were little-known album cuts that didn't make much of an impression. Whether that was due to the nature of those collaborations or to the fact that Mick Jagger and Keith Richards didn't give up credit easily on the really good ones is a question that would probably get different answers from each of the band members. For example, Bill Wyman, one of The Stones who has never been shy about his accusations of credit-hogging by The Glimmer Twins, has contended that "Paint It Black" should have been given a Nanker Phelge credit.

In any case, of the songs that were actually credited to Nanker Phelge (Nanker being the band's name for the funny faces made by Brian Jones and Phelge the last name of a Stones acquaintance), "Play with Fire" stands out as the finest. The odd thing is that it seems clearly to have been a Jagger/Richards composition, especially considering that they were the only two official band members to play on the track.

According to the legend, a recording session one night in January 1965 dragged on into the wee hours of the morning, prompting Jones, Wyman, and Charlie Watts to fall asleep. Jagger and Richards, ever the troopers, stuck it out, along with the pretty impressive substituting duo of session man par excellence Jack Nitzsche on harpsichord and tam-tams and Phil Spector, the Wall of Sound master producer, on bass (actually a tuned-down electric guitar). Richards adds acoustic guitar, and Jagger provides the vocals and tambourines.

This ad hoc quartet produced a recording of dark, stark beauty. Richards's opening licks seem to herald something sweet and lush, à la "As Tears Go By," only to suddenly veer toward ominous territory as if a sudden eclipse of the sun had taken place. Nitzsche's harpsichord part does a lot of the rhythmic work, almost mechanical in its lockstep melody, allowing Richards and Spector to poke around with commentary in the gaps.

Jagger delivers a chilling vocal, demonstrating early on in the band's run that he could pull back when needed to modulate his performance in accordance with the material. In a 1995 interview with *Rolling Stone*, he looked back with wonder at his effort on the track. "Play with Fire sounds amazing—when I heard it last," he said. "I mean it's a very in-your-face kind of sound and very clearly done. You can hear all the vocal stuff on it."[21]

By "vocal stuff," Jagger means the way he sings the verses quietly, as if fearful of trampling on the delicacy of the musical backing. In the refrains, even without shouting, his singing intensifies and loudens with the threating lines "But don't play with me / Cause you're playing with fire." This was far from the tender, tame stance that was the wont for most pop stars in their pleas to the fairer sex. You can almost picture Jagger glaring as he delivers the chorus, practically daring a would-be game-player to step up and take her chances.

In the verses, the narrator stays out of it, instead detailing the comings and goings of a high-society girl and her mother. While the subtleties of the difference between Stepney and Knightsbridge might have been lost on audiences outside the United Kingdom, Jagger makes it clear through context that there is a definite demarcation between the social face that this family wants to display and the lowly places they'll go to get their kicks.

The Stones relished playing this role in the early days, the irreverent punks who could see through the thin façades of the supposedly respectable upper class, the same class who tended to harshly judge the band and its music. The band, thanks to that elusive Nanker Phelge character, certainly exacted a delicious bit of revenge on that upper crust with "Play with Fire."

53. "Following the River" (from *Exile on Main St.* bonus disc, 2010)

When The Rolling Stones reissued and remastered *Exile on Main St.* for a 2010 release thirty-eight years after the original double album dropped, they added a wonderful bonus for their fans: an extra disc containing ten songs. A few of these ten songs were alternate versions of classic songs that ended up on the finished album, but the majority were tracks that were begun in the rough time period of the *Exile* sessions by the band but never finished.

To finish up these tracks, the band had to return to the studio to add overdubs and polish everything up. The immediate question that arises is: How can men nearly four decades older get back into that head space and recreate the magic of *Exile*? In an interview with the BBC at the time of the reissue, Mick Jagger, the band's principal lyric writer and thus the man who should have been most bedeviled by this quandary, shrugged it off as just another problem that a musician has to solve in the course of his work.

"Of course it's totally different," Jagger said when asked about trying to write new lyrics for music written decades ago. "But you can put your head in a 'mood.' That's what any writing is like. You've got to be able to." He continued, "And so, with all this, you're playing a part. And in a way, I suppose, I was playing the part of myself in 1971."[22]

Jagger may have felt that he sunk back into that mindset well enough (and he did on another standout track from the reissue, "Plundered My Soul"), but the ballad "Following the River" certainly seems like the twenty-first-century version of Mick belting over the top of a 1970s piano piece by Nicky Hopkins. Not that there's anything wrong with that though, because the song turns out to be a compelling hybrid of two eras and just flat-out moving no matter whence its origin.

It's not that Jagger circa 2009, which is when he went into the studio to do the vocals for "Following the River," sounds markedly different than he did when the song was first composed. If anything, his vocals might be even stronger these days, so he has no problem delivering all the power and poignancy the gospel-flavored track requires. His outlook in the lyrics is where the divergence seems to take place.

Even on the slower numbers, there's a reticence to any sort of sentimentality on the songs on the original *Exile*. You can say that "Shine a Light" or "Loving Cup" are benevolent in their outlook, but there's still a kind of decay at the heart of those narratives. What Jagger delivers on "Following the River" is an exceedingly mature, heartfelt send-off to a lover. He holds no ill will toward her; if anything, he sees a time when he'll regret his decision.

Early on, the narrator hints that this girl doesn't deserve his indiscretions: "There's been some others in this room with me / We're really quite a crowd." So he sits her down and does his best to sugarcoat the blow, not because it's the easy way out for him, but because her devotion genuinely means a lot to him and, therefore, she warrants the gentle goodbye.

He also suggests that whatever's inside him that must cut loose of her will ultimately be his downfall. "I'll be lost," he sings about what will happen if she ever tries to locate him, but the line serves a double meaning, suggesting the emptiness of his ultimate destiny. In the chorus, he makes it clear why this breakup will eventually be much harder on him: "I'll be thinking about you all the time / Cause you always saw the best in me." It's a heartbreaking admission that he can't really live up to that finest version of himself, but the nobility in it makes him a far more sympathetic character than some of his debauched counterparts on the original *Exile*.

Hopkins's piano work is truly stirring here, balancing deftly between gospel uplift and downhearted balladry. Backing vocalists Lisa Fischer and Cindy Mizelle take things heavenward in the refrains, while the strings arranged by David Campbell add grandeur and sweep. Taken all together, it's somewhat in the mode of Elton John showstoppers like "Tiny Dancer" or "Levon," which might not be what one would expect of The Stones but is nothing to sneeze at either.

So maybe a little bit of a kinder, gentler Mick Jagger worked its way into "Following the River." Part 1971, part 2009, this song is timeless all the way.

52. "Bitch" (from *Sticky Fingers*, 1971)

Considering the title, if you'd never heard "Bitch" yet knew it was from The Rolling Stones, you might expect something deliberately provocative along the lines of "Some Girls" or "Star Star." Maybe the title does throw down the gauntlet a bit to anyone expecting the salacious side of the band to run amok, but this powder keg of a rocker from *Sticky Fingers* in 1971 provokes not with its lyrics or subject matter but rather with the relentlessness and potency of its groove.

Early attempts to record the song were going along sluggishly until Keith Richards stepped in and turbo-charged the tempo. The end result is a track that's tight but still sways, thundering along on the strength of its main riff, which gets a workout from guitarist Mick Taylor, bassist Bill Wyman, and horn players Jim Price and Bobby Keys.

The horns were in many ways a defining characteristic of *Sticky Fingers*, an album that saw The Stones, following up the twin-shot masterpieces of *Beggars Banquet* and *Let It Bleed*, operating at stratospherically confident levels. Much of that swagger comes from the horns, which here take a song that starts out as dirty rock and seamlessly convey it into the realm of the sweatiest soul and R&B workouts.

By essentially quadrupling down on the groove with practically every melodic instrument at their disposal, The Stones call into attention just how torrid it is. Charlie Watts's beat is a marvel of precision and pep, his snares snapping the music along. Richards gets to freelance on lead guitar, at first offering angular notes that jut off the edges before going on a frenzied run in the "Hey, hey, hey" finish. It's no surprise that "Bitch" fades out rather than just stops; a screeching halt might not have been possible with the momentum that the players achieve.

With such a distinctive thrust in place, it would have been easy for the band to simply mail in the words and call it a day. "Bitch" still would have been a winner in that instance, but Mick Jagger adds a set of lyrics that maintain the music's intensity without getting overly serious. With the sense of fun that the horns bring to the table, a come-down story might have been too jarring a contrast anyway.

So even though the narrator seems harried, his problems are what you might call uptown problems. This cat realizes that he's in love with a woman, but the torment he suffers when she's away tends to outweigh the bliss he feels in her presence. Jagger's off-kilter sense of humor shines through in the verses. For example, his bemoaning that even a horse-meat pie can't satisfy his hunger when she's not around references the old cliché "I could eat a horse" in comically oversized fashion.

Jagger also works in a reference to Pavlov's dog, presenting the listener with the striking image of Mick salivating whenever this temptress calls out his name. And when he calls out, "My heart is beating louder than a big bass drum," and Watts is thumping right alongside of him, it's a standout moment in a song full of high points.

In the chorus, Jagger lets us know that love is the bitch to whom he's referring, and while it's easy to make the leap to the more offensive connotation of the word when you hear it, it does seem like he wants it to mean that love is a hassle or a frustration. The preceding line ("Yeah, you got to mix it, child, you got to fix"), which conjures imagery of drug abuse, would seem to speak to the addictive quality of the kind of all-encompassing desire on display here.

This being The Stones, you can always take things down a bit more controversial path if you really wish to do so, but "Bitch" really doesn't seem to be purposely courting such infamy. This one just comes down to that groove, which sounds effortless in The Stones' capable hands yet is so distinctively thrilling that there's likely only one rock band who could have pulled it off.

51. "No Expectations" (from *Beggars Banquet*, 1968)

Context can sometimes rewrite a song unexpectedly. "No Expectations" was essentially a love-gone-wrong ballad using the blues idiom of a train leaving a station and expanding on that to hint at a more existential malaise suffered by the narrator. Yet the circumstances of the song's recording, coupled with what happened not too long after it appeared, turned it into a kind of swan song for Brian Jones.

Jones's connection to the band he helped to form was all but severed by the time The Stones sat down to record the songs that would become *Beggars Banquet* in 1968. His abuse of drugs and alcohol and his alienation from core members Jagger and Richards meant that his contributions to any one song tended to be minimal if there were any at all. Yet in "No Expectations," he seemed to connect to the loneliness of the lyrics and delivered an acoustic slide guitar part that both harkened back to his more productive times with the band and rendered the song fathoms deeper.

As Jagger remembered in a 1995 interview with *Rolling Stone*, the contribution was essentially the final significant one Jones would make to a Stones recording. "We were sitting around in a circle on the floor, sitting and playing, recording with open mikes," Jagger said. "That was the last time I remember Brian being totally involved in something that was really worth doing. He was there with everyone else. It's funny how you remember—but that was the last moment I remember him doing that, because he had just lost interest in everything."[23]

In June of 1969, about a year after "No Expectations" was recorded, Jones was informed by the other members of The Stones that they would be carrying on without him. Less than a month later, he was found dead in his swimming pool. So it's understandable that many fans latch onto this performance as Brian's touching goodbye, even if that's never what it was intended to be by any of the parties involved.

The real significance of the track, besides it being a truly outstanding song and wonderful recording, is that it was a new kind of slow song for the band. *Beggars Banquet* is often thought of as a return to basics for the band, but The Stones were actually breaking new ground in the way they were honoring their original influences. The up-tempo songs had more of a dangerous, serious edge to them than even their swampiest blues from the early days. And "No Expectations" demonstrated that the band could handle a ballad that didn't rely on a flowery melody or ornate production to get it across.

As opposed to melody-driven slow ones from The Stones' recent past, like "Ruby Tuesday" or "As Tears Go By," this is a song whose tune is somewhat nondescript, loping from verse to verse (without any real chorus) in straight-line fashion. And long gone are the violins or sitars or recorders that the band had used on some of their earlier changes of pace. "No Expectations" is as much about the open spaces in between the notes as what's actually being played. It's filled with desolate atmosphere, which makes sense on a song of such heartsickness.

Jagger sings the song without ever betraying how he feels about the words, almost stone-faced in his rendering of the sad lyrics. He instead lets Jones carry the emotional weight, and it's the right choice. Jones's slide work careens around almost to the point of sloppiness, but it hits home. The way he takes on the main melody, veering suddenly from the doldrums into a soaring sigh, sounds like someone who can't help reaching for the sky, even after he's been kicked to the dirt time and again.

Keith Richards provides the unassuming rhythm on acoustic guitar, Charlie Watts clicks along on claves, and Bill Wyman comes in now and again with a thump or two on the bass. Eventually Nicky Hopkins enters the fray with piano chords that are as stately and resigned as Jones's licks are unkempt and yearning. It's a mesmerizing contrast.

The lyrics, on paper anyway, are pretty basic stuff. Jagger gets off a couple evocative similes, such as "Our love is like our music / It's here and then it's gone." Mostly it's just a bereft guy heading out of town knowing he'll never be back again to reclaim his love. But what seems simple on the page becomes elementally sad in the midst of the sympathetic accompaniment.

The Stones practice the same type of hauntingly direct songcraft here that their blues idol Robert Johnson perfected so many years prior. "No Expectations" benefitted greatly from this change in the band's approach to balladry, even as it signaled the end of an era as pretty much the last song to feature the inimitable instrumental wizardry of Brian Jones.

50. "She Smiled Sweetly" (from *Between the Buttons*, 1967)

The reputation of The Rolling Stones' 1967 album *Between the Buttons* suffers a bit from middle child syndrome. It followed up the group's unmitigated triumph in *Aftermath* and preceded *Their Satanic Majesties Request*, which was a failure but a bold enough failure that it still fascinates folks. *Between the Buttons* was more or less a pop record, one without any huge hits on it, unless you count the US version, which was goosed by the inclusion of the mega-hit double-sided single "Let's Spend the Night Together"/"Ruby Tuesday."

On top of that, Mick Jagger constantly rips the album whenever he's asked about it in interviews, saying that he wasn't keen on Andrew Loog Oldham's production and that the songwriting wasn't up to snuff. If all that causes fans to overlook the album, they might overlook in turn some unheralded gems like the lovely and thoughtful "She Smiled Sweetly," which would be a shame.

This was the time period when the band, particularly the songwriting duo of Jagger and Keith Richards, was exploring its gentler side, usually on album cuts. What they found was that they could write melodies that were every bit as fetching as any of the top pop acts of the day, even The Beatles, their biggest rivals for chart success.

Where "She Smiled Sweetly" stands out among the other slower songs from The Stones of this period is in the way it delivers its tune. The Stones often turned to their resident jack-of-all-instruments Brian Jones to add some kind of flourish to these ballad-type songs, which was very much in keeping with the experimentalism that ruled the day in the mid-1960s pop world. Yet Jones sits this one out (as does Bill Wyman), and this unassuming track sticks to basic combo instruments: guitar, bass, piano, organ, and drums. And yet it still manages to beguile with its pretty music and sneakily effective lyrics.

Charlie Watts's shuffling beat deserves a lot of credit, as he manages to keep things light-footed even with a snare-heavy approach. Jagger's tambourine adds a little percussive color, while Richards handles every other instrument besides piano, which is played with quiet feeling by Jack Nitzsche. (It should be noted that Richards claimed in 2002, while The Stones were working on a live version of "She Smiled Sweetly," that he played piano on the track. A Jagger quote from 1967, the year the album was released, cites Nitzsche, so we're going with the recollection from closer to the actual event as the accurate one.)

On the surface, this song seems to be about a troubled young man who is constantly soothed by the calming nature of a girl. In that manner, it's not all that different from the *Black and Blue* ballad "Fool to Cry." Yet the gospel flavor of Richards's organ hints that there might be something more momentous at play in this seemingly simple track.

Jagger starts the narrative by asking, "Why do my thoughts loom so large on me?" That opening query immediately flies in the face of the common assumption by the establishment that The Stones had no thoughts in their heads at all. Regardless of that, the narrator finds comfort in the glory of the girl's smile and her command of "don't worry."

In the second verse, the narrator becomes mystified by the inner calm this girl possesses. "Where does she hide it inside of her?" he asks. "That keeps her peace most every day." When the bridge arrives, with Watts kicking up the intensity and Jagger singing with fervor, the girl is there with cosmic advice that the narrator takes to heart: "There's nothing in why or when / You're here, begin again."

Suddenly it becomes apparent that this girl might be more than just the average person who lives down the street. "I understood for once in my life," Jagger sings in the final verse. "And feeling good most all of the time." He sees the light, because this is no mere romantic attraction. He has been touched by something beyond his earthy concerns, beyond even reason. The only thing you can call it is faith, a notion seconded by Richards's churchly organ accompaniment.

It's probably a stretch to assign any specific religious significance to the song, since it never gets overt enough about its otherworldliness to warrant that. It could even just be the songwriting wish fulfillment of rock stars under pressure. But it's hard to deny that there's a greater power lurking above "She Smiled Sweetly," and it's not just the power of The Stones to charm with their soothing softness.

49. "Stray Cat Blues" (from *Beggars Banquet*, 1968)

Some folks will probably never get past the subject matter of "Stray Cat Blues." While other pop and rock stars of the 1960s era tended to couch libidinous urges and sexual tawdriness in innuendo or winking asides, The Stones came right out and articulated it without any filter on this song. So those who judge a song based on the morality of its content probably won't abide it.

The Stones were following up in the blues tradition of broaching lustful topics that generally weren't considered proper for public discussion. What pushes "Stray Cat Blues" even further toward the borderline of musical decorum is the fact that the narrator is lusting after a girl who is just fifteen years old.

Still, the nature of art allows us to inspect even the most untoward behavior even if we might be repulsed by the actual practicing of it in real life. That The Stones go after this song with unapologetic gusto only challenges us more. If "Stray Cat Blues" crosses the line for you, you can move on to the next song in the list. If not, what you'll discover is one of the band's most powerful blues efforts ever.

Remember that *Beggars Banquet* was an album that saw The Stones going back to the roots music that first enthralled them but doing so with far more edge than their original efforts in 1964 and 1965. In those early years, they weren't doing much more than an expert imitation of the music they loved. By the time 1968 rolled around, they had imbibed all of those influences but were now filtering them through the unique experiences they had amassed as world-conquering rock stars. They emerged with a perspective on the material that was fresh and dangerous, making even the most well-worn sounds seem vibrant and novel.

It also seems to be no coincidence than the band's run of success with this type of material began in conjunction with their hiring of Jimmy Miller to be the band's producer. Miller, a musician himself, had a knack for meshing sounds together into a kind of thick stew. Even the vocals, which in pop music were always at front and center, were treated like just another instrument and were mixed accordingly. The overall effect was what mattered, and on songs like "Stray Cat Blues," that effect was bracing.

The flickering guitar opening was borrowed from the Velvet Underground's "Heroin," and although Lou Reed's band probably would have approved of the taboo topic, The Stones' path quickly diverges from there. After all, the Velvet's bottom end never swung as recklessly as what Bill Wyman and Charlie Watts pull off here. Nicky Hopkins joins in with a piano part that's so ominous it practically stalks the main melody instead of mimicking it.

Jagger has played the lothario role many times in song, but rarely with as much openly lewd intent as he manages here. In the verses, he sings in his lowest register, sounding almost sinister, before exploding for joyous shouts in the refrains. If you're going to go down this avenue, you've got to commit to it, and Jagger certainly goes after it with abandon.

For a good part of the song, there's no indication that the girl is even privy to the narrator's come-ons, since he's upstairs lurking about and she's just going on her way. Only in the final verse does she seem to acquiesce, promising to bring along a friend to ratchet up the depravity. And how does this degenerate justify his actions and attempt to convince this girl in the same breath? By shrugging off just how wrong the consummation of this flirtation would be: "It's no hanging matter / It's no capital crime."

Jagger uses animal terms to distinguish what's going on here from the civilized actions of normal humans, comparing the narrator to a bear and the girl to a "strange, stray cat." Yet that's as close to judgment as he comes. As the song progresses, the narrator practically begs to be caught:

"I bet your mama don't know you can bite like that / I bet she never saw you scratch my back."

In those final lines, the narrator seems to be warning uptight society that there are more like him ready to tarnish innocence in order to satisfy their desires. As the band plays a furious, conga-laden jam to the finish, the unease of those words still hangs in the air. "Stray Cat Blues" doesn't shy away from the nastiness, an adult kind of nastiness that's far more deviant than the bad-boy posturing of some of the group's earlier songs. You can shy away from that nastiness, or you can confront it and hear a thrillingly fearless piece of music in the process.

48. "I Got the Blues" (from *Sticky Fingers*, 1971)

The Stones left practically no genre of music unexplored on *Sticky Fingers* in 1971, and they showed that they had mastered just about all of them. There was sad country ("Wild Horses"), rambling country ("Dead Flowers"), grooving rock ("Bitch"), boogie rock ("Brown Sugar"), and, maybe regrettably, jam rock ("Can't You Hear Me Knocking") and, of course, the blues ("You Gotta Move.") These were not mere homages. This was a band so fluent in the respective styles and yet so confident in their own musical personality that their identity shined through the material even as they displayed stunning versatility.

Soul music, particularly the kind of heart-wrenching, sweaty ballads perfected by the likes of Otis Redding, was another genre that captivated the group as young men. On *Sticky Fingers*, they pay their respects with the gorgeously woebegone "I Got the Blues," featuring a lusciously sad horn-filled arrangement and a tour de force effort from Mick Jagger.

The shimmering guitars of Mick Taylor and Keith Richards are the first thing you hear, one playing slow-motion arpeggios and the other winding around those notes like a vine. It doesn't really matter who of them is doing what, because they are one in this performance. Bill Wyman and Charlie Watts are minimalists here, just making sure the song gets from point to point and staying clear of the horns of Jim Price and Bobby Keys. It has been noted throughout this book how much the horns added to *Sticky Fingers*, but it's also worth mentioning that Price and Keys proved nimble enough to find their footing in whatever stylistic scenario the band threw at them.

Here they, like the guitarists, are in unison, harmonizing their parts and adding just the right balance between resigned sighs and anguished bleats on their horns. Billy Preston delivers the knockout blow with an organ solo that doesn't hold anything back, which is okay, because the band clears the space for this showcase. Preston's peripatetic career path took him to stops with the two leading lights of the British Invasion. His work with the Beatles on the *Let It Be* project was colorful embellishment, but The Stones tended to give him a lot more leeway. What he brings to "I Got the Blues" is essential.

That leaves Jagger. He wisely discards his larger-than-life Mick Jagger persona here. That persona certainly serves its purpose for some of the band's more attitude-driven numbers, but it wouldn't have delivered here. He simply sings "I Got the Blues" from the heart, and it's one of his most on-point efforts, hitting all the devastating lows and yearning highs without fail.

We meet the narrator pining away for the woman who left him behind, for reasons to which we're not initially privy. Even as Jagger modulates his way into the bridge, his narrator still earns nothing but our sympathy, as he prays that his former love will be happy with whomever she finds in the future. But his wish that she find a guy "who won't drag you down with abuse" implies, without saying, that he was less than kind to her when they were together. Jagger sounds positively bereft as he barely manages to spit these words out.

In the final verse, Jagger waxes philosophical, a strategy that is usually the last resort of the desperate. "In the silk sheet of time, I will find peace of mind," he sings. But his next line is a more direct shot to the heart: "Love is a bed full of blues." Whether Jagger came up with it himself or found it in some old blues song, that line is as evocative as it gets.

The final moments of the song once again honor the soul-man tradition. Jagger improvises his way through a series of laments, the horns bringing him to a seeming conclusion at the end of each line, only to rev it up and do it all again with Watts clearing a path. It's reminiscent of the way that James Brown, yet another soul legend who made a significant impact on Jagger, would start to leave the stage only to shake off his handlers and rush back to the mike to utter a few more pained words. Even after doing it multiple times, this gambit by the band is so successful that no one would have minded if it had gone on indefinitely.

The Stones, like all great purveyors of soul, know just when to leave us wanting more. "I Got the Blues" transcends tribute to become a performance to which tribute is owed.

47. "Back Street Girl" (from *Between the Buttons*, 1967)

We're back once again on the unheralded *Between the Buttons* LP with another Stones ballad that balances sweet music with sour sentiment. "Back Street Girl" dares the listener to decide which of those extremes actually wins the day, whether you're supposed to believe that The Stones are condoning or bemoaning the behavior described in the song.

Too many folks write this period in the band's career off. Histories of The Stones often make it seem that they leapt right from "(I Can't Get No) Satisfaction" to *Beggars Banquet*. The interim includes some of the band's most reflective character studies and heartfelt laments. Maybe they weren't breaking new ground, The Beatles always one step ahead of them (and everybody else for that matter), in terms of pop mastery. But Mick Jagger and Keith Richards were proving they could hang with the best songwriters, even Lennon and McCartney, while doing so on their own irreverent, noncompliant terms.

Whenever they would do one of these ultramelodic numbers, they would turn to their instrumental secret weapon, Brian Jones, for some sort of idiosyncratic contribution. On "Back Street Girl," Jones plays the vibraphone, just a couple sad notes here and there that sound like stray teardrops splashing from the downturned eyes of the spurned girl of the title. One thing about Jones is that he never played these turns in a showy manner, preferring to support the emotional tenor of the song with whatever might have been needed.

In this case, the accordion part played by guest Nick DeCaro is actually the most prominent instrumental part. He gives the song the melancholy flair of a French chanson. Richards's acoustic guitar part is extremely tender, all the better to confuse audiences when the sting of the lyrics unexpectedly arrives.

It might be jarring to hear such callous lyrics being sung against such a lilting melody, almost lullaby-like in its gentleness, were it not The Stones and Mick Jagger doing the singing. Stones fans have almost been conditioned to expect as much from Jagger, almost to the point where it can skew the meaning in unexpected ways. It's hard to give him the benefit of the doubt that he might be using the music to actually betray something deeper roiling inside him than the heartlessness he displays on the surface of the lyrics.

That's why sometimes a cover of a song can be informative. Bobby Darin, the legendary crooner who crossed over deftly in the beginning of the rock-and-roll era, released his version of "Back Street Girl" not too long after it appeared on *Between the Buttons* in England in 1967. Darin caresses that song in the special way that he had, and the narrator suddenly sounds strikingly sympathetic, even when he's serenading her with lines like "You're rather common and coarse anyway."

When you hear the song that way and then go back and listen again to The Stones' version, Jagger's character doesn't sound so bad either. As a matter of fact, Mick spills a lot of emotion as he delivers the lines, at least once your ears are open to hearing it. What emerges from the song then is his façade of hardness and obstinacy crumbling in the face of a girl who has genuinely touched his heart.

The heartbreak in the song comes from the fact that he can do nothing about it. When he sings, "Please don't you bother my wife," it becomes clear that his marriage, which can't be on very romantic ground considering that he messed around with the girl in the first place, is a stabilizing force in his life, something that he couldn't forgo even if he wanted.

Hence, he puts on his meanest airs in an effort to scare her out of loving him. Maybe he's looking for her to leave because he doesn't really have the strength to set her free, tough words notwithstanding. The music tempers any of the lyrics' lingering harshness. This isn't "Stupid Girl," which doubles down on its insults with taunting rock and roll. The accordion and the vibraphone and the tumbling melody here are the aural equivalent of a giant pillow attempting to break a violent fall.

"Please take the favors I grant," Jagger sings at the end of the song. "Curtsy and smile nonchalant just for me." Even though the chorus suggests that he can maintain a clandestine affair with "Back Street Girl," there is the sense that this arrangement won't satisfy either party; it sounds like it's all or nothing. Take a close listen to this quiet beauty, and you're likely to hear an anguished adieu rather than a flippant farewell.

46. "Honky Tonk Women" (from *Through the Past, Darkly [Big Hits Vol. 2]*, 1969)

"Honky Tonk Women" became one of The Rolling Stones' biggest hits on its release in 1969. One of the last Stones songs to be released as a stand-alone single and not be included on a studio album, it was a smash practically everywhere it was issued and shot to No. 1 in the United Kingdom and United States. That's not bad at all for a song that came about as a lark when Mick Jagger and Keith Richards were pretending to be cowboys while taking a holiday on a Brazilian ranch.

What Jagger and Richards created back on that South American jaunt was something a little bit closer to the song "Country Honk." That acoustic track, embellished by Byron Berline's fiddle, was a nice, unassuming piece of country-tinged filler on the band's 1969 album release, *Let It Bleed*, which came out a few months after the "Honky Tonk Women" single.

The Stones' approach to country material was very often tongue-in-cheek, sometimes too much so. That kind of gentle mocking can come off as condescending to the material when pushed a bit too far. "Country Honk" doesn't go quite so wayward down that road, but there's a distance between the players (especially Jagger) and the material that keeps it from truly reaching its peak.

"Honky Tonk Women," the song that would emerge from "Country Honk" once newly minted Stone Mick Taylor started messing with it in the studio, doesn't suffer from those problems, because the band manages to put a distinctive stamp on it that separates it from any single genre. Although you can still hear some of country echoes in the song, mainly in Jagger's exaggerated accent, it also encompasses plenty of barroom boogie and rhythm and blues, the former provided by Ian Stewart on piano, the latter by saxophonists Steve Gregory and Bud Beadle.

In addition to all that, there are still plenty of hard rock edges jutting about this fascinating arrangement. Richards and Taylor take turns stabbing at each other with their instruments before joining up every once and a while in if-you-can't-beat-'em, join-'em harmony. This interplay is accentuated by the decision to leave Bill Wyman's bass out of the verses, a tactic that allows every note and chord of the two guitarists to really make a mark.

There's also something interesting going on with the percussionists. Charlie Watts explained in *According to The Rolling Stones* how the odd intro that he and producer Jimmy Miller on cowbell contrived was an unrepeatable piece of studio magic. "We've never played an intro to 'Honky Tonk Women' live the way it is on the record," Watts remembered. "That's Jimmy playing the cowbell and either he comes in wrong or I come in wrong—but Keith comes in right, which makes the whole thing right. It's one of those things that musicologists could sit around analyzing for years. It's actually a mistake, but from my point of view, it works."[24]

The relative starkness of the verses also comes in handy when the whole band, horns and all, kick in for the choruses. It's not quite soft-to-loud, since those guitars certainly make their presence felt early and often; it's the contrast of the music's open spaces in those verses against the rich, full propulsion of the refrains that does the trick here, especially when the female backing vocalists and Richards come in howling over the top of Jagger on the refrain.

You could go on and on about the seemingly limitless nooks and crannies hidden in the one-of-a-kind music of "Honky Tonk Women." That's a good thing, because the lyrics are somewhat of an afterthought here. It almost goes without saying that there are somewhat tawdry references to women and drugs that the band would never quite outgrow, but there's nothing in the words that's too revelatory. It does indeed sound like the work of two urbanites trying to play cowboys for a bit only to get pulled back by their urges out of the prairie.

In fact, one of the reasons that "Country Honk," which is essentially the same song albeit in a vastly different arrangement, doesn't work as well is because the music is so tame that you almost have to pay attention to the words. By contrast, the inventive and vibrant music of "Honky Tonk Women" invites you to shout those words out without once giving thought to their meaning. Sometimes that's all you need in a single, and this doozy is one of the most instantly unforgettable ones The Stones have ever delivered.

45. "Ventilator Blues" (from *Exile on Main St.*, 1972)

The story goes that the basement where The Rolling Stones recorded much of their 1972 double album *Exile on Main St.* wasn't exactly brimming with fresh air. When you consider the state of the musicians who inhabited that dank basement for hours on end and the different methods they used of propping themselves up to play, such as booze, pills, and hard drugs, one could get asphyxiated just imagining the stench emanating from that place.

Hence it was only natural that a song called "Ventilator Blues" should have emerged from those sessions held in the bowels of Nellcôte. The Stones may have stumbled onto the metaphor because it was anything but a metaphor for them at the time, but the line "Everybody's going to need a ventilator" turns out to be a pretty resonant koan for anybody living through suffocating times.

There are many songs where The Stones affect a menacing vibe. "Ventilator Blues" is one where they seem to be the menaced ones. Mick Jagger seems to force out his vocals while being choked. The instrumentalists move along at a measured pace as if afraid their next step will trigger the trap door lurking constantly beneath them. The claustrophobia that the band must have felt in those environs is evident in every single moment of the song.

You probably have to credit some of that to Nellcôte itself, which exerted its haunting influence on the track. The band hasn't performed it live since shortly after its release, perhaps because they knew that the setting produced lightning in a very stuffy bottle. "We always rehearse 'Ventilator Blues,'" Charlie Watts mentioned in 2003. "It's a great track, but we never play it as well as the original."[25]

"Ventilator Blues" is also unique in that Mick Taylor gets a songwriting credit along with Jagger and Keith Richards, the only one he would ever receive in his time with the band. Oddly enough, Taylor doesn't make much of an impact on the song until his lyrical soloing toward the end. Richards is responsible for the odd riff, reminiscent of a rusty old lawnmower being yanked into action, that kicks off the song and staggers intermittently throughout it.

Charlie Watts plays a start-and-stop beat that nudges the song forward with some trepidation. Nicky Hopkins starts out on the low end of the keyboard before switching to some screeching high notes as the song progresses. Bill Wyman's bottom end scrapes the center of the earth, while the horns of Bobby Keys and Jim Price don't get a chance to celebrate here, instead harmonizing in insinuatingly low tones.

There have already been several mentions about the production work of Jimmy Miller and its role in the high-water mark of The Stones' career from 1968 to 1972. His efforts in pulling everything together on "Ventilator Blues" are particularly noteworthy. Not only is Jagger, in all his double-tracked agony, buried in the mix at times, but even Taylor's solo, which would have been a typical money shot in most rock songs, stays below the fray. Miller's intent here is to keep everything beneath the surface, almost struggling to be heard. The song doesn't even get a proper fade-out, instead suddenly blurring into the mysterious "I Just Want To See His Face." These risky techniques provide the song with oodles of ominous atmosphere.

Jagger is on top of his game as a lyricist with lines that expertly convey creeping dread. Spines crack, hands shake, and butts break. Just don't expect any mercy: "Ain't nobody slowing down no way / Everybody's stepping on their accelerator." What's worse is that he implies that this kind of horribly fetid destination in life could have been avoided if his narrator knew a little better: "Ain't going to ever learn."

"Everybody's trying to step on their Creator," Jagger sings, a piercing image of heartlessness that a timid soul couldn't hope to withstand. But The Stones are anything but timid, and the defiance that rises in the song's closing moments offers a sliver of light into this unmitigated parade of darkness. "What you going to do about it?" the narrator asks, before immediately providing the answer: "Gonna fight it."

Jagger repeats that mantra as the song goes its less-than-merry way toward its sudden conclusion. That bit of cathartic spunk keeps "Ventilator Blues" from being unrelentingly bleak. Still, the threatening music seems to say, "You might have the guts to fight it, but it doesn't mean you'll win."

44. "Dandelion" (from *Through the Past, Darkly [Big Hits Vol. 2]*, 1969)

When The Rolling Stones released *Their Satanic Majesties Request* in 1967, it was largely seen as a disappointing effort by the band to latch onto the flower-power psychedelia that was sweeping the rock world at that time, a style of music epitomized by The Beatles' triumphant *Sgt. Pepper's Lonely Hearts Club Band*. Truth be told, it wasn't the style of music that hampered the band at that time, since they executed it well enough, even if it was hard to reconcile the peace-and-love vibes with the band's rabble-rousing public image, and even if they lacked a George Martin—type producer at the time to harness all the wild-flung, drug-fueled energy.

What hurt that album was a dearth of memorable songs. With the exception of "She's a Rainbow" or "2,000 Light Years from Home," there were no songs on *Request* that were memorable beyond the exotic approach to recording them. The Stones could have rectified this problem somewhat and improved the album exponentially by including both sides of the single that they released in the summer of 1967, a few months before the LP's release.

The A-side, "We Love You," seemed to both embrace the beads-and-flowers generation and satirize it, all while doing so with a mind-bending arrangement that featured trippy instrumental flourishes from Brain Jones and skewed far more spooky than summery. The B-side was even better: the gorgeously yearning "Dandelion," which seemed to suggest that the positivity and good vibes that hung so lightly in the air at that time seemed destined to blow away in the wind like the petals of a delicate flower.

"Dandelion" manages to marry the melodic wistfulness of the era with some solid rock thrust. The latter likely occurred because the song, as originally conceived by Keith Richards, began life as a Searchers-like riff rocker tentatively titled "Sometimes Happy, Sometimes Blue." By the time The Stones polished it off, the forward momentum was already in place, delivered by the burbling bass of Bill Wyman and the rumbling toms and snapping snares of Charlie Watts. The group embellished on that foundation with the help of Nicky Hopkins, who plays the tickling harpsichord part that accompanies Jagger as he hop-scotches through the verses.

The cosmic harmonies that float through the song's ether provide even more sustenance for a hungry listener. Although they couldn't be credited, it seems likely that John Lennon and Paul McCartney joined in with Richards and Jagger to provide backing. The Beatles and Stones were always friendly rivals, and it makes sense that John and Paul would be pitch in on this, the most Beatlesque of Stones songs. Brian Jones, who once played the sax on a Fab Four song (the oddity "You Know My Name, Look Up My Number"), uses the instrument here to give the bridge a further melodic boost, as if it needed one.

The lyrics touch on the child's game of picking off a dandelion's petals as a way of making a choice between several alternatives. Jagger's words, when combined with the pretty melody and the lilt of the harpsichord, do a wonderful job of evoking that kind of childlike innocence and wonder. The singer even sounds like he's bounding skyward with each line.

Those good feelings are somewhat held in abeyance in the refrains though, as the melody takes a turn for the serious. The stakes seem raised, as if the choices now have real-life consequences. It's symbolic of the shift from childhood to adulthood, and it renders this song a bit weightier than your average love-promoting lullaby. "Dandelion don't tell no lies," Jagger sings, the implication being that the grown-ups do. "Dandelion will make you wise," he goes on, as if to say that the grown-ups are too busy trampling on the things in some mad, futile pursuit to notice their sage advice.

These intricacies are brought out in the music, which creates a bittersweet undertow attempting to pull the listener out of youthful reveries of romping in fields, when life's choices were indeed simple enough to be picked from a flower. With "Dandelion," The Stones prove they could do the whole Day-Glo pop thing as well as anybody, even as they maintain some latent skepticism that the trippy tenor of the times would lead to anything but their beloved blues.

43. "19th Nervous Breakdown" (from *Big Hits [High Tide and Green Grass]*, 1966)

The Beatles famously took several of Ringo Starr's offhand comments and turned them into song titles for hits like "A Hard Day's Night" and "Tomorrow Never Knows." The Rolling Stones followed suit with "19th Nervous Breakdown," which borrowed a phrase that Mick Jagger uttered during a particularly stressful time in the band's brutally busy schedule.

Released at the start of 1966 as a stand-alone single, "19th Nervous Breakdown" proved to be another smash hit for The Stones, hitting No. 1 in the United Kingdom and just missing, at No. 2, in the United States. Many of the kids listening might have only heard the jumpy guitars and catchy refrain and not given a second thought to the song's meaning. This was an early effort by the band to add a little social commentary to their rock, something that was still relatively rare at the time in that idiom.

While The Beatles had begun to branch out in this rough time period into character sketches both vague ("Nowhere Man") and specific ("Eleanor Rigby"), those characters weren't necessarily intended to represent a larger strata of society, unless you count lonely people as some kind of unified group. Other bands at the time were still sticking mostly to the topic of young love in all its permutations. Among The Stones' British Invasion contemporaries, perhaps only The Kinks were aggressively taking aim at the bigger picture with songs like "Well Respected Man" and "A Dedicated Follower of Fashion," sneaking Ray Davies's wry cultural observations through to the listening public via pop hooks and choruses.

"19th Nervous Breakdown" is close in spirit, at least lyrically, to Bob Dylan songs of that time period such as "Just Like a Woman" or "Leopard-Skin Pill-Box Hat," songs where he wields a scalpel to cut through the hypocrisies of high society. The Stones' song steers clear of Dylanesque surrealism and, in direct, biting language, picks apart a well-off debutante and exposes her for what she really is: a scared, lost kid with a few more creature comforts than the norm.

Jagger wastes no time in digging deep, as the first line accuses, "You're the kind of person you meet at certain dismal dull affairs." The narrator strives to be sympathetic, suggesting that her wastrel habits have been acquired via a lifetime of parental negligence and spoiled privilege. The girl's mom and dad come across as buffoonish, one on the hook for a cool million in taxes, the other with a mind-numbing sealing wax obsession. With this withering portrait, Jagger pokes at the generational divide in the midst of the class warfare.

In the bridge, the narrator implies that he has tried to wake this girl up from her opulent stupor to no avail. His reward for his effort: "On our first trip I tried so hard to rearrange your mind / But after a while I realized you were disarranging mine."

The refrain is brilliant in the way it suggests that these dramatic crises of hers crop up on the regular. Maybe that's why Jagger sings as though he's joyously anticipating the next one instead of warning the girl of its approach.

This is no dire message, à la "Mother's Little Helper." The effervescent music won't allow it to be. With Keith Richards's free-spirited jangling and Charlie Watts's nimble high-hat-heavy approach setting the tone, the mood is far more celebratory than cautionary. You get the feeling that the narrator doesn't care if she avoids her next breakdown or not.

He just wants to call her out for sucking him so often into her insane vortex.

By song's end, with Bill Wyman sliding down the neck of his bass in taunting fashion as if he's sticking out his tongue at this hapless girl, there is no doubt where the band's sympathies lie. They join the narrator in chiding her for thinking that just because she's well-connected and well-off that she should also be the center of attention. And, in doing so, they slyly slam all those other rich folks who feel that their wealth earns them the same kind of special treatment.

For one of The Stones' first stabs at this kind of material, "19th Nervous Breakdown" is strikingly accomplished. Jagger gets his point across in short, potent strokes, while the band strikes hard with the glee they take in her comeuppance. Not only was the group breaking new ground among their pop peers with the topical stuff, but they were also setting a high standard for it with this top-notch single.

42. "Losing My Touch" (from *Forty Licks*, 2002)

Has there ever been a band so often anthologized as The Rolling Stones? They truly represent the perfect storm for record companies wishing to compile greatest hits. After all, they've been around forever, have been pretty prolific over their long career, especially in the early days, and, even on their weakest albums, usually provide something of import for their fan base and the music world at large. The fact that they've never been afraid of trying different things means that the option exists to round up their songs by style just as easily as by time period.

Anyone claiming to be peddling the definitive Rolling Stones collection is stretching the truth, unless they're holding a flash drive with every song the band ever recorded. Still, as these things go, 2002's *Forty Licks* wouldn't be the worst thing to play if you had a couple of hours to explain the band to an invading Martian or something like that. It has the benefit of touching every part of the band's career (with the obvious exception of 2005's *A Bigger Bang* and anything else that might come in its wake), and while it's light on classic album tracks, it's a solidly thorough hits retrospective.

It also adds the bonus of four tracks that the band recorded specifically for the project. Three of the four are afterthoughts, but "Losing My Touch" is a stunner that prevents this compilation from seeming superfluous. Written and sung by Keith Richards, it's wisely placed at the end of *Forty Licks*, joining the proud group of Richards's ballads that act as sober mornings after to balance out the decadent songs of the night that populate most Stones albums.

If you ever doubted what Keith Richards could do as a torch singer, you won't know what hit you after hearing "Losing My Touch." Richards's singing style has always been marked by various tics and asides, which, while endearing and now almost trademark, can sometimes distract from the material. He keeps them to a minimum here, singing in a deep croak with the tenderness and vulnerability of a guy who needs love but knows he couldn't hold on to it, even if fell into his arms.

Another winning aspect of "Losing My Touch" is how the players respond to the jazzy demands Richards makes of them. Charlie Watts, whose side projects outside The Stones tend to be anything but rock related, plays his part on the drums with restraint and touch, while Ron Wood's pedal steel guitar simmers just below the song's surface and doesn't speak out so much as wistfully sigh. Meanwhile Chuck Leavell's piano dances quietly with Richards's acoustic. It's the last dance of the night, the last dance of the whole affair.

One of the reasons Richards's ballads strike such a chord is that they present such a contrast to the caricature of Keith as a tipsy, cackling skeleton man who either outsmarted or plain outlasted God to survive this long. "Losing My Touch" shows a guy who's aware of his mistakes and paying the price for the ones that can't be amended. While it's always tricky to assign the feelings promoted in a song to its creator, certainly these wounded emotions feel like a more truthful representation of Richards than anything found in a pirate movie, especially when the guy sings them out so movingly.

You can call this song autumnal, but winter is probably nigh. Richards sounds like a guy close to the end of his journey, at a time when regrets and laments tend to pile up. The events of the song are minimal, just a narrator who appears to be planning a quick meeting with a former love before he hurriedly heads out of town. There doesn't really need to be a narrative when the feelings come across so clearly, which they do thanks to economical lyrics that still find room for some typical Keith Richards flair. When he describes things being in a "lockdown," it seems to refer to both the difficulty he's having making his getaway and to his petrified emotional state.

In the refrain, Richards yanks himself into a slightly higher register to sing, "I'm losing my touch way, way too much." As messages sent during the dark night of a soul go, that one is refreshingly direct and bravely honest. Now that everything can be had online, you don't need to pony up for *Forty Licks* to hear "Losing My Touch." If you had to though, this one would make the expenditure worthwhile.

41. "It's Only Rock 'n Roll (but I Like It)" (from *It's Only Rock 'n Roll*, 1974)

Who knew that The Stones were so sensitive? "The idea of the song has to do with our persona at the time," Mick Jagger said in 1993 of his inspiration for the 1974 hit "It's Only Rock 'n Roll (but I Like It)." "I was getting a bit tired of people having a go, all that 'oh, it's not as good as their last one' business."[26]

The good thing about being in a rock band with a recording contract is that you can usually get in the last word on grumpy critics and assorted naysayers. Ironically enough, the defensive title of the song provided fodder for endless journalists looking for a ready-made headline for articles about The Stones. In listening to the song, however, one can easily tell that the mood of the song is a bit more defiant than defensive.

"It's Only Rock 'n Roll (but I Like It)" features one of the oddest genesis stories of any Stones track. Mick Jagger was doing some work with Ronnie Wood in the latter's home studio for a Wood solo album a few years before Ron would join The Stones. David Bowie was also there at the time and provided some backing vocals for a demo of "It's Only Rock 'n Roll," which was filled out by the rhythm section of Willie Weeks on bass and Kenney Jones on drums. (Jones was a fellow member of The Faces with Wood; he would later replace Keith Moon in The Who.)

Wood's contribution gained him an "Inspiration by" credit once The Stones finished up the track, a process that consisted of Keith Richards wiping out all of Wood's efforts, with the exception of his twelve-string acoustic, and overdubbing new electric parts. Richards also left the rhythm section of Weeks and Jones on the finished track, meaning that the only Stones who participated were The Glimmer Twins. (In another ironic twist, the video for the song, which finds the band in sailor suits frolicking in soap suds, includes Mick Taylor, even though he's not on the finished track. He would, of course, be replaced in The Stones a few years later by Wood. You sometimes need a program to tell the players when you're talking about this band.)

This unorthodox method of recording the track actually works in its favor. Richards's guitars seem to be on top of the rhythm section, cutting in rudely at strange angles with serrated authority. His solo late in the song is like a sludgy Chuck Berry homage, while his chugging rhythm parts owe a debt to glam rockers T. Rex. It all comes together in an unkempt, undignified, yet unstoppable way, seconding the song's message about rock music being battered but refusing to break.

Like Bob Dylan in "Idiot Wind," which was released around that same time, Jagger splits his disdain between the press, with their pens like daggers, and a woman who never seems to be satisfied with the actions of her man. The singer seems to relish the role of the put-upon victim, asking to what extreme he could possibly go to impress his persecutors.

It's important that the music keeps up the bravado though, or else this song could have seemed a bit defensive. (Paul McCartney's similarly themed "Silly Love Songs" falls into that trap.) The shouted chorus sneers and jeers at these would-be critics, suggesting that all that matters is what the performer thinks about the finished product. And Jagger's salacious refrain of "I like it" in the breakdown and coda leaves no doubt that he thinks he and his band are doing just fine with this material.

Jagger may have claimed that the song was aimed at the press, but Bianca, his wife at the time, was rumored to have little affection for the music her husband played. It seems likely that Mick's inclusion of a demanding woman in the narrative was more than just a way to make the song resonate with nonrockers. That part of the song likely hit close to home.

"It's Only Rock 'n Roll (but I Like It)" was the title track for an album generally regarded as one of the band's least inspired, which, in retrospect, gives this song an extra dollop of meaning. The Rolling Stones, as mentioned earlier in this book, were at a time period where they were struggling in the wake of the ultradynamic run of music they put together in the five-year stretch from 1968 through 1972. So while the album that contained it may have given the detractors a bit more fodder for their barbs, the song itself proved that the title was a bit of false modesty, because rock and roll, when performed with this much sass and vigor, never needs defending.

40. "Laugh I Nearly Died" (from *A Bigger Bang*, 2005)

There are a whopping sixteen songs on 2005's *A Bigger Bang*, which, at press time, stands as the most recent full album of material from The Rolling Stones. That seems excessive, especially when you consider that *Exile on Main St.* contained eighteen songs in 1972 and was a double album. The CD era allowed artists more space, which they usually filled regardless of whether they had enough product to do so.

That's not to say that *A Bigger Bang* is bloated with filler. But what tends to happen on overstuffed albums like this one, which was a solid affair, if lacking a high number of truly revelatory songs, is that the best material has a hard time rising to the top, because there's so much stuff blocking its path. "Laugh I Nearly Died" is a fine example of this. In terms of quality it should be listed among The Stones' classics, and yet it's largely unknown outside the hardest of the hardcore fans.

It's also not a song likely to gain its reputation through live performances. It went unplayed by the band even when they toured after the release of *A Bigger Bang*, and it's doubtful that they'll dig it up down the line to be inserted into their hits-heavy set. The song probably would have suffered in live rendering anyway, because large arenas and stadiums would only stifle the intimacy of the suffering conveyed.

"Laugh I Nearly Died" is instead a marvelous studio concoction, one that seems to have been largely the brainchild of Mick Jagger. Jagger not only sings here but also plays guitar and keyboards on the track while adding percussion as well. Keith Richards is also on board on guitar while the rhythm section of Darryl Jones and Charlie Watts comes along for the ride. It's a Spartan effort in terms of personnel and relatively stark in terms of execution, but what's in there packs a wallop.

What's neat about the song is that it's so effective without really resembling any other classics from the band's vast catalog. The closest thing to it might be the brooding *Emotional Rescue* track "Down in the Hole." Both songs lock into a repetitive, trancelike groove over which Jagger emotes. But "Down in the Hole" stays in a kind of one-note rut throughout, whereas "Laugh I Nearly Died" thrillingly explodes out of its groove to cut loose some raw emotions.

With guitars flickering around him and Watts thumping along ominously, Jagger recounts a sort of miserable travelogue in the verses. Greece, Rome, Africa, Arabia, and India all fly by, but none provide any sort of succor, only adding to the angst of the narrator. Of course it's a woman causing all this trouble, and Jagger sings with his wounds exposed to the world even as the instrumentalists behind him keep their composure.

When the groove shifts with some thudding guitar notes toward the chorus, Jagger stops listing his itinerary and starts to detail the depth of his pain. His voice conveys not just sadness but also a kind of righteous indignation at the way he's been treated. "I feel pushed aside," he barks, almost in disbelief that this should be his fate. Playing up the sorrow would have been easy, but Jagger's work here covers far more emotional range and feels just right for someone suffering in this manner.

In the final verse, the narrator's destinations turn from specific to abstract. "Living in a fantasy but it's way too far," Jagger sings, suggesting that maybe all his previous stops were just part of a fever dream his subconscious formed to escape harsh reality. Now he's completely at sea: "I lost my direction and I lost my home."

It all leads up to one more return to the chorus, as the narrator relates the ultimate hurt he was forced to endure: "When you laughed, laughed / I almost died." The song plays out with Mick multitracked to form an a cappella group that sounds like a chain gang, all the better to symbolize the figurative prison in which the narrator will reside for eternity regardless of his actual wanderings.

"Laugh I Nearly Died" stands apart from much of *A Bigger Bang* in terms of its ambition and scope; it feels epic without consciously trying for it. Maybe The Stones overloaded the album a bit, but this wondrous downer deserves to be separated from the pack and appreciated by a much larger audience.

39. "Mixed Emotions" (from *Steel Wheels*, 1989)

While the early 1980s were generally a hard time for many of the best rock-and-roll acts of the previous two decades, the latter half of the decade found many of those same acts regaining their mojo. Paul Simon, Peter Gabriel, Steve Winwood, and pretty much every member of The Traveling Wilburys fired back from the brink of obsolescence with albums that reminded us all of what made them great in the first place.

In that same time period, The Rolling Stones not only had to overcome the slump that had enveloped them, typified by the bummer of their

1986 album, *Dirty Work*, but they also had to reunite after some ugly private and public sparring between the group's two leaders, Jagger and Richards. Even though some of their peers had come back strong, there was no guarantee that their own reentry into the rock-and-roll world would go as smoothly.

Considering all of that, "Mixed Emotions" is not just a great song but also one of the most important ones in the band's history. Released to herald the arrival of their 1989 album, *Steel Wheels*, the song was a reassuring blast of upbeat rock and roll that found the band sounding surer of themselves and their place in the culture than they had in nearly a decade. Even on some of the band's best tracks from the early 1980s, the strain was audible. "Mixed Emotions" teems with confidence and harmony, even as it hints at the problems that brought the band to the precipice of extinction.

By all accounts, Richards had the music for the song intact when he and Jagger convened in Barbados for a songwriting session early in 1989. There is some debate based on various interviews as to whether Keith had most of the lyrics intact and got a finishing touch from Jagger or if Mick handled the bulk of the words. (Richards has even contradicted himself on that matter over the years.)

It seems pretty safe to hypothesize that Jagger was responsible for the hook: "You're not the only one with mixed emotions." After all, Richards had been far more vocal in the press with his displeasure with Jagger during their enmity, even going so far as recording a "How Do You Sleep?"–style swipe at his musical partner with the solo song "You Don't Move Me." That line in the chorus certainly seems to be Mick's way of saying that he had felt the same type of anger and hurt during that tumultuous period in the band's history.

"Mixed Emotions" need not be heard as a conversation between the band members to work. You can simply hear it as a guy trying to convince a reticent girl to put the problems they suffered in the past behind and enjoy the overflowing possibilities waiting in the future. "So get off the fence now, it's creasing your butt," Jagger sings hilariously.

But we know better than that. We know that this was a bit of rocking therapy for these two longtime collaborators. The rest of the band did their part as well, with Charlie Watts setting the peppy, steady-as-he-goes pace, Bill Wyman getting in some funky bass riffs in the play-out, and

Ronnie Wood joining Richards for some raggedly propulsive guitar interplay.

"Mixed Emotions" manages to rise above a mere workmanlike reaffirmation of the band's strengths thanks to a couple moments that, within the context of the band's long history of ups and downs, really tug the heartstrings. From the unmistakable urgency of the chorus in contrast to the breezy verses, to Jagger and Richards harmonizing on the bittersweet lines in the refrain, to the way a thrilling squall of guitar accompanies Jagger as he shouts out, "Let's rock and roll," heading into the final chorus, the song goes way beyond nostalgia and achieves deep feeling, what one might even call love seeping from every note the band plays.

It's easy to pin the song's Top 10 success on the public's relief to have The Stones back in their lives, but that would short-change what an excellent song "Mixed Emotions" is, even when stripped of all its real-life associations. It brilliantly set the tone for the band's late-period career. More importantly, it served the dual purpose of both assuring the public they wouldn't have to endure a world without The Rolling Stones and reminding them what a horribly dull place such a world would be.

38. "As Tears Go By" (from *December's Children [and Everybody's]*, 1965)

In the midst of his landmark interview with Jann Wenner in 1971, John Lennon was asked by the *Rolling Stone* founder about his feelings on those other Rolling Stones. Let's just say he didn't hold back: "I would like to just list what we [The Beatles] did and what The Stones did two months after on every f***in album. Every f***in thing we did, Mick does exactly the same—he imitates us. And I would like one of you f***in underground people to point it out, you know *Satanic Majesties* is *Pepper*, 'We Love You,' it's the most f***in bullsh**, that's 'All You Need Is Love.'"[27]

Mind you, this all came at a time when Lennon was a bit peeved at Mick Jagger for comments he had made about The Beatles, even though Lennon was far more critical of his old band in the same interview. It is surprising, however, that the acerbic Beatle didn't attempt to strengthen his case by mentioning the fact that "As Tears Go By" followed close on the heels of "Yesterday" in 1965.

The two songs share obvious similarities. Both deviate from the normal rock-and-roll formula by featuring just acoustic guitar with strings as backing. Both hold off on introducing those strings until the second verse. And both even feature the singer, Paul McCartney in The Beatles' case and Jagger for The Stones, humming his way to the song's completion.

These are all valid points, but The Stones do have a pretty good argument in their defense. "As Tears Go By" was actually written a year before McCartney literally dreamed up "Yesterday." In fact, it was one of the first songs that Jagger and Keith Richards wrote, with a little help from producer/manager Andrew Loog Oldham, who, according to legend, forced the two into a room and wouldn't let them out until they emerged with a song.

They came out with "As Tears Go By," which they deemed far too tame and sappy to actually record. So they handed it off to a relative unknown up-and-comer named Marianne Faithfull, whose middle-of-the-road take on the song scored her a hit on both sides of the Atlantic. Faithfull would go on to be Mick Jagger's paramour just a few years later, inspiring many more Stones classics before their rollercoaster relationship ran its course.

So the claim that The Stones heard "Yesterday" and immediately cranked out "As Tears Go By" to cash in on the classical-pop bandwagon doesn't hold. Yet the band's eventual recording and release of the song in late 1965 as a successful US single and as a part the US-only album *December's Children (and Everybody's)* did indeed come in the wake of the mammoth success of "Yesterday." Richards played some gently plucked acoustic guitar, Jagger sang in an almost unrecognizably dreamy voice, and Mike Leander, who later would go on to arrange the strings on The Fab Four's "She's Leaving Home," took care of the orchestration.

The problem with blaming The Stones for all of this is that their version of "As Tears Go By" is undeniably moving. Just because The Beatles had beaten them to it, the approach that they took was still what suited the song best. Another way to look at it is to understand that "Yesterday," for all the innovation in terms of the arrangement, was still right in The Beatles' melodic comfort zone. By responding with "As Tears Go By," Jagger and Richards proved that they were far more than just blues enthusiasts and that they could hang with Lennon and McCartney at the highest levels of pop songwriting.

Regardless of this debate, "As Tears Go By" is a lovely effort. Maybe Richards was just trying to come up with a tune that sounded like a radio ballad, but he ended up revealing his tuneful chops in the process. In a similar fashion, Jagger might have written words that he thought were palatable to a large audience, but he inadvertently demonstrated startling sensitivity and wisdom far beyond his years, not to mention a sympathetic streak that felt genuine, despite the irreverent indifference he often chose to display as a public face.

So maybe John Lennon's complaints in that long-ago interview hold a little bit of water when it comes to "As Tears Go By." What matters here is that The Stones' song can go toe-to-toe with "Yesterday" or any other ornately arranged pop song of that era.

37. "Emotional Rescue" (from *Emotional Rescue*, 1980)

The criticism often laid on "Emotional Rescue" is that it's not "Miss You." When it was released in 1980, it was immediately compared to the band's previous foray into disco-tinged pop/rock, which had been a huge smash just two years earlier.

In terms of chart success, the difference was somewhat negligible. "Miss You" hit No. 1 in the United States and No. 3 in the UK, while "Emotional Rescue" reached No. 3 and No. 9, respectively, in those charts. In terms of quality, "Miss You" is better, but it's better than a large percentage of The Stones' excellent catalog of songs, so there's not much shame in that.

What rankled a lot of people was the similarity in styles between the two, the syncopated drums and prominent bass line emphasized over rock guitars. Folks never seemed to tire of the band's never-ending stream of blues-based rockers. Yet in this case, it seemed as if it was okay for the band to dip into the disco well once for a single, but twice was pushing it. Maybe fans were worried that they'd never be able to get back to their traditional sound.

Even Keith Richards bad-mouthed "Emotional Rescue" for years after its release. Richards may have been critical due to the fact that he had little to do with the song's creation or recording, as he added just a few electric guitar parts to the coda. Mick Jagger, Ronnie Wood, and Charlie Watts worked the song out in the studio one day, Jagger on electric piano, Wood on bass, and Watts on drums. Bill Wyman played some synthesizer on the finished track, but you can hear in the finished track how that main trio sort of drives the bus.

Watts is brilliant, laying down a sleek beat through persistent high-hat and martial snares. Wood meanwhile proves to be a funky bassist, popping his head up now and again with rubbery fills that grease the way from bar to bar. Bobby Keys provides the saxophone, here as more of a supporting player than the lead role Mel Collins played on sax in "Miss You." Keys's laid-back improvisations are in keeping with Jagger's hepcat patter.

Jagger's falsetto here shades toward the comical. But that's okay, because the stakes here are never too high. "Emotional Rescue" doesn't trade in urgency or itchy energy like "Miss You" did, although it shares the same urban feel, even when Mick's riding through the desert. This is a feel-good number that gets a long way simply via the engaging sound the players make when it all comes together, a tantalizing timber, if you will.

Jagger dives into the role of a would-be savior to a girl whose life in a rich man's arms doesn't turn out the way she thought it would. Or at least that's what we surmise from the narrator's pleading; since the girl never gets to tell her side of the story, it could be just his fertile imagination conjuring her loneliness, the same imagination that compares her to a Pekingese and creates Lawrence of Arabia fantasies.

The silky groove persists while the instruments surge and wane around it, eventually leading to a spoken-word section, Jagger laying it on as thick as he can. "I will be your knight in shining armor coming to your emotional rescue," he intones, enunciating every word for maximum passion. His falsetto now replaced by a somewhat creepy deep drawl, he then breaks into a salacious refrain of "You will be mine, you will be mine, all mine."

In these moments, the tables seem to turn, and we start to wonder if this girl wouldn't be better off hanging out with the rich dude. You could delve really deep and say that Jagger's exaggeration of the soul-man shtick is his way of saying that these songs sometimes reduce women to damsels lacking a point of view or decision-making capability of their own, that they can be simply swayed by the guy with the best rap. But that's probably more of an in-depth reading than the band intended. They seem to have been trying to create a song that sounds great—end of story. Mission accomplished.

In 2013, The Rolling Stones began performing "Emotional Rescue" live for the first time in history. The fact that it snuck into set lists seems to be an indication that Richards either softened toward it or simply gave up the fight, while the rapturous response it received proved that fans were ready to accept it as the classic it always was. It's no "Miss You," but then again, a lot of Stones songs must accept that they're no "Emotional Rescue."

36. "She Was Hot" (from *Undercover*, 1984)

When perusing the career of The Rolling Stones, one is hard pressed to find many flops among the songs they released as singles. Although they're probably considered by most folks to be more album oriented than singles oriented, the group certainly posted a pretty high ratio of singles to hits, at least while they were competitive in the pop game. (The fact that they had no big crossover hits after "Mixed Emotions" speaks more to the way pop radio simply began to exclude rock artists of a certain age than to any letdown in the accessibility of the band's singles in their later career.)

"She Was Hot," however, flailed on the charts, failing to reach the Top 40 on either side of the pond. The reasons? Well, it was definitely a drastic departure from "Undercover of the Night," the single that preceded it from 1984's *Undercover*. That song courted pop audiences more directly with an exotic, danceable beat. "She Was Hot" is a more traditional driving rocker that's in line with the band's previous triumphs but maybe seemed out of step in those heady days when MTV-courting pop songs ruled.

Speaking of MTV, another reason "She Was Hot" may have faltered could be the video for it, which attempted to be risqué but instead came off as laughably lousy. Bad acting by the band and a concept that may have seemed like a good idea at the time but crashed and burned on execution combined to produce a clip that definitely makes the list of so-bad-they're-good videos. (On the bright side, the video may provide the only known evidence of Charlie Watts changing his facial expression from his trademark sleepy-eyed half smile.)

Such things mattered to audiences back in the day, so "She Was Hot" sank without leaving much of a dent on the audience at large, making it a relative rarity among Stones singles. (Heck, even "Harlem Shuffle," a

throwaway R&B cover from 1986 with some Ralph Bakshi–style anima-
tion in the video to liven it up, soared to the Top 10.) It's a shame though,
because those who simply accept this track as a flop without actually
judging the song on its merits are missing a rip-snorting rocker that actually represents one of the band's artistic peaks in the 1980s.

"She Was Hot" comes on like yet another in a long line of Chuck
Berry–inspired rockers from The Stones. Keith Richards starts things off
with a blast of guitar that's like a morning alarm. Watts then kicks everybody out of bed with a propulsive beat in the verses, joined eventually by
Ian Stewart's right-hand boogie on the piano. The song could have stayed
along those lines and been just fine, if maybe somewhat forgettable.

But the refrains are a different animal, more mysterious and intan-
gible. The instruments initially drop back into the atmosphere and leave
Jagger pretty much on his own to emote his tale of an unforgettable one-
night stand. Soon the tension and momentum starts to rev up along with
the instrumental backing until Mick releases it all with a scream in the
final line. It's not too much of a stretch to hear the build-up and explosion
here as an aural representation of the sexual experience the narrator is
reliving.

The lyrics create a similar contrast. In the verses, the narrator bemoans
cold and loveless scenarios in New York and Detroit, only to drift back in
the connecting sections to that one unforgettable dalliance. Sweat pouring, clothes ripping, limbs flailing—Jagger doesn't skimp on any of the
torrid details, easily melting away any of the chill lingering from the
verses.

He eventually defends his actions as the only normal reaction a hot-
blooded male in a cold climate can have: "Always take the passion where
you find it." The final portion of his reminiscence suggests that the passion he found that "cold and rainy night" was such that it transcended the
actual environs and willed into existence sultrier surroundings. "Melted
snow" gives way to a "molten glow," and the narrator eventually travels
"Down the avenue, into the lost bayou / Into the tall bamboo, into the
human zoo."

The band stays on this seductive plane for the remainder of the song,
and we leave Jagger still in the midst of his reverie, chanting the word
"hot" over and over with lascivious gusto, refusing to call it a night. One
can never tell why some songs connect with a large audience and some
don't. "She Was Hot" never made the Top 40 back in its day, but the fact

that it earns its spot on this far more illustrious list of the best of The Stones speaks to just how steamily sensational it is.

35. "Monkey Man" (from *Let It Bleed*, 1969)

The intro to "Monkey Man," a daringly dynamic track The Rolling Stones laid down for *Let It Bleed* in 1969, is elegant and mysterious, an alluring entreaty to the listener to enter this dark alley with the band and see what transpires. What does transpire is violent and thrilling all at once, a mélange of machine-gun drums, edgy guitars, and maniacal vocals that suggest that even though you might have been better off to turn around and run, you've only really begun to live in the midst of this tumult.

It's no wonder that "Monkey Man" has been the stuff of movie soundtracks for years, since it effortlessly sums up the kind of scuzzy, noir atmosphere that directors of R-rated dramas often wish to convey. Indeed, this song sounds like it anticipated the career of Martin Scorsese, the master of the American gangster film, years before Scorsese actually broke through in a big way. (He would use many Stones songs in his movies, with "Monkey Man" doing the honors in his masterpiece *Goodfellas*.)

The song was recorded during a brief period between the Brian Jones and Mick Taylor eras in the band's history, but The Stones pack quite a wallop as a quartet with a little help from select special guests. Nicky Hopkins provides some piano, which lends a bit of incongruous elegance to the extended instrumental portion of the song, while producer Jimmy Miller adds some tambourines.

Whereas Brian Jones was usually the one to provide Stones songs with a bit of instrumental color during his time with the band, Bill Wyman comes up big on "Monkey Man" with the chilling vibraphone bit at the start of the song. The track could have easily begun with the thrust of the guitars and drums, but the quiet moodiness of that intro allows Keith Richards and Charlie Watts the opportunity to make even more of an impact on guitar and drums when they finally bust down the wall.

Jagger's lyrics are marvelously wacky and probably not nearly as bleak as what some would interpret. The early mention of "junkies" often makes folks want to hear "Monkey Man" as a kind of drug song, but that doesn't seem to be the ultimate intent. Instead, Jagger and the band seem to be having a bit of a laugh not only with how the public perceives them but also with the dark and dastardly image they tended to promote at that time.

Right off the bat, Jagger dares everyone to believe in what he's saying at their own risk. "That's not really true," he sings after claiming that he's a "flea-bit peanut monkey" whose friends are all junkies. Once he's established that he likes to stretch the truth, how can you trust anything that follows?

In the second verse, Jagger takes the litany of suffering he detailed in "Jumpin' Jack Flash" to a comically exaggerated extreme. "I was bitten by a boar, I was gouged and I was gored / But I pulled through," he sings. He also hints at a life of squalor: "I'm a sack of broken eggs, I always have an unmade bed." He then asks, "Don't you?" This question insinuates that maybe the audience that would gawk and gape at his antics might just be witnessing a part of themselves that they try to keep hidden away.

"Well I hope we're not too messianic or a trifle too Satanic," Jagger apologizes, referencing the polar opposite views it was possible to take of the band. His next line is probably the only one you can accept at face value ("We love to play the blues"), but the simplistic way that he phrases it implies that trying to narrow the band down to any categorization is at best limiting and at worst inaccurate.

As if to prove that point, the band then enters into an instrumental jaunt that encompasses both a kind of protofunk embodied by Watts's busy beat and claustrophobic psychedelia courtesy of Richards's woozy slide guitar. Jagger comes back in to choke out his assertion that "I'm a monkey" as the band boogies its way to the fade-out.

"Monkey Man" is impossible to pin down, zigging every time you expect it to zag, and yet it never feels erratic or needlessly complex. The impact, no matter what portion of the song is holding court, never wanes, which is why you can cut and paste just about any bit of it onto a film and get the desired boost. Many, including Scorsese, have done just that. But you don't need any accompanying pictures to bring out the best in this song. "Monkey Man" conjures up a vivid world, both intimidating and intoxicating, all by itself.

34. "Worried about You" (from *Tattoo You*, 1981)

All bands wish they had a scrap heap as impressive as the one possessed by The Rolling Stones. That a whole album full of gems like "Worried about You" were lying around in 1981 proves just how prolific the band was in its heyday. *Tattoo You* may have been a kind of desperation move at the time by a band licking its internal wounds, but it managed to toe the line between artistic solidity and wide-range accessibility as deftly as any Stones album you might care to name.

The first side of the album, which features up-tempo numbers, is a bit bumpier from track to track, giving away its grab bag nature more readily. But the second side, despite featuring songs begun for a wide array of albums and by an ever-changing cast of characters, is a pretty seamless set of ballads. That's because the core of The Stones' slow stuff, consisting of the band's innate soulfulness and touch and Mick Jagger's knack for piercing his preening façade to reveal what's roiling inside of him, stays intact regardless of the ephemera of specific recordings.

"Worried about You" originated in that odd time in the band's history when they were essentially using an album's worth of songs (1976's *Black and Blue*) to determine who should join the band as another guitarist. Wayne Perkins was one of those contenders, and his probing, aching solo on this track is one of its defining moments. That he would lose out to Ronnie Wood seems to have been more a matter of personality than any fault in his actual playing, which here and elsewhere on *Black and Blue* was outstanding.

Why "Worried about You" missed the cut in 1976 is a mystery, but there's no doubting that the finished product is a marvel. The variety that the band demonstrates within the song is quite impressive. In the beginning, Billy Preston on after-hours electric piano, Charlie Watts on patient high hat, and Bill Wyman on meandering bass each wends his own solitary path from bar to bar as Jagger's falsetto moans in their midst. Yet as he heads toward the chorus, the band members, joined by guitarists Perkins and Keith Richards, fill out the emptiness around him, giving the song a bit more acceleration than your average ballad.

Watts then snaps off a snare drum break to start the chorus, and Jagger heads back into a lower register that betrays the urgency of the narrator's plight while Richards joins in for wounded high harmonies. This kind of push and pull between stark and dense is evident throughout the song, as the band members build up and tear down the track with exquisite timing and undeniable feeling.

Jagger's ability to dictate how much he holds back and how much he cuts loose allows the vocals to hang right with the music. His falsetto may be a bit shaky at times, but that only drives home the uncertain precipice on which his narrator balances. The snarl he unleashes in the final verse feels like the response of a man who can't keep his composure anymore. And when he soars into those choruses, his emotions threatening the boiling point, the track goes beyond a typical my-love-is-gone lament. It epitomizes the kind of boundless torment that one might have to endure if worry was a constant and not just a temporary thought or impulse quickly doused.

The title phrase can be deceiving. When you hear the words "worried about you," it's natural to think of someone showing concern for another human being. But the title leaves out the fact that the narrator is worried about what she can do to him, the havoc she can wreak in him, whether she's staying away from him or gracing him with her presence. He imagines being able to find someone else, someone more benign to his nervous system, but only after being put to the ultimate test: "Sure as hell burns, I'm going to find that girl someday." After where he's been in his current relationship, that burning hellfire shouldn't even be that daunting.

The Stones push the song past the five-minute mark, well beyond what you would expect for a typical ballad. Yet every second is worth it, since the song leaves no emotion unexplored. Jagger is at his best here, and the ad hoc band is in perfect synch with each other and the song's emotional content. "Worried about You" may have needed six years to come to fruition, but it's somewhat apropos, since it takes its own time, slowly yet inevitably piecing together a heartsick whole.

33. "Happy" (from *Exile on Main St.*, 1972)

History has proven that when you're a Rolling Stone and inspiration strikes, it's best to grab whoever happens to be milling about in the studio at the time and get the darn thing on tape. Since the band members are known to be less than rigid about arriving at their scheduled studio times, it's probably unwise to wait for a complete band lineup to polish up the track. You might just be waiting a long time.

Had Keith Richards not followed this basic rule, the world might have missed out on his shambolic anthem "Happy" from 1972's *Exile on Main St.* During a session for the album at his Nellcôte villa in France in 1971, Richards stumbled onto a guitar riff that he quite liked. The only ones hanging around at the time were producer Jimmy Miller and saxophonist Bobby Keys, neither of whom was an official band member.

But that didn't stop Richards, who wrote the track on the spot and put the basic demo together by overdubbing bass and guitar while Miller played drums and Keys laid down some extra percussion. Joining that trio when the recording was finished in Los Angeles were Mick Jagger on backing vocals, Nicky Hopkins on electric piano, and Keys and Jim Price on horns. Thus the song that would kick off side 3 of *Exile* received no contributions from three of the five band members, and yet it stands as one of The Stones' most indelible feel-good party starters.

It's also the first time that Richards delivered the lead vocal on a rocker for the band. His previous partial or full leads came on ballads "You Got the Silver" and "Salt of the Earth" and the novelty "Something Happened to Me Yesterday." Here he sinks his teeth into an up-tempo track with not only humor and attitude, which you might expect, but also with a great deal of heart, which allows the song to linger long after the initial kick of listening to it wears off.

That opening guitar salvo sort of creeps up to make its case, before settling into the circular riff that persists throughout the song and is eventually seconded by the horns of Price and Keys. Richards's solos briefly stab their way through Miller's dense production net, only to get yanked back under by the frenetic locomotion of the walled instruments.

Of the song's lyrics, Richards had a typically idiosyncratic take in *Life*, written with James Fox. "There has to be some thin plot line, although in a lot of my songs you'd be very hard-pressed to find it," he wrote. "But here, you're broke and it's evening. And you want to go out, but you ain't got sh*t. I'm busted before I start. I need a love to keep me happy, because if it's real love it will be free! Don't have to pay for it. I need a love to keep me happy because I've spent the f***ing money and I have none left, and it's nighttime and I'm looking to have a good time, but I ain't got sh*t."[28]

It's probably for the best that Richards didn't use quite the same wording in the lyrics he wrote. What "Happy" charmingly captures is the difficulty of keeping one's individuality while also admitting the need for companionship. The narrator admits to blowing all his money, messing about in school, and running like the wind from any regular job. He basically shuns anything routine as well as every sound piece of advice ever given to him. The end result is a life lived on his own terms that he clearly wouldn't change for anything.

And yet the chorus spells out that there's something missing, or else it would be missing if he didn't have that special someone who meant more to him than countless Lear jets lined up on an infinite runway, the one to whom he always "can fly way back home." "I need a love to make me happy," he sings, Jagger joining him in a show of solidarity. Without that love, any amount of iconoclasm that he might wish to display isn't going to keep him from fragmenting into tiny, hollow pieces.

In the song's closing moments, Richards backs off into the whoosh of the band and allows Jagger to do some vamping on the main title. It's as if he's made his point and need not embellish it any more. For a song that started with a ragged three-man crew, "Happy" blossomed into joyous fullness. It's a song that says that you can stay true to what you are, as long as what you are isn't alone.

32. "I Am Waiting" (from *Aftermath*, 1966)

If you're looking for existential ponderings, you don't usually turn to The Rolling Stones. If anything, you might expect the band to sneer at such lofty pretensions in favor of the earthier concerns and pleasures that their blues-based rock and roll so effortlessly conveyed. And yet there was a time in the mid-1960s when the band's chief songwriters, Jagger and Richards, were open to such subject matter, essaying it quite fetchingly as a matter of fact on the 1966 winner "I Am Waiting."

The year 1966 was a prime time for rock and pop artists who wanted to express something a little bit more than the standard boy-meets-girl, boy-loses-girl (or vice versa) themes. It was also a time when such artists were experimenting with joining these heavier topics to formal, antiquated musical settings. In some cases, they were willing to adopt instrumentation more appropriate to medieval madrigals than to rock songs.

Whenever The Stones went down this path, they usually turned to Brian Jones. Jones had the ability to make whatever he played on whatever instrument he chose ring with emotion that dovetailed with the tenor of the particular song. In the case of "I Am Waiting," he manages to capture the idle feeling expressed by the lyrics on the Appalachian dulcimer, which he plucks in concert with Richards's acoustic guitar. The two instruments are played so delicately that they wouldn't wake a snoozer in the next room, and yet they evoke undeniable yearning that deepens Jagger's somewhat quizzical statements in their midst.

The Stones demonstrate on "I Am Waiting" exactly how to utilize the restrained nature of those quieter sections, with Richards and Jones flickering like candles nearly extinguished each time Charlie Watts strikes his toms, to contrast a more modern pop-folk rumble in the refrains. In lesser hands, these two distinct musical approaches could have sounded like different songs jammed together haphazardly. Yet Watts's snare shots signal the transition from the tranquil acceptance of the verses to the urgent striving of the choruses, which introduce significant Jagger/Richards harmonies to further boost the intensity.

Jagger is also aware of this contrast and plays it up in his vocals as well. He sings the melody of the verses as if completely removed from any emotional attachment to them, drawling out each word with exaggerated diction as if trying to twist the meanings. Those words don't add up to much on the page, just repeated assertions of anticipation. All we know is that the narrator is "waiting for someone to come out of somewhere."

When the refrains erupt, he takes on a much more frenzied tone, emphasizing both the inevitability of what he's describing and the seriousness of his warning. Against what he's warning us is never quite described in any detail. But its impact is undeniable. Although we'll try to avoid it ("It's censored from our minds"), its arrival will cause great consternation. "Stand up coming years escalation fears," Jagger sings, his mixed-up syntax belying the clarity of his plea. "Like a withered stone, fears will pierce your bones," he insists. "You'll find out."

Once this chorus hits, the verses are then retroactively colored by the knowledge of his vague threat. Suddenly it's clear that the narrator isn't waiting for some reward or boon; he's waiting for the other shoe to drop. The song ends in the quiet section, with Jagger moaning out, "Oh we're waiting," pulling the entire audience onto the imagined cliff with him so that everyone can plummet together.

The Stones are able to slip the song's inherent despair past us because it's so damn pretty. And maybe that's the point of "I Am Waiting." Maybe the boys are suggesting that people get caught up in the superficial pleasures of the world around them and never see what's ready to pounce at any minute.

"I Am Waiting" made a memorable appearance in the film *Rushmore*, where it's used to perfection by director Wes Anderson, who seems to be quite fond of the melodic, restrained side of the band that had its heyday in 1966 and 1967. This song may have needed a little boost from an outside source to garner its share of the spotlight, mostly because its subtlety renders it a bit of a wallflower next to more forceful tracks from the band's catalog. Once it has your attention though, you're not likely to ever forget this wistful, wonderful track.

31. "Plundered My Soul" (from *Exile on Main St.* reissue, 2010)

Exile on Main St. yielded a ridiculous amount of heady pleasure on its release in 1972, two albums of material filled with practically every genre of roots-based music squashed into a stew seasoned with The Stones' blend of instrumental gusto and strung-out swagger. Who knew that there was still marvelous stuff it had held back from our ravenous musical appetites? The album, ever the mischievous, unruly child, was still misbehaving all these years by keeping some classic stuff to itself.

The 2010 reissue of the album featured a passel of bonus tracks from around that period, and this was no mere cutting-room floor detritus. For just one shining example, "Plundered My Soul" not only easily could have slotted into the track list of the original album seamlessly; it could have also been a radio song from an album almost defiantly inaccessible. All that could have happened if only the band had found the time to finish the track all those years ago.

"Plundered My Soul" began with the grooving trio of Keith Richards, Bill Wyman, and Charlie Watts laying down rhythm guitar, bass, and drums respectively. That basic track isn't all that dissimilar to "Tumbling Dice," which would go on to be the main single from *Exile*, so maybe that's why it was shelved. In any case, the swaggering rhythm made the song a perfect candidate for rediscovery when the band looked back at the tapes for the 2010 project.

Mick Jagger took over from there, writing a melody and lyrics that blend heartbreak and sass in much the same way that the bluesy chord patterns and rhythmic stutter-stepping do. Jagger also effortlessly taps back into the yowl he fashioned back on the original album, capturing not only the timber of his vocals from that time period but also the attitude, that unique mixture of lusty brio and dejected weariness that somehow sums up the whole *Exile* ethos. It's an album full of characters feeling deep emotions in spite of their extracurricular efforts to numb themselves, and "Plundered My Soul" nails that vibe.

Much credit also goes to Don Was and The Glimmer Twins team of Jagger and Richards for the production work they did in melding the recent overdubs with the original recording captured by *Exile* producer Jimmy Miller. Instead of brightening things up and putting an extra crispy gloss on everything as rock productions circa 2010 tended to do, they locked into Miller's style of subjugating individual sounds in favor of the meshing of the whole. The added parts, which include Jagger's vocal, Bobby Keys's sax, Mick Taylor's electric guitar, and the backing vocals of Lisa Fischer and Cindy Mizelle, each have an opportunity to speak their minds, but ultimately they all cede the spotlight to the soulful stop-and-go of the Richards/Wyman/Watts foundation.

Jagger's lyrics strike just the right balance between genuine regret for his actions, deep hurt at the way he's been treated by the woman in the song, and the warm feelings that she still engenders in him, even if she's now just a memory. These are two wayward souls whose paths briefly intersected but were always too erratic to produce anything but divergence.

There are many things to love about "Plundered My Soul." Consider the way the tentative electric guitar opening is quickly overridden by Watts's sure hands as he shifts the song directly into classic Stones territory. Or the way the music drops away briefly in the refrain, leaving just Wyman rumbling underneath Jagger's moans, until that main groove kicks back in with Keys huffing and puffing the whole ensemble onward. Or the way Taylor rains guitar notes that are equal parts honey and teardrops in his welcome return to the band's fold. (Say what you want about the ruthlessness of The Stones in terms of how they treated some of the subordinate band members, but inviting Taylor back for this song showed a lot of class.)

It is tempting to wonder what "Plundered My Soul" might have sounded like had the band finished it when it was started. But the track as it eventually appeared so seamlessly combined the old and the new that it's hard to imagine that any other version recorded at any other time could have improved on it too much. *Exile on Main St.* turned out to be the gift that keeps on giving, with this track being the biggest prize from the album's latest bestowal on rock fans.

30. "Jigsaw Puzzle" (from *Beggars Banquet*, 1968)

The oft-repeated storyline concerning The Rolling Stones is that the band lost its way amid the psychedelic trappings of *Their Satanic Majesties Request* in 1967 only to regain their mojo by returning to the blues-based approach of the single "Jumpin' Jack Flash" and the album *Beggars Banquet* in 1968. That version of the story only glances off the truth, which in reality was a little more complex than that and encompasses a multitude of intricacies within the band's music at that time.

A good place to start exploring just how difficult it was to pigeonhole the band circa 1968 is the fascinating track "Jigsaw Puzzle." It can be found on the same *Beggars Banquet* album that was heralded as the band's triumphant return to their roots in the blues, and yet there's nothing about the song that really resembles your basic twelve-bar rumble. If you were to attempt to categorize the song, and good luck with that, you could probably call it psychedelic folk boogie. Of course, those three words put together make the song sound ridiculous, yet "Jigsaw Puzzle" is anything but.

One other important element of the storyline that gets omitted too often is how The Stones began to devote more attention and time to their lyrics in 1968, in terms of both degree of difficulty and cleverness. "Jigsaw Puzzle" can get away with being such a bizarre mishmash of musical styles in large part because it is driven, quite well as a matter of fact, by Mick Jagger's lyrics.

Like everybody else, Jagger was beholden to Bob Dylan for the latter's willingness to tackle just about any type of subject matter in a song, with the absolute exception of the typical theatrics of young romance that dominated the pop charts. And Jagger clearly is trying to set a grand-scale scene here in much the same way that Dylan did on classics like "Visions of Johanna" and "Desolation Row."

But Jagger manages to strike his own path by interspersing detailed, real-life observations with flights of fancy. In the song's final verse, the narrator describes a wild confrontation between dying pensioners and a vengeful queen that plays out like a fevered nightmare. On the other hand, his descriptions of a gangster living a double life of domesticity and violence (anticipating *The Sopranos* in a way) and of his bedraggled band (the musically unflappable rhythm section is depicted as nervous, Keith Richards and Brian Jones as "damaged," and Jagger himself as an entertainer fed up with entertaining) are lived-in and astute.

Dylan, for the most part, carried most of the weight of adding extra dimensions to what he had written on the page. Jagger has the advantage of a crack band to help him on that quest. And so it is that "Jigsaw Puzzle" benefits from the distinct talents of every Stone. Watts won't let Jagger ponder too long on anything, nudging him along with his kicky beat. Richards keeps things rich with his acoustic guitar but also plays up the askew nature of the lyrics with steel guitar fills that go off on weirdly dissonant tangents. Bill Wyman gives the song a funky, nimble bottom end that gooses the melody. Jones chips in with a droning, high-pitched mellotron part that sounds like some sort of exotic bird swooping high above the messy human stew below him. And Nicky Hopkins helps out on piano, coming to the forefront during the section where Jagger describes the band members, as if the others are too busy listening to what Mick has to say about them at that point and so they let Hopkins take the lead.

Perhaps no Stones song has ever been as aptly named, not just because the narrator is trying to make sense of the disparate folks who walk through his life every day, futilely trying to put them together into a cohesive whole. "Jigsaw Puzzle" is an apt description for all of the musical elements, both straight edged and curved into all kinds of strangeness, that The Stones jam into unholy unison here. These pieces really have no business fitting together. They do though, creating a track that realizes its grand ambition in ways that rival another *Beggars Banquet* song, a little number called "Sympathy for the Devil."

More on that one to come.

29. "Thru and Thru" (from *Voodoo Lounge*, 1994)

In the previous entry on this list, "Jigsaw Puzzle," it was mentioned that some of the song's lyrics seemed to anticipate the central character of the groundbreaking HBO drama *The Sopranos*. Well, *Sopranos* creator David Chase returned the favor to The Rolling Stones by closing out the second season of the show with a montage set to "Thru and Thru," a track off the band's 1994 album, *Voodoo Lounge*.

Written and, for the most part, performed by Keith Richards, "Thru and Thru" was intended as one of those after-hours closing tracks that Richards has perfected over the years with The Stones. (On the original vinyl album, it was the last song on *Voodoo Lounge*. The CD version and subsequent releases included "Mean Disposition" as a kind of bonus track, but "Thru and Thru," with its brooding music and reflective lyrics, was clearly intended to finish things off.) Chase latched onto the song's ability to shift at will between atmospheres ranging from mournful to sweet to ominous and found a perfect summation of his everything-at-once show.

Some songs need a little exposure and context to put them across. In the case of "Thru and Thru," it may have been just a case of Richards's somewhat unique time-release talents as a writer and performer hiding the song from all but the diehards, talents that, according to Keith, sometimes need to grow on people. "I know these songs," he said in *According to The Rolling Stones* in 2003 about his writing style. "I'm not writing them to hit you between the eyes, right now—you can do that with a shooter—but to see if you get it in a bit, once you've had a couple of babies and you've laid down with a babe."[29]

In other words, Richards's songs are not all about instant gratification in terms of hooks or refrains or whatever. The unspoken implication in that quote seems to be that his musical partner, Mick Jagger, is more concerned with hitting the bull's-eye right away with his songwriting efforts. While that might be an oversimplification of Jagger's approach, it can't be denied that Richards's songs have a way of insinuating themselves under a listener's skin with their vulnerability and ready emotion. "Thru and Thru" projects all that with minimum effort and maximum heart on Keith's part.

In the beginning, "Thru and Thru" is just Richards on electric guitar and vocals, promising the same kind of loyalty in love that customers can expect from reliable businesses in terms of service. Yet the words are almost immaterial compared to the nooks and crannies of the playing and singing. He plays the riffs a little bit differently each bar, sometimes punching them out almost offhandedly and sometimes drawing them out for a little more impact. Keith then sings the way he plays, adding notes that deviate from the basic melody because he knows that such deviations often reveal the lyrics in poignant ways.

When Richards, backed with silky, soulful vocals by a group including Ivan Neville and Bernard Fowler, sings, "I'm waiting on a call from you," there is more than a little desperation in his statement. The same goes for when he sings, "I'm your lover, baby, thru and thru." There may be bravado somewhere in those words, but not the way Keith sings them.

In the final verse, the lyric changes from the assurances the narrator made earlier to documentation of some kind of news that has left him angry, stupefied, and bereft. Even as he spews curses in a kind of lashing out, his voice betrays the sheer depth of the blues through which he's suffering. As if to demonstrate the majestic pain of this poor soul, Charlie Watts erupts with drums that rip through the contemplative night. Watts achieved the enormity of the drum sound on the song by playing his instrument at the bottom of a stairwell, creating the effect of a violent disturbance in a tranquil setting, somewhat akin to what Phil Collins pulled off on "In the Air Tonight."

Lest you think that this narrator is going to wallow for too long, Richards leads the band on an extended coda of murky, steadily mounting intensity. If he's going to achieve catharsis, he's going to do it on his own terms, not by striving for some sort of redemptive light but by burrowing through the darkness with a battering ram.

These tonal shifts don't make "Thru and Thru" the easiest song to wrangle, but they do gird the song well for repeat listens, which truly reward those looking for an unheralded track from The Stones. Kudos to David Chase for recognizing the brilliance of this one, although anybody who gives it half a chance will likely find it out soon enough.

28. "Dead Flowers" (from *Sticky Fingers*, 1971)

The somewhat macabre idea of giving someone dead flowers, as occurs in the chorus of this memorable foray by The Rolling Stones into countrified rock or rock-tinged country, depending on the side of the tracks from which you hail, apparently came from an actual incident in the life of Gram Parsons. That's apropos, because the song itself probably wouldn't have been possible without Parsons's interaction and influence on the band.

Parsons is one of those guys whose influence on music casts a shadow longer than his recorded legacy, which features time with The Byrds, The Flying Burrito Brothers, and two standout solo albums recorded right before his overdose death at the age of twenty-six in 1973. His inability to maintain his sobriety for very long and his penchant for self-destruction meant that he was always wearing out his welcome with his musical companions; only on those two stunning solo albums did it all truly come together, as he mashed together the genres of country, rock, and R&B, using his teardrop-stained vocals as the glue, and came away with the prototype for the alt-country movement that would take hold many years later, with Parsons as its patron saint.

He befriended The Stones, particularly Keith Richards, in the late 1960s, gaining a spot in the band's retinue on and off until he was uncere-moniously ejected from Richards's French estate while the band was recording *Exile on Main St.* in 1971. In that time, he ignited Richards's passion for classic country music, which would then in turn show up in the band's repertoire, most notably on a pair of killer tracks on *Sticky Fingers*, "Dead Flowers" and "Wild Horses."

The former of the two songs, even as it details some pretty harrowing stuff in the lyrics, is the more lighthearted and rambling of the two tracks. It's also one of the band's catchiest songs, as they locked into a country-flavored acoustic rhythm but added just a bit of boogie to keep things from bogging down. Pianist Ian Stewart is largely responsible for this bit of pep with his tinkling runs in the lead-up to the refrains.

The other musical MVP on this track is Mick Taylor. For much of the song, his electric fills add a little melodic counterpoint to the steady going of the rest of the band. In the instrumental break, his solo is a marvel of economy, as he almost mathematically plucks out different combinations of the same limited series of notes to create something somehow both bouncy and bittersweet.

With those aforementioned elements lending a touch of Stonesy atti-tude to the basic country-rock foundation, it's left to Mick Jagger on vocals to truly bring the song into the band's territory. He does this with a tale of hedonism, heartbreak, and decay that would have sounded right at home in the midst of fuzzed-out guitars and booming drums had the band chosen to play it that way. Yet here, amid those country chord changes, the whole take sounds more sorrowful than spiteful, regardless of the cheap shots in the lyrics.

Jagger's exaggerated drawl that he overdid on some of the band's country numbers is tempered here (except for maybe when he drags out the pronunciation of "Kentucky Derby day"). His narrator is burying his sadness in indulgence while lashing out at his ex before he dives full-on into a numb, drug-addled stupor. He wants the girl to think that he's moving on to another and that he knows that her new, haughty lifestyle is just a front for her baser desires, yet he also indirectly betrays just how low he's sunk in her absence.

In the chorus, Richards joins in on harmonies as the narrator sarcastically tells her to send along dead flowers, since that sums up just how black and cold he views her to be. In response, he'll be right there to bedeck her grave with roses, with the nasty insinuation being that he'll be glad when she's dead.

Again, this is where the choice of music, the humor, and the overall catchiness come in handy, because those factors leaven those harsh sentiments. As we'll see as the countdown progresses, "Dead Flowers" is probably closer in musical style to what Parsons was doing, while "Wild Horses" is closer in sentiment, since that plays the sorrow much straighter. In any case, Gram may have planted the seed, but Richards, Jagger, Taylor, and the rest of The Stones supplied the versatility and talent necessary for them to add country music to the list of American musical genres they effortlessly conquered.

27. "Angie" (from *Goats Head Soup*, 1973)

"Angie," the lead single from the 1973 album *Goats Head Soup*, was a vast departure for The Rolling Stones from the music they produced on their previous album, *Exile on Main St. Exile* was messy and murky, requiring listeners to get down in the dirt with it to truly appreciate its myriad virtues. "Angie" is clean and pristine, all bright colors that radiate even as the song expresses unmitigated sadness.

The latter approach tends to be one that plays well on the radio, and "Angie" was a smash, No. 1 in the United States, Top 5 in the United Kingdom, and a huge seller in countries all over the globe. Some rock critics were less than amiable to the crowd-pleasing ballad, however; *New Musical Express*'s Nick Kent called the song "atrocious."

It seems to be human nature for people who have grown accustomed to one style of music from an artist to feel a sense of betrayal when that artist makes a significant change in that style, so that's probably where some of the rancor emanated from. Perspective is hard to achieve in the moment; songs like "Angie" tend to engender suspicion simply because of their immense popularity, since there are so many other immensely popular songs that are absolute drivel.

Yet here we are, some forty years after its release, and "Angie" has not only stood the test of time; its profundity and wisdom seem to deepen. It's a song about admitting that a relationship is spent, that devastating moment when it's deemed by one of the parties involved that it's better to cut losses than persist in a tarnished version of a love once immaculate. Maybe such sentiments sounded odd coming from the pens, mouths, and instruments of The Stones, but damn if they don't ring true and powerful.

Keith Richards is responsible for the song's beautiful melody. Accounts differ, as they often do with this band, but the general consensus is that he wrote the song at around the same time his daughter Angela was born, hence the title. It also seems pretty certain that Richards left much of the lyric writing to Mick Jagger, who simply utilized the name and took the song in a different direction than an ode to a child. (The creation of "Wild Horses" features a similar story.)

The song starts off on a high point musically when Richards's plaintive acoustic guitar starts to blend with the gorgeous piano work of Nicky Hopkins. Note how the two play off each other, one receding whenever the other comes forth, creating a tender dance. The other instrumentalists are similarly simpatico, Mick Taylor joining Richards on acoustic guitar, Bill Wyman typically unassuming yet integral on the bass, Charlie Watts's drum fills always right on point. Nicky Harrison arranged the strings with that same kind of awareness of the other elements of the song, until the whole thing resembles ensemble playing at its most generous and affecting.

"Angie" also represents one of the most heartfelt musical performances in the recorded career of Mick Jagger. Jagger just sings this one rather than playing the part, and, as such, the emotion that bends some of the notes from their rightful place in the melody is palpable. He nails the extremes like a conspiratorial whisper and a pain-wracked howl, but it's the overall weariness and futility he projects that really captures the tone of the lyrics.

The narrator of the song keeps asking "Angie" questions like a benevolent prosecutor, trying to nudge her to see his side of things, even as she clings to the faltering relationship. It's refreshing to hear a breakup song free of rancor or recriminations. We can assume that stuff is there, but it would have shattered the tone had it surfaced. Instead, this is all about wanting what's best for the person you love, even if that means saying goodbye.

He tries to find hollow victories in the efforts that they gave and the obstacles they overcame just to reach this point. But the ever-encroaching clouds on the horizon, which symbolize the poverty, shattered dreams, and waning love that now characterize their relationship, are impossible to ignore.

In the closing verse, he tries one more time to give her solace. "Ain't it good to be alive?" he asks, and the heartbreak comes from the fact that we know she might answer in the negative. "They can't say we never tried," he concludes, grasping at consolation in the face of the future without her.

Maybe "Angie" wasn't what everyone was expecting of The Rolling Stones in terms of style. But who wants a band who delivers the same thing every time out? Anyway, in terms of the lofty standards The Stones have set time and again, regardless of the style they utilize, this beauty of a ballad meets and even exceeds them, and that's all that really matters.

26. "Shine a Light" (from *Exile on Main St.*, 1972)

Two days after the death of their former bandmate Brian Jones, The Rolling Stones performed a memorial concert on July 5, 1969, at London's Hyde Park. At the beginning of the concert, Mick Jagger read an excerpt from Percy Bysshe Shelley's "Adonais," which itself was a tribute to the fallen poet John Keats. In the poem, Shelley essentially argues against mourning the dead since they are the ones blessed with peace, while the living "lost in stormy visions, keep / With phantoms an unprofitable strife."

As touching as Shelley's words might have been, Jagger's own subtle tribute to Jones, "Shine a Light" from 1972's *Exile on Main St.*, captures the essence of The Stones' founding member even truer. It's all the more moving for not shying away from the demons that Jones faced in his tumultuous life. Nor does it skimp on Jagger's honest frustration at his friend's degradation and demise, even as it rallies to offer him heartfelt well wishes in his next journey.

The song was actually begun while Jones was still alive; many of the lyrics would make it intact to "Shine a Light," as Jagger bemoaned Brian's slow capitulation to both his own impulses and those who would prey on him in his weakness. There was definitely more of a bite to this early version, called "Get a Line on You," especially in referencing Jones's attraction to "high school girls." But that basic feeling of watching a friend disintegrate before your very eyes is undeniable even in that early take, perhaps demonstrating a bit of haunting foresight by Jagger, albeit foresight enforced by Jones's steady slide before his death.

"Shine a Light" didn't take its finished form until Jagger accompanied Billy Preston to church in Los Angeles. Hearing the gospel performances at the church inspired Mick to complete the song with the benevolent, heavenly refrain that provides the uplift to balance the sour story of the verses. That same uplift also affects the vibes on *Exile on Main St.*, since "Shine a Light" is the penultimate track on the double album. Even as it sums up the consequences of all the debauchery detailed on *Exile*, it asks for a bit of forgiveness for even the most wayward of the songs' souls.

And the music is so convincing that you believe that forgiveness is merited. It begins with Preston's sad piano chords and Jagger in a voice heartbreakingly small and distant. From that humble beginning, the track opens up into a veritable orchestra conveying equal parts lowly sorrow and unfettered joy. Preston eventually breaks out in spirited sprints on piano and organ, while a chorus of backing vocalists joins Jagger in sending the song heavenward. In stark contrast, Mick Taylor busts into a guitar solo so bluesy and pain wracked in the thrilling instrumental break that even those angels who appear out of nowhere must have wept a bit.

That's not too bad for a song in which Jagger and Taylor were the only Stones to actually contribute: Keith Richards sat it out; Taylor played bass instead of Bill Wyman (it should be noted that Wyman has also claimed credit for bass on the song in interviews, as has Taylor, whom the album credits also list); and producer Jimmy Miller subs for Charlie Watts on drums.

Jagger takes only two lines to paint a devastating portrait: "Saw you stretched out in room ten-o-nine / With a smile on your face and tear right in your eye." The protagonist's penchant for "Berber jewelry" clearly resembles Jones's own. So too, sadly, does the following assertion: "Well you're drunk in the alley, baby, with your clothes all torn / And your late-night friends who leave you in the cold grey dawn."

That's the point in the song where Jagger grants Jones a soft landing in death that his plummeting downward spiral in life wouldn't seem to warrant. Angels appear smiling, "beating their wings in time," and Jones, ever the charmer, wins them over: "Oh, I thought I heard one sigh for you."

In the chorus, Jagger repurposes Shelley's "Heaven's light forever shines" for his old pal: "May the good Lord shine a light on you." And, even more important, considering Jones's undeniable talent in life: "Make every song your favorite tune."

In a way, that last line sums up what Jones brought to the table with the band, his ability to take any instrument off the shelf and wield it to give The Stones' songs, which were often harsh or unsentimental in tone and spirit, a bit of idiosyncratic, out-of-the-blue beauty. No one ever quite did get a line on Brian Jones, but, with "Shine a Light," Mick Jagger and friends at least gave him a glorious fare-thee-well.

25. "Salt of the Earth" (from *Beggars Banquet*, 1968)

Rock artists generally operate on one of two wavelengths in respect to their audiences. Some try to write and perform on the level of their fans, hoping they'll be relatable to the common man and woman in this way. Others simply relay their own experiences, which, if the rock star is successful enough, tend to be vastly different than those of the common man or woman.

Both approaches can work if handled correctly. The first approach relies on the performer's ability to understand and convey the problems, concerns, joys, and pains of their fans. In the second approach, the performer relies on the fans' willingness to vicariously experience another kind of lifestyle and its resultant highs and lows. These are admittedly huge generalizations that don't account for nuance or versatility, but if you try it, you can usually stick artists into one of these two categories.

The Rolling Stones have always been firmly among that second group, the ones who write how they live and let the audience respond to the sheer otherness of it all. Yet on "Salt of the Earth," the beautifully realized closing track from 1968's *Beggars Banquet*, the band pays tribute to how the other half, or, let's face it, the other 99 percent lives, all while still admitting their fans seem as alien and distant to the band as the band does to most of their fans.

"Salt of the Earth" was one of the band's first attempts at an anthem that worked toward uplifting an audience. *Beggars Banquet* is, for the most part, an unforgiving kind of album, brutal and unsparing about the realities of the world and full of behavior that ranges from self-serving to heinous. "Salt of the Earth" gives us a bit of a break from all that, showing a sympathetic side to the band at the last possible moment. Putting it at the end, especially with the stomping, double-timing, gospelized coda closing out the song, was an inspiring way for the band to give fans just a glimmer of hope at which to grasp.

While the music yields warm good feelings via the combination of Keith Richards's speedily strummed acoustic guitar; Charlie Watts's booming, connecting drum breaks; Nicky Hopkins's piano and its transformation from contemplative to hard-charging; and the Los Angeles Watts Street Choir, who simply take over the proceedings at the end and leave The Stones hustling to stay in stride, the lyrics don't skimp on the hard truths. Richards gets the first word with the simple plea of "Let's drink to the hard-working people / Let's drink to the lowly of birth," his untrained, moaning vocal seeming to rise right out of the "wavering millions."

Mick Jagger brings a different type of attitude once he takes over the lyrics, one that seems to doubt that the pleas the band makes throughout the song will ever be answered. The people "need leading but get gamblers instead," he sings, some biting criticism sneaking out of this otherwise sober song. He then takes on the sorry lot that passes for elected officials, telling of how the common man's "empty eyes gaze at strange beauty shows / And parades of gray-suited grafters / A choice of cancer or polio." The Stones aren't known for such political broadsides, but Jagger zings the powers that be pretty well there.

Even though he can sympathize with those "uncounted heads" who stare at him every night from the seats below and all around and feel frustration at how they're being played, it doesn't mean he can stand in their shoes. He describes them as "A swirling mass of greys and blacks and whites / They don't seem real to me / In fact they look so strange." It's a stunning admission in the midst of this heartfelt song of encouragement that, while he may wish these people well, he is at too far a remove to truly understand them.

That kind of honesty may make this less of a feel-good rouser, but it adds another dimension to the track. Jagger's admission seems sad somehow, as if he wished he could somehow be at eye level with the majority of the world, but fame and riches sailed that boat long ago for him.

Following the tragedies that befell the United States on 9/11, Jagger and Richards, who at that time were suffering through one of their periodic bouts of animosity toward each other, got together on the stage at Madison Square Garden for the Concert for New York in front of a crowd consisting of firefighters, policemen, and many others who would be considered "Salt of the Earth" and whose lives were deeply affected by the events of that fateful day. With the house band behind them, they put aside their differences and delivered the thirty-three-year-old song, tweaking the lyrics a bit to remove some of the spikier edges, allowing it to be the uniting balm it needed to be on that night.

But that was really only a one-night thing for this fascinating track. In its original rendering, The Stones might have huddled the masses, but they did it from a million miles away.

24. "Beast of Burden" (from *Some Girls*, 1978)

Part open-hearted plea from a man to a woman, part interpersonal band politics, "Beast of Burden" melded those elements together with nary a hitch and turned into a huge hit for The Rolling Stones. It was the second single off *Some Girls* in 1978, and, like its predecessor, "Miss You," it roared into the US Top 10. The common view is that the band hit their artistic high point in the late 1960s and early 1970s, but, in terms of chart success, the stretch they put together from *Some Girls* to *Tattoo You* would be hard to top.

It's also somewhat funny to think that *Some Girls* is often referred to as the band's response to the tougher sounds of punk, especially when you consider those two singles. "Miss You" was suave disco and "Beast of Burden" was straight-up soul testifying, and neither had an ounce of punk in its DNA. Look further on the album, and you'll find a little bit of sneering attitude and songs with frenetic pace, but *Some Girls* is actually as varied in its attack as the best Stones albums tend to be.

"Beast of Burden" stands out as one of the first chances most fans had to hear what a Stones lineup with Ron Wood might sound like. Wood's first full album with the band was *Some Girls*, and since "Miss You" was largely devoid of rock guitars, the second single provided a taste of the guitar-weaving techniques that he and Keith Richards would employ from that point onward.

You can hear those intertwining guitars well on "Beast of Burden" because the leisurely pace and open spaces of the production allow them plenty of room. So fluid is their chemistry that Wood and Richards seem to swim through the song, making it hard to believe that this was the first time they had worked full-time together in the band. At one point, Wood rises up for a quick, sky-bound solo before returning to his interplay with Richards while Charlie Watts keeps things at a steady trot, albeit with some typical head fakes thrown in to keep everybody guessing.

Richards came up with the main idea for the song and allowed Mick Jagger to fill in a lot of the lyrics on the spot. Jagger, understanding that a song as leisurely and laid-back as this one probably couldn't bear the brunt of wordy lyrics, wisely keeps things light and improvisational throughout. Jagger's instincts in these soulful songs have always been spot-on, and "Beast of Burden" is no exception. Listen to the way he alternates between an anguished croon, a playful coo, and a defiant bark depending on what emotion he's choosing to show to the girl he's addressing.

Of course, some Stones fans believe that it's not a girl who he's addressing at all but rather his longtime buddy and bandmate Richards. Richards has hinted as much in interviews, suggesting that some of the emotions he was feeling as he was trying to reinsert himself into the hierarchy of the band after his years of heavy drug use were probably spilling out. You can certainly hear a bit of that if you choose, although the whole thing gets a little muddled by the fact that it's Jagger singing these feelings that could be attributed to Keith.

That's probably why it's best to enjoy the song on the level of so many other great soul songs, which is as a man pouring his heart out to a woman in an attempt to salvage a relationship. In the case of this story, what's causing a rift is the amount of effort the narrator has to put forth to keep her in the fold. "My back is broad, but it's a-hurting," Mick sings early on, and that theme is repeated throughout the song.

He's willing to endure the constant trials and tribulations she throws his way, because the rewards seem to be worth it. "All your sickness, I can suck it up / Throw it all at me, I can shrug it off," he dares her. Certainly these lines could represent the Jagger/Richards dynamic at that time, but, again, the song works on a visceral level without the need for reading deeply into it.

For as put-upon as this guy claims to be, the song projects such warmth that you always feel like there's going to be a positive outcome for him. The harmonies of Jagger and Richards certainly help that cause, giving the feeling of a friendly gang pleading with this girl on their leader's behalf. "Beast of Burden" is The Stones in their element, showing off their love of and talent for soul music while adding heaping helpings of their own charming quirks to the thing. Maybe Keith wrote it about Mick, and maybe Mick was singing it about Keith, or maybe it's just that the kind of codependent relationship that band members sometimes form aligns pretty well with the give-and-take between two lovers. Whatever it is, it works beautifully here.

23. "Get Off of My Cloud" (from *December's Children [and Everybody's]*, 1965)

"If the last one didn't do as well as the one before, that meant you were out, you were sliding out. I mean, it was a state of mind. So each one had to be better and do better, it didn't just have to be better. I mean, you could make a better record each time but if it didn't do better as the other one or at least as good, it was a sign that you were declining. You know, it was just real pressure to come up with a red-hot song that says it all in 2 minutes 20 seconds every eight weeks."[30]

That quote came from Keith Richards in 1982, recalling the ultracompetitive pop scene in the mid-1960s. We like to think of that era as a simpler time in music, but due to the reliance on singles as the ultimate arbiter of success, it really was an age when artists, even ones as formidable as The Rolling Stones, couldn't afford to let down at all. And how is it possible to not let down following a single as monumental as "(I Can't Get No) Satisfaction"?

The Stones rose to this imposing occasion brilliantly late in 1965 with the crackling single "Get Off of My Cloud," which followed "Satisfaction" to the top of the charts in the United States, the United Kingdom, and several other countries all over the world. These back-to-back smashes would have been viewed as an incredible accomplishment by any artist, but considering the fact that Mick Jagger and Keith Richards wrote both those hits a little more than a year after they attempted penning their first songs together, these songs are especially amazing.

What's more impressive is how the band found a way to do all this without compromising an iota of their attitude or sensibility. Both songs are itchy and angsty, with rage boiling slightly below the surface ready to bubble up at any time. From a musical standpoint, they're propulsive and edgy, triumphs of force and friction more so than tunefulness and tenderness.

Yet even though "Get Off of My Cloud" often is lumped in with "Satisfaction," it is by no means a sequel or rehash. Musically, "Satisfaction" is largely built off that unforgettable riff, but "Cloud" gets the job done in a lot of different ways. The guitar hook that Richards created and Brian Jones played on the song is a quizzical thing, scratching its head at its surroundings. Charlie Watts provides the oomph with his killer intro and relentless snares while Bill Wyman probes with his bass. Richards takes the role of rhythm guitarist, clawing away during the verses before really ripping it up heading into the chorus. The production of Andrew Loog Oldham on the song has been maligned by critics and band members over the years, but the claustrophobia of it, whether intended or not, actually works in perfect concert with the complaints of the lyrics.

Mick Jagger once again embodies a bugged protagonist dealing with concerns that seem trivial when taken individually but when added up make for one giant hassle. His apartment is barraged with unwanted visitors and endless phone calls, so he decides to take a wee-hours drive. In the midst of this banging rock and roll, it's interesting to hear Jagger singing, "It was so very quiet and peaceful, there was nobody, not a soul around." They had only just become worldwide superstars, and already all the noise and nonsense seemed to be getting to the band, hence the desire for some sort of temporary oasis.

The narrator's dream is quickly interrupted by an avalanche of parking tickets, which sends him rocketing back into the furious chorus. The call-and-response vocals allow us to indulge in the defiance with the band, since we all at various times in our lives long for solitude and normalcy in a world designed to crowd and craze. "Don't hang around, 'cause two's a crowd," Jagger sings, tossing any would-be hangers-on off his cloud like flies off his shoulder.

It's easy to hear the song as a metaphor for the band's own pressure-cooker lives, what with a ruthless schedule and a record company breathing down their necks. That they were able to solve their problem while getting digs in at their oppressors must have been vindication, at least for the few moments until someone else came knocking at their door to make some other demand.

"Get Off of My Cloud" works on that micro level, but it persists as a rock classic because of how it resonates with anyone frazzled and frustrated by life's daily, ever-encroaching nuisances. Belt out this song, and for those thrilling two minutes and thirty seconds, you'll be at cacophonous peace.

22. "Wild Horses" (from *Sticky Fingers*, 1971)

Gram Parsons's influence on this burned-out love song from *Sticky Fingers* was so strong that it led to some speculation over the years that he might have written it. (The fact that his own version with The Flying Burrito Brothers predates The Stones' release of it helped to cause the confusion.) In fact, "Wild Horses" is one of many songs by the band that Keith Richards originated with one idea in mind, only to have Mick Jagger take it over and take it in an entirely different direction. In this case, the differing motivations and strategies of the two men added up to create a triumphantly tearful ballad.

For three days in December 1969, The Stones stopped into Muscle Shoals studios in Alabama and managed to lay down three songs, one of which was "Wild Horses." ("Brown Sugar" was one of the other two, so you could say it was a productive stint.) The composition was begun by Richards, whose first child was born in August 1969, causing Keith regret about going out on the road and leaving the boy behind.

"It was one of those magical moments when things come together," Richards wrote in his autobiography about the song's genesis. "It's like 'Satisfaction.' You just dream it, and suddenly it's all in your hands. Once you've got the vision in your mind of wild horses, I mean, what's the next phrase you're going to use? It's got to be couldn't drag me away."[31]

So Richards wrote the music, using a twelve-string acoustic guitar to really draw out the melancholy in those chords and the chorus. He then handed the song off to Jagger to complete the verses. And that's when the track took a turn away from Marlon, the name of Richards's little boy, and veered toward Marianne, as in Faithfull, Jagger's on-again, off-again lover of that era.

Or at least that's what everyone assumes. Jagger had a different recollection in the liner notes to the 1993 Stones anthology *Jump Back: The Best of The Rolling Stones*: "I remember we sat around doing this with Gram Parsons, and I think his version came out slightly before ours," Mick said. "Everyone always says it was written about Marianne, but I don't think it was; that was all well over by then. But I was definitely very inside this piece emotionally. This is very personal, evocative, and sad. It all sounds rather doomy now, but it was quite a heavy time."[32]

That heaviness hangs in the air throughout the song. You can hear it in the lazily strummed guitars of Richards and Mick Taylor, in Richards's just-right electric solo, in Charlie Watts's thudding fills. Jim Dickinson filled in on the tack piano when Ian Stewart famously begged off playing the sad chords. As for Jagger, he holds back the histrionics and plays it relatively straight, his fatigue and frustration mingling seamlessly with his unshakable devotion to the wayward girl he's addressing.

The opening lines hint at a simpler time in the couple's life together: "Childhood living is easy to do / The things you wanted I bought them for you." As time passes, however, they become inseparable in anguish as well: "I watched you suffer a dull aching pain / Now you've decided to show me the same."

As bad as things get, the narrator's loyalty never wavers. "You know I can't let you slide through my hands," Jagger sings at the end of the first verse. Perhaps alluding to the drama in her life, he uses the metaphor of the stage to describe his steadfastness: "No sweeping exits or offstage lines / Could make me feel bitter or treat you unkind." And there's that chorus, Richards joining in for heartbreaking harmonies with Jagger to transcend the cliché and make you believe that no amount of horsepower could sway them from their intent.

The final chorus of the song ends with Jagger changing the kicker line. Instead of the horses dragging him away, he sings, "We'll ride them someday." Some might say it's a hopeful ending, but it also sounds like the kind of thing someone would say as parting words to a loved one they won't be seeing again. This kind of poignancy isn't what we often consider when we think of The Rolling Stones. Yet "Wild Horses" demonstrates that the songwriting of Jagger and Richards can fragilely glow just as well as it can bombastically glimmer.

21. "Tumbling Dice" (from *Exile on Main St.*, 1972)

"Tumbling Dice," the Top 10 single that ably represented the notoriously elusive *Exile on Main St.* to the world, very much sounds the essence of ease and languor whenever it's cued up by some classic rock DJ. In actuality, it was the song on the album that required the most battle and strain on behalf of the members of The Rolling Stones to eventually whip it into its amiably amorphous shape.

The song originated as a different tune called "Good Time Women," which you can hear on the bonus disc of the *Exile* reissue released in 2010. The chord changes of the songs are the same, but the original take was played at a much faster pace with much more grit than polish. Mick Jagger's lyrics in the early incarnation are barely formed, but the band saw enough potential to keep after it.

Somewhere along the line, and it was apparently a very long line consisting of endless takes, the song acquired the strolling pace that released its untapped potential. And somewhere along that same line, Jagger scrapped his original lyrics for a new set inspired by a conversation with a gambling-savvy housekeeper. (Let's hope Mick paid her well enough to allow her the disposable income for her hobby.)

And so the "Tumbling Dice" that we know and love was born. It should be noted at this point that not an ounce of that effort is audible on the finished record. From the moment that Keith Richards's guitar jerks the song into life, it emits an undeniable aura of self-confidence. It knows just where it has to go and will get there in the way it chooses, and it damn well knows you're going to follow it every step of the way, because it's that good.

This is another Jimmy Miller production that skimps on crispness in favor of an instrumental cohesion. When Phil Spector created his so-called Wall of Sound, he managed to do it by giving each instrument a crystalline spotlight in the mix. Miller liked to put all of the instruments into a blender, where they swirled around each other, some flavors stronger than others, but none overpowering.

In the case of "Tumbling Dice," the brass parts of Bobby Keys and Jim Price are reduced to a distant blare on the bottom end, where Mick Taylor's deft bass prances around. Richards gets a bit of a solo and a recurring riff but mainly goads the silky rhythm along. In another sign of how this song struggled to life, there were two drummers on board:

Charlie Watts, who played the majority of the track, and Miller, who took over in the coda when Watts couldn't get the feel. All hands needed to be on deck on this album.

The song is a bit of an oddball throughout. There is a blast of "ooh-ooh" backing vocals even before Jagger says his first line. The refrain comes after three verses, then after two more, and then after just one at the end, an asymmetrical construction that somehow makes perfect sense. Frankly, none of it is textbook, but that's the beauty of the whole *Exile* project. The textbook was either burned, thrown out the window, or had something even more untoward done to it, and the resulting chaos, harnessed just so by The Stones, was revelatory.

Jagger's tale of a gambling man who has crapped out at the table but always finds a little bit more luck in temporary romance isn't anything new, but the portrayal is caddishly charming enough that the lack of novelty is an afterthought. The bottom line is that he seems able to convince women in every town to take him in before rolling him on his way. Years later, Jagger would return to the theme with diminishing results on the 1984 solo track "Lucky in Love." That one followed all the rules for what a hit single should be (and, to be fair, did reach the Top 40) but doesn't have a fraction of the magic of "Tumbling Dice."

Then again, few songs do. It's one of those songs where it's useless to try and put a finger on the whys and the wherefores. Take the refrain: "You've got to roll me and call me the tumbling dice." It doesn't appear to make much sense, but when sung by Jagger, those backing vocalists coming in at every angle, it's endlessly profound.

Little miracles like that abound in the song; it all just works. And the bottom line is that "Tumbling Dice" proves that you're allowed to try real hard to get a song right, as long as the end result doesn't sound like you did.

20. "Start Me Up" (from *Tattoo You*, 1981)

If you stick around long enough in the public eye, you're bound to become a caricature. Nuance takes time to translate to an audience, so the press seizes on outsized characteristics or repeated actions to present a portrait of an artist that often resembles something that might be done by somebody for twenty bucks on the boardwalk.

The Rolling Stones made the interesting decision at some point to embrace their collective caricature. You'll hear various stories from friends of Keith Richards about how The Stones' guitarist will be engaging them in an erudite conversation with perfect diction until a camera or a microphone comes into the picture, at which point he cocks his head and reverts into tipsy, slurring Keef mode. Mick Jagger gives interviews that tend to be polite to the point of yawn inducing, only to get on stage and transform into a preening, prancing rooster who mesmerizes audiences for two-hour stretches.

These strategies have worked for them because it's somehow reassuring to their fans that The Stones stay youthful and irreverent in image, even as their actual ages suggest they should be off somewhere collecting their pensions. On "Start Me Up," the band managed to capture the caricature on record, and it's a wonderful thing. It's all there, from the blatant sexual references to Jagger's emoting to the back line's stoicism to the raw and raggedly evocative guitars of Richards and Ronnie Wood. You can see this song as much as you can hear it, the lips logo embedded in your mind's eye as the music rocks your ears.

The ironic part is that this song that so defines that calcified image of the band almost was left on the scrap heap. The Stones started fooling around with what would become "Start Me Up" at the sessions for *Some Girls*, only they were insistent in doing the song in a kind of reggae strut. You can hear the evidence of these attempts with a little online searching; the differences aren't all that severe from what would become the finished song, although those earlier takes had a bit more hitch in their giddyap.

When The Stones couldn't be bothered to write new material for an album for 1981, producer Chris Kimsey came up with the idea to dig through the band's seemingly limitless cutting-room-floor material to see what could be salvaged. He distinctly remembered a take of "Start Me Up" with a bit more rock edge to it, and this basic track would form the basis for the eventual song. Kimsey's archaeological find also convinced the band that a whole album of found material would be viable, which is how *Tattoo You* came to be.

Maybe it's because we've heard the song so many times now that the instruments and vocals are inseparable in a way, but it seems, if Richards's indelible opening guitar riff could be translated into actual words, that it would definitely reveal the phrase "Start Me Up." The rest of the band takes the baton from there and pushes the pleasure levels to strato-spheric heights. Never before have Charlie Watts's drums sounded so overpowering, while Bill Wyman, clearly influenced by the reggae ver-sion, fills in the gaps on the bass with head-bobbing elasticity. That bit of bounce helps to balance the thunder of the guitars and drums and keeps the song limber enough for Jagger to slither about it without getting steamrolled.

For those who prefer their Stones G-rated (if there are such people), you can really stretch your imagination into believing that Jagger is sing-ing about his exploits as a motorcycle racer. The rest of us know that Mick is brazenly flaunting the libidinous desires he has for a particularly hot paramour. To call it innuendo would be giving his approach here more credit than it deserves or even wants, what with references to tops blowing and oil spreading and things leaking and, well, if you can't catch this drift you should just flip to the next track and see how you do with that one.

Jagger's buddies Wood and Richards don't just keep the engine churn-ing with their guitars; they also add some ingratiating harmonies to make this sound like a collective seduction rather than a single-minded pursuit. In the final moments, Mick drops all the pretense with the borrowing of an old blues line: "You make a dead man come." No use in pretending anything but the obvious at that point.

And that's the brilliance of "Start Me Up," really. It feels like The Stones are beating all the critics to the punch line. If that's what everyone expected of them, they showed just how thrilling fulfilling those expecta-tions could be and why that caricature, oversimplified though it may be, has been so captivating for all these years.

19. "Let's Spend the Night Together" (from *Between the Buttons*, US version, 1967)

"Let's Spend the Night Together" continued an incredible run of singles for The Rolling Stones that began with "(I Can't Get No) Satisfaction" in 1965. Time and again, the band proved their ability to make raucous, uncompromising music a staple of the pop charts. In the United King-dom, this track soared to the Top 3. Its ascent in the United States was stalled by the fact that radio stations shied away from the suggestiveness of the title, preferring to play the gentler and equally worthy flip side,

"Ruby Tuesday," instead. (US audiences would be compensated somewhat by the fact that "Let's Spend the Night Together" appeared on their version of The Stones' 1967 album *Between the Buttons*; it was left off the UK version.)

By 1967, The Stones were confident enough in their standing that they no longer felt the need to couch their feelings and desires in innuendo and latent messages, as was the case with the concealed sexual bent of "Satisfaction." It's all right there in the title with "Let's Spend the Night Together," and the desire is made even more explicit by the urgency and intensity of the music. Not only was the band unafraid to put this sexually charged message across without any kind of buffer, but they were also demonstrating through the tenor of the song just how important it was to them. And it's still refreshingly frank even after many years of cultural lightening up.

Hard-charging piano replaced air-clearing electric guitar as the band's weapon of choice on the song. The band had recently attempted a piano-driven single with "Have You Seen Your Mother, Baby, Standing in the Shadows?" Alas, this song was ruined by a ham-handed brass fanfare that overwhelmed it and made it sound like some kind of Vegas blowout. They must have learned their lessons from it, because the piano thrust here is undeniable. (Richards has stated in interviews that he played piano on the track, but it's also possible that Jack Nitzsche, a common Stones collaborator at that point, played some piano in the final mix as well.)

Besides the piano, the other two standout elements here are Charlie Watts's trouble-starting drums and the unforgettable "ba-da-da . . ." backing vocals that form an irresistible hook. There's not much letup on this track, with the exception of the dreamy bridge. That bridge is brief, but it serves the purpose of highlighting the gusto of the main groove once it kicks back in.

Speaking of that bridge, there is a bit of a Beach Boys vibe to the way the "doo-doo-doo" vocals lap around each other lusciously. That doesn't seem like a coincidence. In 1966, the Boys had a hit with "Wouldn't It Be Nice," a song that also expresses the desire for a couple to spend the night together, only it does so much more politely and under the guise of a marriage that would make the cohabitation permanent.

The little homage (or maybe it's a parody) in that section of "Let's Spend the Night Together" clearly seems intended to show the differences in the two approaches. There's also a vast difference between the way Brian Wilson sings his song like a friendly suitor and Mick Jagger attacks his with abandon and untethered emotion. Which approach is better, in terms of music or seduction, is a matter of taste, but the point is that The Stones couldn't be bothered with subtle hints. They were going to lay it on the line, judgment or criticism be damned.

The way they pulled off "Let's Spend the Night Together" seemed to render any arguments against its morality awfully hard to hear. Jagger's convincing whether he's shouting out barely disguised bedroom come-ons or simply reveling in the thought of the girl's eventual capitulation. (Listen to the pure delight in his "my, my, my" refrain.) In the song's final verse, he even throws it back to "Satisfaction" in a way: "I'll satisfy your every need, your every need / And now I know you will satisfy me."

The Stones performed the song on *The Ed Sullivan Show*, and Jagger was famously forced to sing the words "Let's spend some time together" by leery network censors. Never ones to be bested, the band's response was handled by Jagger, who rolled his eyes in comical fashion every time he got to the word "time." The Rolling Stones' refusal to compromise on issues like this is its own form of integrity, and they would help lead the charge toward the collapse of the staid, restrained culture of the generation older than the band in the years to come. None of that tangential stuff would have been possible without the chops and the songs though, and "Let's Spend the Night Together" delivers brilliantly on both of those levels.

18. "Slipping Away" (from *Steel Wheels*, 1989)

It's odd to think now how integral the lead vocal contributions from Keith Richards have become to the albums of The Rolling Stones when you consider that it took him five years into the band's recording career to finally step up to the mike and go solo on "You Got the Silver" from *Let It Bleed* in 1969. Think of all of the wonderful ballads we would have missed, many of which made this list (and a few others, like "How Can I Stop?," "Sleep Tonight," and "This House Is Empty," that weren't that far off).

The Stones often place these Richards-led numbers at the ends of their albums, a wise strategy since their after-hours, bluesy ambience is the perfect come-down after the hard-driving rock and roll that usually precedes them. "Slipping Away," which closed out 1989's quasi-comeback album *Steel Wheels*, is both the quintessence and the best of these songs.

"Slipping Away" is one of the first songs in the band's history that acknowledges the passing of time. There were other ballads prior to it, like "Memory Motel" or "Winter," that nodded to the past, but only in terms of a young man looking back at a love from when he was a younger man. (Oddly enough, "As Tears Go By," written by Richards and Jagger when they were still ridiculously young, might be the closest thing to an old-age rumination in the band's catalog up to the point of *Steel Wheels*.)

One wonders if the band paused a bit before committing this song to tape. After all, "Slipping Away" was an admission of sorts that these seemingly eternally youthful rockers with the energy of those a third of their actual age actually could feel the ravages of time. If there was a strategy involved in the song's release, it paid off. Since that time, similarly bittersweet reflections that included the calendar's brutal march as subtext would appear with regularity on the band's records, often courtesy of these Richards' showstoppers, and their presence deepened these records immensely.

"Slipping Away" delivers this shock to the senses of Stones fans right in its title. In the verses, the narrator rues that the inevitable erosion he perceives in himself is beyond his control, taking pieces of him when he sleeps or even breathes. It's almost needless to say that the loss of love exacerbates this phenomenon: "Just as you have touched my heart / I wake up, baby, and we're apart." Even when he tries to wax philosophical about time, he inadvertently betrays the futility of fighting its effects: "First the sun and then the moon / One of them will be round soon."

On many of the songs that Richards had performed solo in the past, there was little to no contribution from Mick Jagger. Yet there's something touching and telling about the way Jagger comes in to harmonize here on the bridge, which snaps out of the laid-back groove of the verses and takes on a more urgent tone: "All I want is ecstasy / But I ain't gettin' much," the pair sings. "Just getting off on misery / It seems I've lost my touch." There is none of the bravado or attitude for which the band is known in these lines, yet there is an infinite amount of honesty and pathos there. This is a side of the band that we hadn't seen, but we quickly realize that it's quite moving.

Richards helps himself a great deal with a pretty melody and then relies on his bandmates and cohorts to deliver the musical goods. The harmonies in the refrains, courtesy of Bernard Fowler, Lisa Fischer, and Sarah Dash, are arranged for maximum tenderness. Charlie Watts provides an unwavering pulse while Bill Wyman, on the last track of the last album on which he would play as a Stone, yields a melodic and sympathetic bottom end. Like in the old days of *Exile on Main St.*, instruments sneak up on you out of nowhere at odd times, a bit of piano here, an acoustic guitar part to complement the electric there, some horns at the end to prop up the soulful coda.

Without ever exerting himself too much, Richards reigns over it all with a resigned sorrow that permeates every croak and moan that slips out of him. As he scats amid the lovely walled backing vocalists in the coda, we hear a man who's ready to face what comes but not without uncertainty and trepidation. The old joke says that Keith Richards, having survived so much in his life, will probably outlive us all. "Slipping Away" argues that even if you're indestructible, you can feel the pain of what doesn't kill you.

17. "Shattered" (from *Some Girls*, 1978)

Sometimes it takes an outsider to really nail the vibe of a place or region. In rock-and-roll terms, think of the way that Canadian Robbie Robertson wrote all of those incredible songs about the American South for The Band. Or the way that Don Henley and Glenn Frey, originally from Texas and Michigan, respectively, captured the hedonism tinged with melancholy that pulsed from Southern California in the 1970s.

To that list, you can add Mick Jagger, who, on "Shattered" in 1978, delivered an incisive snapshot of New York City, summing up The Big Apple of that era better in less than four minutes than cultural historians could hope to do given a book's length. *Some Girls*, the album that produced the song, is the band's most urban record by far; even the one foray into country on the album ("Far Away Eyes") is so wrongheaded that it could only have come from city slickers. It isn't until "Shattered" appears as the last song on the album that we can retrospectively hear *Some Girls* as a concept album of sorts about life in a city that never sleeps or takes prisoners.

Some Girls is often considered to be Jagger's record, considering Richards was dealing with the legal ramifications of a drug arrest at the time of its making. Yet "Shattered" wouldn't be what it is without Richards's contributions, which includes the burping main riff, achieved by adding a phaser effect to his guitar, and the unforgettable "Shadoobie" refrain, which somehow speaks volumes about the nonsense that the city throws in your face every single day.

Keep in mind that New York City in 1978 was a far cry from the shiny-surfaced, *Today Show*–ready haven it is today. The promise of something big waiting around the corner was accompanied back then by crime and squalor. It's that NYC that Jagger describes, and he does so while nodding to rap, then in its relative infancy, with the way he speak-sings the lyrics and punk, if not so much in musical execution, then at least in we're-screwed attitude.

He's abetted in this journey by Charlie Watts's tough drums and Ronnie Wood's high, stinging guitars, which contrast the low burble of Richards. "Shattered" is another example of the band taking other genres and making them their own. What was impressive here is that the genres in question were relatively new, and yet the band sounds completely at home in their midst.

In The Stones' rendering, the city is a voracious living entity, fed by a heady mix of love, joy, sex, dreams, laughter, loneliness, sex and sex and sex, pride, greed, dirty dreams, and (just in case you didn't hear Mick the first nineteen times) sex. The narrator is taking the worst of it though: "And look at me, I'm in tatters."

Some of the descriptions play up the surreal nature of the surroundings: "People dressed in plastic bags, directing traffic." At other times, Jagger easily slips into the town's lingo to play up this guy's frustration: "All this chitter-chatter, chitter-chatter, chitter-chatter 'bout / Shmata, shmata, shmata, I can't give it away on Seventh Avenue." The clever repetition of words hints at the excess of everything available to the city's denizens.

Jagger delivers this murky monologue brilliantly, his been-there, done-that cool giving way to itchy tension. "Don't you know the crime rate is going up, up, up, up, up?" he bellows. Things get really ugly as the song progresses: "We got rats on the west side, bed bugs uptown." "Go ahead, bite the big apple, don't mind the maggots," Jagger dares the listener. His final line suggests that it's best to just go along for the tawdry ride rather than rail against the squalor: "Pile it up, pile it up / Pile it high on the platter."

Whether the "it" in that closing salvo refers to food, money, or drugs, the implication is that too much of it, while it might be pleasurable for a while, will eventually catch up to you. "Shattered" is one of The Rolling Stones' most memorable depictions of street life, all the more remarkable considering that the streets in question weren't their native ones.

16. "Mother's Little Helper" (from *Aftermath*, UK version, 1966)

Benzodiazepine was discovered in 1955 and began being sold in 1960. The most popular brand of this new drug was Valium, which soon began being prescribed for short-term psychological problems like insomnia or longer-term issues like anxiety. Most current assessments by medical professionals and conductors of studies are in consensus that it was probably overprescribed, especially considering its highly addictive nature.

The fact that the drug was already on the radar of The Rolling Stones in 1966 when they released "Mother's Little Helper" is an indication of how quickly it rose to prominence. Whether Mick Jagger read about it in some newspaper piece or they ran across it on their travels, the band realized that housewives, frazzled and frenzied from their nonstop efforts to maintain their homes and families, were the ones most likely to partake of this new medication. The term "Mother's Little Helper" has since become synonymous for any drug used by a wife or mother to help them get through the mounting problems of a single day. The song's insinuation is that those single days pile up into weeks and years, until dependency on the drug is inevitable.

Of course, The Stones would never say it with that kind of righteousness or clinical coldness. Give credit to Jagger, who wrote the lyrics, for making the protagonist of his song a kind of amalgam of all women, thereby highlighting the breadth of the problem. By keeping her tale relatively general but still imbuing it with telling insight, he makes it easy for us to substitute any harried mother in her place.

He sings his tale over a bed of music that is brooding but not without color. For a change, Bill Wyman's bass powers the song, generating a steady rumble that moves the track stealthily along. Charlie Watts bangs away with a bit more abandon than one might expect from what is essentially a folk song, but it works, and his connecting fills when the music briefly drops away are always interesting. Keith Richards, who wrote the music, provides the cackling, almost macabre riff on a twelve-string electric guitar that stands out amid the low drone. (It should be noted that some sources list Brian Jones as the one who plays the twelve-string; Richards gets the benefit of the doubt here though, because he provided a pretty detailed remembrance of playing the part in interviews about the song.)

Jagger gets the song rolling before his compatriots can even join him, mewling out the immortally obvious opening line, "What a drag it is getting old." "Kids are different today, I hear every mother say," he sings, so attuned to the jargon of moms that you'd think he was part of their daily tea meetings. He also doesn't waste any time in seeing through this woman's need for Valium: "And though she's not really ill," he sings, "there's a little yellow pill." (Although the brand name is never mentioned and there are other brands of benzodiazepine as well as other drugs that performed similar functions, we're going with Valium here since that was the one that had heavily permeated the culture by 1966.)

The ominous thrum of the music lets you know that this woman won't be getting "through her busy day" without some sort of consequence. As the song progresses, we find out that it's not just the kids bringing these moms down. Husbands aren't what they used to be, either. The normal demands of cooking and cleaning are mentioned, but there's a sexual subtext, par for the course with The Stones. How else can you read lines like "They just don't appreciate that you get tired" and "They're so hard to satisfy" than to see them as barely veiled complaints about the bedroom demands of an insensitive husband?

In the bridge, which features Jagger's voice overdubbed so he can perform some nifty close harmonies with himself, the mother steps forward to beseech the local physician for some medication. "Outside the door, she took four more," he confides, the drugs only exacerbating her problems instead of solving them.

We know where this is headed, although Jagger spares us an actual overdose, only warning of one. In the final verse, the mother confesses that it's not just that her work is hard; it's that it's also boring. There's a bit of feminism in that admission, something you wouldn't ever associate with The Stones, but it's there nonetheless and well ahead of its time to boot. It also sounds like the band is sending a message back to all those who would bemoan the depravity of the rock-and-roll lifestyle, contending that suburbia breeds its own brand of discontent and misbehavior.

The final "Hey" in "Mother's Little Helper" is intended as a wake-up call, but, if we're to believe the song, the mothers in this song might be in too much of a stupor to hear it. The Rolling Stones were certainly wide awake to the problem though, even if they were the last band you'd ever expect to deliver a cautionary tale.

15. "Miss You" (from *Some Girls*, 1978)

"Miss You" just wasn't fair. No rock-and-roll band should have been able to ease into the disco milieu without showing any strain whatsoever or losing their identity in the process. But that's exactly what The Rolling Stones managed to do, sashaying away with a No. 1 US hit in the process (it went to No. 3 in the United Kingdom) and a song that now, despite its dance-floor-ready origins, is a classic rock staple.

Close listeners of the band's output knew that, by 1978, dance music had been on the band's radar for several years. Album cuts like "Fingerprint File" and "Hot Stuff" showed that The Stones could background melody in favor of rhythm, even though the rhythms in those songs were more funk infused than anything else.

"Miss You" was the first single on *Some Girls*, a highly publicized album introducing a new band lineup (Ronnie Wood had replaced Mick Taylor), so the spotlight, or strobe light as the case may have been, was on the song. The fact that a song that embraced the four-on-the-floor rhythms of disco coincided with this fresh incarnation of the band may have had some purists fearing that these rock-and-roll poster boys were abandoning the Good Ship Chuck Berry.

That was far from the case, of course, and, what was more important, The Stones on this record sounded like they were once again invested in fighting for the title of the world's greatest band after years of coasting a bit following the heady highs of the late 1960s and early 1970s. That they could do this while striking out into modern sonic territory and not relying on past glories was nothing short of miraculous.

"Miss You" starts, like so many great Stones songs, with a great riff. But it's not long after the first iteration of that riff that the differences start to come to the fore. Watts's suave, Studio 54–flavored kick drum is quickly accompanied by Bill Wyman's pogoing bass line. Wyman took inspiration for his part from Billy Preston, who helped Jagger conceive the song in Keith Richards's absence in 1978. Richards was a bit player at times on the *Some Girls* album, in part because of legal troubles surrounding a drug arrest in Toronto. It's easy to wonder if a song like this would have come to fruition with a more active Keith and his traditionalist leanings in the fold.

In any case, Wyman and Watts effortlessly play the slinky rhythms as if they were second nature and not something they were both learning on the fly. They receive ample help in constructing the overall sound of the song from Richards and Wood, who stab at the deadpan elegance of the beat with jagged guitar fills; Ian McLagan, whose electric piano sneaks into the picture in the song's second half; and Sugar Blue, who takes over harmonica duties from Jagger and provides soulful commentary throughout.

Jagger keeps the lyrics simple, conversational, knowing that any flowery touches might sink the overall feeling he's seeking here. These words have to sound like they're flashing right from his gut into his brain with no filter. And he sings masterfully as well, holding in his emotion in his early verses, parceling bits of it out only in the "Ooh-ooh" falsetto cries. The early restraint only makes his eventual capitulation to his overwhelming desires that much more effective.

Urgency begins creeping in during the bridge ("Baby, why you wait so long?"), the narrator's pain audible for the first time. Partying friends and potential replacement girls don't offer him any solace. By song's end, he's out in Central Park stalking the night as if he's deranged, "Ooh-ooh"-ing himself right into lust-infused madness. His cool façade shattered, he admits he's been "lying to myself, it's just you and no one else" and that she's been "blotting out my mind, fooling on my time."

Mel Collins splits the night air with a jittery sax solo, and Blue adds the coup de grâce with a quick romp that sounds almost like it was played by a violin, so lyrical and nimble are the notes. All of the moving parts contribute without getting in each other's way, and that beat just keeps pounding away, mimicking either the narrator's head about to explode or his heart about to implode.

The Stones manage to locate the sensuality of the disco beat while still adding the messier energy inherent in the best rock. If there is one quality about this band that most of its peers must envy, it's versatility. It's at the forefront on "Miss You," as they dip their foot into the pool of disco and damn near blow everyone else out of the water.

14. "Under My Thumb" (from *Aftermath*, 1966)

What an interesting coincidence that "Under My Thumb" should be just a notch ahead of "Miss You" on this list of the greatest songs of The Rolling Stones. It's not likely that too many people would categorize these songs together, considering that they were released a dozen years apart, which is practically eons on a rock music scene, where things seem to change so fast. Yet when you play the songs back-to-back, you begin to realize just how similar they are.

Both are built around an irresistible groove carved out by Bill Wyman and Charlie Watts. Both feature slinky, insinuating riffs; electric guitar and harmonica do the honors on "Miss You," while Brian Jones plays the riff in "Under My Thumb" on the marimbas of all things. Both songs are sleek and restrained for much of their duration, only uncoiling a bit for effect as they progress. Listening to them one after another, one a classic rock and oldies staple and the other the band's supposed foray into disco, makes the whole act of trying to herd certain songs into genres seem like a pointless exercise. Great bands like The Stones dance across those stylistic lines so deftly that they pretty much eradicate them.

Where the two songs differ is in their lyrical approaches. Where "Miss You" portrays a guy almost helplessly in lust with a female whom he can't possess, "Under My Thumb" turns that scenario on its ear in a fashion that has caused more than a little controversy over the years. Feminists, in particular, have taken umbrage with the narrator in the song for calling his girlfriend a "squirming dog" and for noting with barely suppressed glee "the way she talks when she's spoken to." The very title of the song could easily be read as a celebration of sexist behavior.

Probably the key factor in whether or not you find the song offensive lies in whether you believe that Mick Jagger is writing through a character or playing a thinly veiled version of himself. If you believe the latter and you have feminist leanings, you're probably none too happy with "Under My Thumb." But that's a bit of a slippery slope. How then would you reconcile Jagger writing "Hang Fire" when he was clearly not on the dole or writing "As Tears Go By" through the perspective of an old man when he was in his early twenties?

The argument against that would be to say that Jagger's playboy lifestyle mirrors the kind of sexual conquest the song describes, but again that doesn't seem fair to Mick. Songs are not documentaries and shouldn't be treated as such, and writers should have the leeway to depict any type of behavior they wish, even if it might be unsavory. The Stones have pushed this envelope time and again throughout their career, and it's to their credit that they've been fearless enough to show a darker side of human nature that pop songs, for the most part, pretended didn't exist in earlier years. It's impossible to imagine the last fifty years of rock and roll without the genre making the leap to address real life, warts and all, and The Stones were at the forefront of that movement.

What makes "Under My Thumb" so fascinating is that it does its job so well that the sly sexual commentary almost slips by as you're listening. There's a reason that this song, which came from 1966's *Aftermath* but was never released as a single, is one of the most oft-played tracks by the band on radio. That killer groove; Jones's marimbas, which morph from conspiratorial in the verses to jubilant in the run-up to the refrain; a shivery solo from Keith Richards in the break; the thrilling sprint to the finish, with bits of fuzz electric guitar from Richards playing off the smoothness of the rhythm and Jagger getting his workout in on the mike—it all adds up to an endlessly satisfying whole that withstands repeat listens without any strain.

All of this musical cohesion gives the message, if it is indeed a message and not just a random story of one particular relationship, of "Under My Thumb" a reason to exist. Compare it to a song like "Some Girls," which seems to have no other reason for being other than to get some tongues wagging and grab some publicity for the band.

"Take it easy, baby," Jagger sings as the song comes to its close. Maybe he was anticipating the negative reaction the song would engender and launching a preemptive strike against any criticism. Or maybe, and this seems more likely, he was just grooving on the track like most everybody else who crosses its path seems to do, without getting too caught up in what was being sung. Even if you're not swayed by the arguments here and still find fault with the message of "Under My Thumb," you still have to marvel at the capabilities of the messengers.

13. "Waiting on a Friend" (from *Tattoo You*, 1981)

In a 2013 *Rolling Stone* article that detailed, among other things, the interpersonal relationships between the members of The Rolling Stones, both Charlie Watts and Keith Richards were quoted as saying that Mick

Jagger and Richards were like brothers. Their point was that it takes a close, almost familial relationship to inspire the kind of arguments and hostility the two have occasionally expressed to each other over the course of their fifty-plus years working together.

Jagger pointedly disagreed. "People always say things like that," he told Mikal Gilmore for the article. "But I have a brother [Chris Jagger], you know? My relationship with my brother is a brotherly relationship, and it's nothing at all like my relationship with Keith, which is more like someone you work with, completely different. With a brother, you have parents in common. You have families in common. We don't have that, Keith and I. We work together. It's nothing to do with it being a brotherly relationship."[33]

This came just three years after the publication of Richards's autobiography, which laid waste to Jagger in a number of ways. Amidst the insults and name-calling, Richards took the time to display genuine hurt at the state of affairs of the relationship. "Sometimes, I think, 'I miss my friend,'" he wrote. "I wonder, 'Where did he go?'"[34]

For any of those Rolling Stones fans still holding on to the vision of an unbreakable bond of friendship and love between The Glimmer Twins, quotes like these are like ice water poured over their heads to jolt them out of a pleasant reverie. And yet the aural evidence of "Waiting on a Friend," The Stones' beloved ballad of bonhomie from *Tattoo You*, offers a counterpoint that's somehow more convincing. While it lilts away, the idea of Jagger and Richards as inseparably bonded for life is impossible to eradicate.

"Waiting on a Friend" was one of the oldest reclamation projects for the *Tattoo You* album; the basic track was recorded in Jamaica back in 1972 when the band was working on *Goats Head Soup*. Although he doesn't receive credit on the album, Mick Taylor did eventually receive royalties for playing guitar as part of the lush instrumental mix. Nicky Hopkins's piano is the foremost factor in the trebly construct, with tinkling runs that make the song glide.

Once the band decided to redo the song for *Tattoo You*, some key guests were added. Mike Carabello plays a variety of percussion instruments to give "Waiting on a Friend" a light and airy rhythm, while jazz legend Sonny Rollins plays saxophone solos in the instrumental break and the outro that jibe with the song's relaxed vibe yet still soar. Jagger's falsetto adds to the dreamy feel.

The lyrics depict a guy who seems to be fed up with female companionship, categorizing the ladies as gossips at best and whores at worst. (Funny that this one didn't raise too much ire from feminists; maybe it just sounds so innocent that it skirted by.) What he needs is something they can't quite provide: "I'm not waiting on a lady / I'm just waiting on a friend."

In the final verses, he elaborates on this exigency: "I need someone I can cry to / I need someone to protect." Those two lines say a lot about friendship, in that they imply that supplying it is just as important to a soul's well-being as receiving it. Other pursuits just don't measure up: "Making love and breaking hearts / It is a game for youth." In that couplet, Jagger both negates the band's love-'em-and-leave-'em reputation and makes a reference to getting older, bold, uncharacteristic moves that somehow strengthen the devotion to friendship he exalts here.

It's hard to separate these sentiments from the video that accompanied the song, one of the band's first and probably their best. There's that great painterly shot of Jagger on the stoop of St. Mark's Place in New York (with reggae great Peter Tosh hanging out there with him), just idling about until Richards comes strutting down the street in his hat and scarf. The two then stagger into a bar where Ronnie Wood, Bill Wyman, and Charlie Watts are waiting, and the feelings evoked by both the sound and the vision are as warm as any the band have ever produced.

Those feelings are potent enough to ultimately win the day concerning the dynamic between Jagger and Richards. So what if all other evidence points to a relationship perhaps irreversibly frayed by the passing of time instead of strengthened? On top of its infinite charms as a song, "Waiting on a Friend" is essential for allowing us all to indulge in the sentimental illusion of Jagger and Richards as brothers for life.

12. "Rocks Off" (from *Exile on Main St.*, 1972)

It says something about the polarizing nature of *Exile on Main St.* that the album, often hailed as the greatest in the history of The Rolling Stones, which, by definition, puts it on the short list for greatest album in the history of rock and roll, often gets put down by one of its chief creators. Mick Jagger has often gone on record to complain about the album's mix, its lack of standout songs, and the haphazard nature of its recording.

In *According to The Rolling Stones* in 2003, Jagger mentioned how difficult it is to play the songs from *Exile* live. "So there's a good four songs off it," Jagger says (referencing "Sweet Virginia," "Happy," "Tumbling Dice," and "All Down the Line"), "but when you start to play the other nineteen, you can't, or they don't work, or nobody likes them, and you think, 'OK, we'll play another one instead.' We have rehearsed a lot of the tunes off *Exile*, but there's not much that's playable."[35]

The funny thing about it is that much of what Jagger is saying is true, but that doesn't negate the brilliance of *Exile*. Maybe the songs can't be replayed properly in a live setting, but that's only because that chaotic atmosphere in which the album was recorded could never possibly be reproduced. The mix is murky, but it only adds to the allure. The album is a rollercoaster and it's unkempt and frustrating at times, but within it lie myriad moments of transcendence that cleaner, more direct rock music never attains.

Just because a song like "Rocks Off" won't ever be played live to the band's standards, that doesn't in any way mitigate its original brilliance, when it served as the bawdy, bounding kick-starter for *Exile*. The song builds from the usual Stones starting point, a dirty Keith Richards guitar riff, and expands into wild and wooly territory, almost spinning out of control on several occasions. It reaches impossible heights in the process and manages to say something about the drudgery of everyday life from the perspective of a million-record-selling rock star that somehow resonates with all of us who've never set foot on a stage or in front of a microphone.

Jagger can deny the song's excellence now all he wants, but his animated response of "Oh, yeah!" to Richards's opening salvo on the record begs to differ. As is often the case with The Stones, what sustains the song once all the disparate elements intrude is the rhythm section. Bill Wyman plays more forcefully here than normal to cut through the din, and Charlie Watts's rolls to the cymbal offer listeners orienting points to help wrap their heads around the whole cacophony. And what a cacophony it turns out to be, with barreling piano from Nicky Hopkins and mariachi-style horns from Jim Price and Bobby Keys.

Jagger drawls out the verses as if barely awake, Richards joining him for the bridges and refrains in high harmony. The refrain of "I only get my rocks off while I'm dreaming" might seem to suggest sexual frustration, but the song hints at a deeper malaise than that. Even as Jagger references a dalliance with a dancer ("I can't seem to stay in step / Cause she come every time that she pirouettes on me"), what really registers are his feelings of ineffectuality that practically render him a ghost in plain sight.

The highs and lows of the narrator blend together into an indistinguishable whoosh: "I'm zipping through the days at lightning speed / Plug in, flush out, and fire the f***in' feed." "I can't even feel the pain no more," he complains, and that feeling of numbness is understandable to anyone who finds life's finer points are being inexorably dulled by the march of time.

As if there weren't enough going on in "Rocks Off," the song takes a kind of psychedelic breakdown about halfway through, with Jagger swirling around in a weightless cloud for a moment. This brief interlude might indicate a drug trip, or it can just be a pleasant reverie that recharges the narrator's senses. In any case, Jagger snaps out of it singing an octave higher, energized but ultimately still frustrated: "The sunshine bores the daylights out of me." Hearing these lines, it seems clear that it's not only orgasmic pleasure that this guy can get in his dreams; pleasure of any kind seems to be severely lacking in his everyday life.

Putting such a depressing sentiment next to the vigor of the music surrounding him turns out to be a brilliant gambit, because it suggests that even the headiest rush can't quite overcome these blues. Of course The Stones couldn't ever hope to play "Rocks Off," or much of the music on *Exile* for that matter, like it is on the record. How would anybody ever recreate such imperfect perfection?

11. "(I Can't Get No) Satisfaction" (from *Out of Our Heads*, US version, 1965)

It has to be a blessing to a band when their signature song also happens to be a pretty great track that's also representative of their material as a whole. Since what becomes a hit or registers with an audience is beyond an artist's control, this isn't always a given.

In the case of The Rolling Stones, "(I Can't Get No) Satisfaction" is still their signature song fifty years since it was released in 1965, and it's not enough to say that it holds up well; it's more accurate to say that it still packs all of its original punch. It is often ranked by critics as one of the greatest hits in rock-and-roll history. Such accolades should not automatically rocket a song to the top of an artist's body of work. "Satisfaction" feels right about here in terms of its merit, even with the acknowledgment that its impact on rock and roll probably outstrips that of any other Stones effort.

Going back to my book on Bruce Springsteen and my discussion on "Born to Run," I noted how evergreen songs that are heard so often on the radio and played a million times in concert are the hardest ones to judge. You really have to force yourself to hear the song anew when you listen to it and catch the nuances and flourishes within it that you might have taken for granted through many years and listens.

"(I Can't Get No) Satisfaction" presents that same problem, especially since you have to subconsciously wade through the mythology around it. Most casual fans know the story, or at least parts of it: Keith Richards writing the riff and then falling asleep, only to hear it on a tape recorder the next morning; Richards and Jagger doubting the song could be a hit single; Richards envisioning the riff to be played by horns. And so on and so forth. Of course, none of that would mean a thing if the end result weren't so thrilling.

Probably the most difficult thing about judging "Satisfaction" properly is trying to feel again the impact of that opening riff as it must have sounded blaring out of speakers in 1965. It's still a powerful thing, no doubt, but, at the time, there was nothing really that compared in terms of brashness and wildness. It was a sound that only rock and roll could make, and it took The Stones and Richards to discover it. That there have been a multitude of imitations of that riff over the years, many by The Stones themselves, shouldn't be held against it. (Nor should it excuse it from being judged against other riffs that may dig even deeper, such as the ones on The Stones' own "Jumpin' Jack Flash" or "Gimme Shelter.")

It also feels sometimes like the riff in "Satisfaction" overshadows the other wonderful elements it contains. Bill Wyman's bass line nimbly sidesteps Charlie Watts's bashing beat, which gets extra juice from Jack Nitzsche striking the stuffing out of a tambourine. Richards also finds a multitude of open spaces within the song to insert all kinds of fills that range from takeoffs on surf music to Chuck Berry strutting. Even though the arrangement essentially keeps repeating itself, the little bits of color that Richards provides outside of his riff keeps things varied.

Most people also tend to hear the words in the refrain and some of the more showy lines in the lyrics without noticing the subtleties that Mick

Jagger provides. It's easy to locate the frustration and alienation in the lines, but there's something like freedom in there as well. By being able to spot the absurdities in advertising, by noting the futility of trying to build a relationship, even a temporary one, the narrator is empowering himself to overcome these nuisances. The music plays up this feeling with its jubilant desecration of the more formal-sounding rock that The Stones' biggest competitor, The Beatles, tended to purvey up to that point.

That difference of approach might be the ultimate reason why "(I Can't Get No) Satisfaction" resonated so much at the time. The Beatles could be idolized, but it must have been hard for a teenager to relate to them on a human level, these perfectly dressed, handsome youngsters who played every note in place, sang like angels, and left tunes behind that were absolutely airtight in their perfection. Here were The Stones, playing guitars like air horns, singing a grammatically incorrect refrain, swearing that life was a big pain, that getting girls required dealing with their cycles, and that the end result of even your noblest efforts was more often than not going to be a big zero. And sounding absolutely liberated in doing so.

That otherness still powers through, no matter how many times "(I Can't Get No) Satisfaction" is played, long after any comparisons with The Beatles stopped having any bearing on the song's effect on listeners. All else aside, it's as good an explanation as any for how the song somehow casts a larger shadow on the history of rock and roll than it does on the catalog of The Rolling Stones.

10. "Memory Motel" (from *Black and Blue*, 1976)

For every excellent life-on-the-road anthem written by rock stars, there are probably about a dozen more that are self-indulgent and riddled with clichés. Some artists stay away from writing such songs altogether, since they don't really relate to the lives of their listeners in any way. Such songs had their heyday in the late-1980s, when hair-metal bands trotted out about one per album, featuring grainy videos of tour buses, planes landing in the rain, and slow-motion concert footage.

The Rolling Stones have written a lot of songs about rock and roll but not too many about the touring lifestyle. Maybe that's because they knew they knocked it out of the park with the stellar "Memory Motel," a life-on-the-road song that succeeds because it brings the rock star down to the level of the fans by concentrating on lost love, a theme that's universal.

"Memory Motel" doesn't exactly have the pedigree of your typical Stones classic. For one, it appears on 1976's *Black and Blue*, an album now mostly known not so much for its music but for its significance as the one where the group auditioned guitarists to replace Mick Taylor. And although there is fine guitar work throughout by Wayne Perkins on tender acoustic and Harvey Mandel on weeping electric, the song is driven by its keyboards: Mick Jagger plays a piano that sounds as if it's been sitting in a hotel bar unused for years but with lots of stories to tell, Keith Richards conjures a whole range of emotions on electric piano, and Billy Preston comes aboard late with synthesizer strings to add another hint of heartache to a song already brimming with it.

Speaking of Preston, he, Jagger, Richards, and Wood form a four-man group to produce some of the loveliest harmonies in Stones history. Whether they're seconding the refrain or singing sweet "Sha-la-la's," they're a big part of the reason why this is one of the most ingratiating recordings in the band's history.

Since there is an actual Memory Motel in Montauk in Long Island, New York, and Jagger used some of his tour itinerary from 1975 for the lyrics, most people assume the "Hannah" who bewitches the narrator to also have been inspired by a real-life love of Jagger. Carly Simon is the most common assumption on this front, especially when you consider the descriptions of her looks in the lyrics ("Her eyes were hazel, her teeth were slightly curved") and the fact that she serenades the narrator with her guitar in hand.

"Memory Motel" doesn't really need any of those associations to succeed, however, mostly because it's easier without them to place yourself in the shoes of the narrator and feel the bittersweet tug of memories that only remind you of what you've lost. So what if you haven't been in fifteen states and stayed in skyscraping hotels like the narrator? You could easily be in the same town as a former love and still feel as hollow in your gut as Jagger does here.

The descriptions are some of the most evocative in the band's catalog. "It took a starry night to steal my breath away," Jagger sings. "Down on the waterfront, her hair all drenched in spray." Those are the kinds of lines that you might expect to be sung by Nat King Cole in a string-laden ballad. That prettiness is balanced out by some of the rawer feelings on display, as Jagger sings of frayed nerves, gnawed bones, and, ultimately, a retreat to alcohol to get away from both the aggravations of the road and the tortures brought on by the thoughts of Hannah.

In between each verse, Richards steps in with a little interlude that's like a completely different song, making "Memory Motel" not too dissimilar from Lennon/McCartney mash-ups like "We Can Work It Out" or "Baby You're a Rich Man," where the personality of each composer shines through. In this case, Jagger's more heart-rending histrionics in the verses are contrasted by Richards's measured appreciation of what makes the girl so special: "She's got a mind of her own, and she use it well."

The narrator keeps coming back to the song that Hannah once sang for him: "You're just a memory / Of a love that used to be." Yet as his own song progresses, it becomes his song as well. Actually, it's their song. Only it's not an old song to which a married couple dances year after year; it's a song that allows these two people, maybe alone, maybe with a new lover who can't compare, to reminisce, to wallow in the luscious misery of the tune.

"Memory Motel" probably sits right next to "Heartbreak Hotel," deep in the heart of "Lonesome Town" in the cosmic world of rock-and-roll real estate. Even as The Stones add their own personal touches, they write and perform the song with the knowledge that we've all been there.

9. "Gimme Shelter" (from *Let It Bleed*, 1969)

It is fascinating to look back and see how some of rock and roll's leading lights responded to the turmoil of the late 1960s and early 1970s, a time when the ideals of the Summer of Love generation seemed suddenly unattainable and the news was all bad. Very few tackled the tenor of the times head-on. The Beatles, in the midst of splintering, sang songs primarily about themselves on *Let It Be* and *Abbey Road*. Artists like The Kinks, The Band, and Creedence Clearwater Revival burrowed their way to some imagined bucolic Eden. Bob Dylan, in many ways, sat the whole era out.

The Rolling Stones dove straight into the maelstrom, unafraid of where it might take them, and ended up making the timeliest and most thrilling music of that time period. In fact, the band enjoyed the artistic peak of their career at this time of world tumult. If you're looking for one song to sum up this phenomenon, look no further than "Gimme Shelter."

"Gimme Shelter" eerily captures that moment when people realized how messed up things truly were. Their leaders could not be trusted. Their children were getting killed in a war that couldn't seem to be won and had questionable reasons for even existing. Their fellow citizens rioted in the streets. Instead of ducking for cover amid all this, The Stones found a comfort zone by addressing the angst of the times and inviting others both to groove on the danger of their music and to find power in acknowledging the encroaching darkness.

For the most part, the song is Keith Richards's baby, one that he wrote while looking out at a tremendous storm drenching London streets. The music was all his, while Mick Jagger chipped in on the lyrics. The end result was somehow both threatening and exhilarating, making listeners aware of all the trouble and daring them to stare it all down.

The opening of the song is rightfully one of the most hallowed in all of rock, as Richards's opening riff is overdubbed in such a way as to create a ghostly effect, which Jagger's falsetto howls strengthen. Producer Jimmy Miller plays the guiro, which makes that exotic scraping sound, while Charlie Watts starts to warm up to signal the oncoming groove. Once he snaps off two snare shots and the band lurches into the main rhythm, it's like emerging from a misty rainforest into the heart of a city in strife.

Storms, fires, floods, and everything short of locusts plague the narrator as he traverses a hellish landscape. The image of the streets in flame "like a red coal carpet" is brilliantly harrowing. "If I don't get some shelter / Oh yeah, I'm going to fade away," Jagger sings. It's interesting that he chooses that phrase "fade away." You might think, considering the magnitude of the threats surrounding him, that he would be destroyed in a quick and painful manner. If, however, the disasters in the song are metaphors for the rampant turmoil of the times, a more gradual erosion of body, mind, and soul is understandable.

The story goes that a last-minute decision to include a female singer on the track led to Merry Clayton being called out of bed in the wee hours to contribute, despite the fact that she was pregnant at the time. She showed up, hair in curlers, and delivered vocals that still can put a chill in the air. "Rape, murder, it's just a shot away," she sings, and her voice cracks with the emotion of someone who's terrified and providing a dire warning. Without her contribution, the song is simply not the same. (The fact that she miscarried after the session is a sad footnote to the recording of this legendary track.)

The music stays fierce throughout. Richards is everywhere with guitar fills that are always right on the money and also plays a brief solo that rips through the chaos. The rumbling riff at the end of each bar of music seems to implode the song each time, only for The Stones to rev everything up again. And Jagger plays a two-note harmonica solo that provides the lightning bolts to go along with the rhythmic thunder.

In the final moments, Jagger makes a 180-degree turn and sings, "I tell you love, sister / It's just a kiss away." Some have taken this to be the band granting a brief glimmer of hope, but it could also be the narrator, knowing that everything is doomed, grabbing for some last-ditch comfort before the night finally falls. It's easy to sing during the good times, but it takes courage to chronicle the times when everything seems to be falling apart. Nobody would ever accuse The Rolling Stones of being retiring flowers though, not when "Gimme Shelter" is out there, still tiptoeing the brink, still weathering that all-enveloping storm that, sadly, never seems to abate.

8. "Ruby Tuesday" (from *Between the Buttons*, US version, 1967)

"It's just a nice melody, really," Mick Jagger told Jann Wenner of *Rolling Stone* magazine about "Ruby Tuesday" in 1995. "And a lovely lyric. Neither of which I wrote, but I always enjoy singing it."[36]

We've already spoken throughout this book about how Keith Richards is a bit of a softie, how a large portion of the songs he writes and sings on the group's latter-day albums are soulful ballads about missed opportunities and broken hearts. But it's still probably a bit of a surprise to casual fans that this ballad, the second half of a monster double-sided 1967 single that also included "Let's Spend the Night Together," as delicate as gossamer and as genuinely touching as anything the band has ever managed, came from his pen.

Well, at least partially his pen. Most accounts have Richards collaborating on the music with Brian Jones, but, as was the band's custom, Richards shared songwriting credit with Jagger anyway. Although it's impossible to say how much Jones actually contributed to the composition, it is clear that the part he plays on recorder is integral to the song's ability to project both the narrator's begrudging admiration for and lingering sadness about Ruby.

Jones isn't alone in this, however. Jack Nitzsche works his piano in tandem with him to give the song that fluttery, elusive feeling in the verses, those high sounds seeming to evaporate even as we hear them in much the same way the title character eludes the narrator's grasp. The ingenious idea to use a bowed double bass (with Bill Wyman holding the strings and Richards plucking them) adds to the baroque vibe. And the melody is just a beauty; even when Charlie Watts's backbeat undergirds the refrains, the soaring and falling of the tune toggles our emotions right along with those of the narrator.

Richards claimed at different times that the lyrics were based on a groupie and on his mid-1960s girlfriend Linda Keith. Given his reputation, you can understand how Keith's recollections might be fuzzy, but what matters is that the inspiration eventually led to an all-time classic weeper. Considering that the song was recorded at a time when Richards had not yet stepped up to lead vocal duties with The Stones, it was left up to Jagger to deliver the vocal. In a way, his distance from its creation works for the song, since he not only has to tell her story but also essentially has to stand in for every poor sap who has ever been or will eventually be left behind by Ruby. He does all this in understated yet moving fashion.

Even though the girl has left the narrator behind, his admiration for her elusiveness shines through. Richards manages to paint a portrait of his wayward muse in just a few short strokes. The very first couplet lays out her worldview: "She will never say where she came from / Yesterday don't matter if it's gone."

As the song progresses, the case Ruby makes for her peripatetic behavior becomes more and more compelling. "She just can't be chained / To a life where nothing's gained / And nothing's lost," Jagger sings. Indeed, if we are "dying all the time" and time is running out on all of us, maybe this girl's way of living, spurning all attachments and moving from one paramour to the next, isn't all that reckless after all.

In the end, the narrator can't hold her back any more than he could hold back the wind, so he bids her a fond farewell: "Goodbye Ruby Tuesday / Who could hang a name on you / When you change with every new day / Still I'm gonna miss you." Through the tears, he can see clearly now that he never could have kept her, but it hurts just the same.

Such sentiments aren't often expressed so eloquently in rock music, let alone by a band and songwriter more known for bluesy abandon. In a way, the song was Richards proving that he could rival The Beatles' combination of Lennon and McCartney in the melodic department, something that most observers of the rock scene wouldn't have thought possible at the time. And behind that music lurked a stirring combination of character sketch and heart-on-sleeve lament. "Ruby Tuesday" is so lovingly rendered and hauntingly performed that, in the little black book of rock-and-roll heroines, she'll always be the prototype for the one that got away.

7. "Paint It Black" (from *Aftermath*, US version, 1966)

It started out as a kind of comedy number, The Rolling Stones' appropriation of what you might hear at a wedding in the Middle East. With a few bits of studio wizardry, some exotic instrumentation, and a deadly serious attitude adjustment, "Paint It Black" became a kind of anti-anthem, a rallying cry for all those who weren't about to have a nice day and possessed an unapologetic affinity for the gloomiest aspects of life. Never before had something so bleak sounded so animated.

The fact that the song shot to No. 1 status in several countries served as proof that radio playlists and pop charts were prepared to include outlooks that were a far cry from sunny or sentimental. It helped that The Stones could slip into this somewhat morose worldview and come out of it with something so refreshingly entertaining. Theirs was a new perspective on the pop/rock scene, and they had the chops to deliver that perspective in a fascinatingly unexpected and effective manner.

Musically the song is a combination of bold instrumental choices that somehow come together and make the song ever better than the sum of those parts, a sum that, frankly, was pretty high to begin with. Keith Richards starts things off with a mysterious little trill that seems to set us up for something restrained. But Charlie Watts blasts through all of that with some double-timed bashing, playing with such abandon that it's hard to imagine his placid demeanor creating such a racket.

The throbbing sound in the verses comes courtesy of Bill Wyman banging on the pedals of an organ, providing a thick enough bottom end to both offset some of the more delicate elements and to rise to the bar of Watts's feral drumming. And Brian Jones steps in with the sitar, which more than anything else defines the sound of the song, tapping into all of the haunted aspects within the lyrics. It's one of the most memorable flourishes he ever provided for a Stones song, which is a high compliment considering his other efforts, so many of which we've already discussed in these pages.

Mick Jagger stays pretty deadpan, almost zombielike in the verses with his vocals, as if no feelings can any more penetrate the morose state he inhabits. But in the connecting sections, he comes firing out of this stupor, allowing the listeners to hear the human heart that has seemingly been calcified by the world's cruelty. The contrast between the Eastern drone of the verses and the Western thrust of the bridges plays like a tug of war between acceptance of one's miserable fate and railing against it, and Jagger's vocals are right in step with this push and pull.

On the surface, "Paint It Black" tells of the death of the narrator's lover, an event that causes him to sink so deep into his depression that it becomes his identity. After this, anything brimming with color, light, and life is offensive to him. Hence his fatalistic wish in the song's closing moments: "I want to see the sun blotted out from the sky." His reaction at her funeral is not to mourn her passing but to wish that the same cloud that has shrouded him will envelop the whole world.

While it's fair to hear the song as a metaphor for the mourning process, maybe it's not a particular death that it is mourning. Maybe "Paint It Black" mourns the snuffing out of the life force that makes us crave joy, that makes us hope for the best for others, that makes us smile. "I could not foresee this thing happening to you," Jagger eerily sings as the music hushes at one point. It's the narrator's admission that while happiness is shared, all suffering must be done alone.

Ultimately the descriptions of his condition matter more here than how or why he got there. Whether it was indeed the death or a loved one or a different triggering factor, "Paint It Black" is far more interested in revealing the method of the mourning than the motive. And, in an odd way, it invites listeners to not be fearful of sadness or depression, implying through the ruthless gusto of the music that there is vigor and spirit to be located even in the deepest throes of despair or the most isolated solitude.

In short, "Paint It Black" is yet another killer Rolling Stones song that doesn't try to outrun the awful or the painful. It confronts it all with spirit, even if that spirit is decidedly downcast, and the act of confrontation itself is a kind of victory.

6. "Moonlight Mile" (from Sticky Fingers, 1971)

Albums like *Aftermath*, *Beggars Banquet*, *Let It Bleed*, *Some Girls*, and *Tattoo You* all may have their backers, but the battle for greatest Rolling Stones album, for most, likely comes down to 1971's *Sticky Fingers* versus 1972's *Exile on Main St.* The best albums tend to have incredible closing songs, so that's one area where *Sticky Fingers* comes out on top in the comparison. Whereas *Exile* bows out with the solid but unspectacular "Soul Survivor," Sticky Fingers exits via the tour de force that is "Moonlight Mile."

The song in many ways encapsulates the differences in approach between the two albums. *Exile* was recorded in chaos, which then seeped into the music and production, but that chaos was often revelatory. *Sticky Fingers* is far more polished and precise, especially in terms of the production by Jimmy Miller, and that really shows in "Moonlight Mile," which is a beautiful studio creation.

At times, it almost seems like Mick Jagger is singing over the score to a film, so intricately and ingeniously arranged is the song. Keith Richards wasn't even a part of the recording, which was largely spearheaded by Jagger, who wrote the bulk of the song, and Mick Taylor, who helped to put together the disparate pieces of music into a seamless whole.

"Moonlight Mile" has some of the hallmarks of a road song, especially the weariness and sadness that seems to hang off the narrator's every line, the persistence of that nagging feeling that he'll never quite traverse that last mile to return to the one he loves. But it's also a "dream song," as Jagger has called it in interviews, long on imagery and hazy on details, a reverie that soothes and enthralls. The music manages to convey both these themes without ever seeming disjoined.

The insistent little acoustic riff that undergirds the song is played by Jagger, and its Far Eastern vibe is probably why the song was titled "Japanese Thing" in its working stages. Charlie Watts embellishes on this theme by going often to the cymbals in the opening section of the song, evoking an Oriental temple somewhere in a clearing in the distance. The narrator can't quite reach this beacon, buffeted as he is by rain, snow, and freezing winds. And, considering some of the possible references to drugs that Jagger's lines contain, his own self-imposed stupor might be holding him back as well.

When the rhythm section kicks into a familiar rock-ballad groove, Jagger reveals that the nuisances surrounding him aren't nearly as picturesque romantic as that opening verse, just a lot of unwanted noise: "The sound of strangers sending nothing to my mind / Just another mad, mad day on the road." "I am just living to be lying by your side," Jagger sings, a sweet sentiment rendered sad by the knowledge that he might never realize this reunion.

His desire for some sort of peace in the middle of the storm comes through in lines that you might not expect from someone known for going on stage in front of a blaring rock band: "I've got silence on my radio / Let the air waves flow, let the air waves flow." The line "I am sleeping under strange, strange skies" is accompanied for the first time by strings, arranged by Paul Buckmaster, which lend majesty to the melancholy enveloping him.

A bit of resilience shows up as he bravely journeys down the road, singing, "I'm riding down your moonlight mile." At this point, the song kicks into a thrilling duet of sorts between Taylor's electric guitar, seeming to increase in potency with each note, and Watts's toms, which batter their way through any resistance. This section releases back into the main part, with Jagger letting out a cathartic cry. "Yeah, I'm coming home," he shouts, and, in that thrilling moment, you believe he just might make it.

As befitting a song of such epic proportions, "Moonlight Mile" finishes strong, with Taylor flicking off notes somewhere in the ether while Jim Price on piano scurries just out of reach. The dream is slowly dissipating as the song ends with one more flourish from the strings, a mesmerizing way to end both the song and the album.

"Moonlight Mile" is gorgeous, utilizing the open spaces in the music to provide moments of tenderness amid all the peaks and crescendos. It's also a brilliant piece of writing by Jagger, with lyrics that rank among his most evocative and psychologically revealing. And Taylor and Miller put it all together for maximum emotional impact. The tendency would be to call it underrated, because it wasn't a single and therefore didn't receive the kind of exposure that other songs did. Yet it's hard to imagine anyone who has heard the song not coming away impressed and moved by this performance of The Stones at their absolute peak.

5. "You Can't Always Get What You Want" (from *Let It Bleed,* 1969)

At the end of a decade, it's natural for people to sit back, contemplate, and try to make sense of everything that has just passed. Was there progress made? Were the promises delivered or broken? Was it all worth it? Songwriters tend to put their perceived answers to those questions into songs, so it's not surprising that The Rolling Stones' efforts on "You Can't Always Get What You Want" seem to evoke something coming to an end. It may be a little surprising though how the song also thoughtfully points the way forward, if not to a new beginning, at least to a hard-earned acceptance.

Many people tie the song in with The Beatles' release of "Hey Jude" in 1968, a year before "You Can't Always Get What You Want" appeared as the B-side to "Honky Tonk Women" and as the closing track on *Let It Bleed.* Both songs are grand musical statements and unabashed attempts at anthemic grandeur, so the connection is reasonable.

But "Hey Jude" was a very personal song that connected with the larger audience, who found a message of hope within that specific tale that resonated in their own lives. The Stones' song has an eye on everything going on around it, the various absurdities and surrealities of life in 1969, a time when foundations that had previously been sound for eternity seemed to be cracking underneath the feet of humanity. And yet Jagger and The Stones suggest that there's always a consolation prize available for those who want it, always something that can get you through when there's no chance of you achieving the ideal result.

There's something telling in the fact that the release of "You Can't Always Get You Want" as a B-side came just a day after the death of Brian Jones in 1969. The song feels at times like an elegy for some sort of loss, especially in the beginning with the children's choir, Keith Richards's sad strumming, and Al Kooper, stepping in as The Stones' multi-instrumentalist on the track because Jones was too out of it to contribute, blowing sad French Horn notes into the wind.

Much like "Hey Jude" evolves from Paul McCartney's man-and-piano ballad into a widescreen, sing-along epic, "You Can't Always Get What You Want" slowly emerges from its somber cocoon into a glorious, all-encompassing workout, with Latin percussion from Rocky Dijon and gospel keyboards from Kooper. Producer Jimmy Miller played the drums when Charlie Watts couldn't capture the rhythm. Miller keeps pushing the song, violently at times, to escape the doldrums of its early moments and come to some sort of deliverance.

While "Hey Jude" might have given The Stones a bit of musical inspiration that they then ran through their own rootsy filters, the closest lyrical cousin to the song might be "The Weight," the centerpiece of The Band's brilliant debut album, *Music from Big Pink*, from 1968. Both songs are episodic in the verses, with narrators bouncing from scene to scene in a daze of frustration and futility. Both also enjoy refrains that shrug off the nonsense with uplifting, harmonized glory. (Mick Jagger gets help in the choruses from a trio of backing vocalists, including Doris Troy, who had a big early 1960s hit with "Just One Look.")

Still, the similarities are mostly structural. "The Weight" takes place in an entirely different world, one of trains and dogs and Bible names and where even the biggest problems seem quaint. Jagger, who wrote the song in full before bringing it to the band to be arranged, drops us in the midst of society weddings with drug-scoring femme fatales, testy street demonstrations teetering on violence, and a stop for soda at a drugstore that ends with an addict yelling the word "dead" at the narrator.

Such scenarios are by no means for the faint of heart, but it's in keeping with The Stones' philosophy that a song that is meant to soothe and strengthen their listeners is still filled with dire omens and ill portent. Even the refrain's fallback plan of simply getting what you need doesn't seem like an easy proposition in this harsh world.

Yet the music keeps buoying our spirits no matter how much blood is spilled in the narrative. Jagger sounds convinced and saved in the spine-tingling instrumental breakdown where Kooper's piano keeps climbing and climbing before the kids' chorus lifts and redeems us once again. Mick lets out a scream of joy at this point, one of the most exhilarating moments not just in the band's history but in the history of rock and roll as a whole.

"You Can't Always Get What You Want" suggests that it might be a bit naïve to think that there will always be a rebound from the darkest times to previous heights. By tempering expectations, the song swears that you can survive in an unforgiving world during the most tumultuous times, and that's triumph enough.

4. "Sympathy for the Devil" (from *Beggars Banquet*, 1968)

Sometimes you can measure a song's greatness by tallying up how many things could have gone wrong with it. Artists have an infinite number of choices to make all throughout a song, any of which made incorrectly could at least damage the song and at worst could sink it like a torpedo. On one with such a high degree of difficulty like "Sympathy for the Devil," the stakes attached to each of the individual choices soar.

The first mistake The Rolling Stones could have made would have been presenting the song in a folk-song format, which is how it was originally written by Mick Jagger, à la Bob Dylan's ambitious long-form tracks from the mid-1960s. The band rightly figured, however, that a rambling acoustic track detailing the devil's appearance on Earth to show mankind just how many times it has messed up over the years could have come off as pretentious or scolding.

Instead, the band toyed with the track until they stumbled onto an unstoppable samba groove, which they handed over to Rocky Dijon to beat out on the congas while Keith Richards strutted along on bass. This easily could have tipped the boat too far toward a celebratory romp, so the muted piano chords of Nicky Hopkins were added to provide the mystery and menace that the lyrics so clearly required.

The end result is a cathartic workout that doesn't skimp on the danger. The "woo woo" backing vocals that start up about halfway through the song yield some extra locomotion. They also seem to reference the trains that make their way through so many rock songs, dating all the way back to the "Mystery Train" that Elvis Presley so powerfully rode. In the case of The Stones' song, however, the destination is never in doubt: this train is headed straight to damnation.

Jagger's decision to embody the devil in the first person is another choice that paid off brilliantly. He was inspired by the novel *The Master and Margarita*, by Mikhail Bulgakov, to put Lucifer in a modern setting. Having him deliver the monologue gives the song more immediacy and urgency than if Jagger had created a narrator to tell the tale. It also dares to make the devil relatable, depicting him as someone with a chip on his shoulder about the respect he feels he deserves and with an arrogance about the havoc he claims to have wreaked. For all his restraint and requests for "some courtesy, some sympathy, and some taste" not to mention "politesse," he ends up ladling out thuggish threats as a way of getting what he wants.

In this way, Jagger humanizes the inhuman, which is really the point of the song. This laundry list of heinous crimes and unspeakable atrocities wasn't committed by the devil at all; it was mankind doing these things to itself. And bringing the deaths of the Kennedys into the picture (Robert Kennedy had been assassinated just months before the song's release on *Beggars Banquet*) may have stoked the controversy surrounding the song, but it was also another correct choice. The Stones were trying to say that we didn't have the luxury of examining this legacy of violence and destruction as if it were in a safely distant past, tsk-tsk-ing as we read our history books from the comfort of our beds. They were putting a mirror up to society in 1968, one that sadly still reflects with searing accuracy the horrors perpetrated at this very moment in time.

One of the other genius moves of the song is how it's structured. The refrain taunts and teases the listener. Even though the identity of the stranger is spoiled by the song title and, even disregarding that, should be able to be discovered pretty early on in the narrative by anyone with a little common sense, he hides himself anyway, because that allows his monstrous revelation at the end of the song to be that much more potent. We may be able to guess his name, but identifying him won't do anything to stop him.

As for the other part of his query ("But what's puzzling you is the nature of my game"), that's the part that the song never reveals, at least not until Jagger slips in the answer in his falsetto scatting at the end of the song: "I'll tell you one time, you're to blame." The devil will go through the motions and play the part of the bogeyman on whom all the world's evils can be pinned. But he knows the real score, and that's why he had to make this one-time appearance, to let us know that he knows.

Plus, while he's here, he gets to enjoy the furious and frenetic musical feast The Stones have concocted in his honor. As Richards pumps squealing notes into the night, Jagger, as Lucifer, grunts and whoops in approval before fading back down into darkness, his job complete.

Of course, there were people who misunderstood and overreacted to the meaning and intent of the song, but The Stones make such a thorough rebuttal in words and music here that those dissents make nary a dent. "Sympathy for the Devil" isn't about worshipping the devil; if anything, it makes an argument that, even if you believe he exists, he doesn't have any more power than any other spirit in the night. The devil inside every one of us is what the song exposes and fears, even if we're too busy grooving along to recognize the part we've played in the carnage.

3. "Brown Sugar" (from *Sticky Fingers*, 1971)

Maybe it's a fool's errand to try and assign any meaning to "Brown Sugar," The Rolling Stones thundercrack of a 1971 single that kicked off their masterpiece *Sticky Fingers*. After all, why should anyone give the words a second thought when Mick Jagger, who wrote the thing, admitted in a 1995 interview with *Rolling Stone* that even he was at a loss to uncover the song's mysteries?

"God knows what I'm on about in that song," Jagger confessed. "It's such a mishmash. All the nasty subjects in one go."[37] By "nasty subjects," he means that "Brown Sugar," on its surface, appears to depict sexual dalliances between a Southern slaveholder and one of his slaves, with a houseboy eventually getting involved in the debauchery as well. There is mention of the slaver whipping the women, while the possibility that he has forced himself on the slave can't be denied. Throw in the fact that "Brown Sugar" was a slang term for heroin, and it's like The Stones have pretty much checked off every box in the vice scorecard on this song.

Considering all that, there are certainly those who would argue that the song shouldn't be praised at all, that it engages in stereotypes and seems to revel in racist and sexist behavior. That such behavior did and does exist in the world is beyond debate, however, so faulting The Rolling Stones for singing about it seems like a foolish endeavor. Had Jagger come out in a press conference and endorsed the song as emblematic of the way he truly feels about race relations, ire would be warranted. The song is at its core a slice of life set in an unfortunate era in American history, and art is powerless if it's too timid to shed light on even the most troubling tableaus.

This brings us back to the question of how effective "Brown Sugar" is as a piece of art, and that's where the musical part of the equation has to be considered. Throughout this book, we've noted how The Stones' brand of rock and roll actively and expertly trades in genres like the blues, soul, and R&B, eventually melding and transcending all of these disparate elements to become something truly unique. That's what the best rock bands do, and The Rolling Stones are one of the all-time greats.

Yet acknowledging that debt means that we have to acknowledge in kind just how indebted the band is to black artists, since those aforementioned genres are primarily their domain. When you consider this and then listen to the music of "Brown Sugar," you can start to hear those lyrics as a kind of veiled tribute by the band, an admission that they couldn't have possibly thrived without the work of the black musicians who predated and influenced them.

That music, which begins with Keith Richards taking a classic Chuck Berry riff and distilling and distorting it into a leaner, meaner form, continually references various forms of black music throughout history. The riff and Jagger's fast-talking poetry are derivations of Berry, while the levitation in the refrain recalls Little Richard. Charlie Watts's walloping bass drum has echoes thousands of miles away in African ceremony and ritual, while Bobby Keys's unforgettably sweaty solo skews a bit closer to home, as it wouldn't have seemed out of place in a 1950s R&B revue.

All of these elements, along with some winning out-of-left-field touches, like Jagger's castanets, lock seamlessly into a massive groove that rolls over everything in its path, even good taste if you take those lyrics literally. Yet if you read them as a white band paying due homage to those who influenced them, they seem a lot more benign.

"Drums beating, cold English blood runs hot," could very well be Jagger's retelling of how the blues once fired up his life. When he sings, "Now I bet your mama was a tent show queen," it could be a way of demonstrating how black people had the power to entertain even as their basic human rights were stripped away. And when, in the final verse, Jagger switches to the first person, embodying the houseboy, and sings, "I'm no schoolboy but I know what I like / You shoulda heard me just around midnight," maybe it's his way of letting us know that he has learned all he can from black music and feels confident enough now to strut his own stuff.

Again, this could all be a bit of a reach, but, in the context of the music, it makes sense. If you choose to read the song this way, "Brown Sugar" isn't heroin or a reference to a sexual act. It's the musical elixir that black artists originated, perfected, and utilized to captivate audiences from even before the days of slavery all the way down to modern times. The injustice, of course, is that only a tiny percentage of those artists were ever properly credited or remunerated for their efforts. "Brown Sugar" can't possibly rectify that history, but, as a rocking and rolling tribute to the towering legacy of black music, it's hard to beat.

2. "Street Fighting Man" (from *Beggars Banquet*, 1968)

The idea that a rock-and-roll song could or should reflect the times in which it is released was still a relatively novel one in 1968, which is when The Rolling Stones released "Street Fighting Man." The Stones had never been a political band prior to that song, and they haven't really been one since—and, come to think of it, they weren't really making a decisive stand on "Street Fighting Man" either.

Inspired by protests in England and France, the song may not take sides, but it does manage to encapsulate, in barely more than three minutes, the romance of being on the front lines of a revolution; the righteous urge to fight injustice by any means necessary; and, perhaps most crucial of all to the song's ultimate success, the futility of knowing that your efforts might not produce anything at all or, even worse, might produce conditions more problematic than the ones against which you rebelled in the first place. As such, it makes more of an impact and remains far more relevant than the vast majority of folk songs written in that era, songs that come off as unrealistic and ineffectual compared to The Stones' single.

Of course, it never was a fair fight, because The Stones were able to set their message to musical backing that reverberated with the nervous energy of the times. So as much as Mick Jagger deserves credit for his succinct brilliance in addressing the boons and drawbacks of revolutionary fervor, Keith Richards deserves equal credit for composing a pulsating, powerful piece of music and then using recording ingenuity to raise the bar on vigor and spitfire even higher.

Richards's best sleight of hand was using a newly minted Philips cassette recorder to lay down the basic track with him on acoustic guitar and Charlie Watts on a kind of toy drum set, instruments that allowed both men to get right up close to the microphone in the recorder. This piece of machinery is responsible for the way the guitars seem to vibrate the air and for the extra-forceful sound of Watts's drums. Richards also handled bass on the track and turned to Brian Jones and guest Dave Mason for the era-appropriate psychedelic touches. Jones hazes up the refrains with tamboura and sitar, while Mason plays the woodwind-like shehani toward the end of the song, sounding a strange alarm.

Richards also structured the up-and-down melody in such a way as to make it sound like a siren piercing the air. Mick Jagger filled in that melody with his man-on-the-street perspective. "Everywhere I hear the sound of marching, charging feet, boy," he sings. "'Cause summer's here and the time is right for fighting in the street, boy." On that last line Jagger makes a play on the 1964 Motown smash "Dancing in the Street" by Martha and The Vandellas, and in doing so, makes the violence seem like just another thing that kids do to pass the time, somewhat undercutting any noble reasons they might have for fighting.

Jagger manages to see both sides of the story throughout the song. In the second verse, he presents the contrasting viewpoints: "Hey, think the time is right for a palace revolution / But where I live the game to play is compromise solution." Notice that he's unsure in the first line, and the cold reality of the second line seems to douse any further hopes.

In the final verse, he appears to make his stand, but it's so exaggerated as to seem comic and ultimately nonthreatening: "Hey, said my name is called Disturbance / I'll shout and scream, I'll kill the kind, I'll rail at all his servants." This doesn't sound like Jagger believes in such a course of action; if anything, it seems like he's paraphrasing the words of a revolutionary firebrand to highlight just how absurdly counterproductive they sound.

The refrains, contrasting the punch and zing of the music, are a testament to the political impotency that someone of Jagger's generation, if being honest, ultimately had to admit. "Well what can a poor boy do / Except to sing for a rock and roll band?" he asks, apologizing in a way for the lack of change that he can enact. The reason: "Cause in sleepy London town there's just no place for / Street fighting man, no."

It's a subtle thing, but notice the way that he omits the article, how it doesn't say, "A street fighting man." By doing this, Jagger makes it sound like such a character can take his place in man's long progression, along with Neanderthal man or Cro-Magnon man, and, like the others, he'll essentially become extinct in favor of a creature more advanced.

This touch is just another clever way in which Jagger hedges his bets. Yet rather than sounding like he's waffling of retreating from the fight, he and his band sound like spokesmen with wise heads on their shoulders, questioning the method of using violence to protest injustice, knowing that it only begets more of both.

As Watts's bass drum thunders like explosives in the night and Richards's walled acoustic guitars, open-tuned of course so he can strum with abandon, shred all resistance, The Stones demonstrate the musical might that would seemingly conquer all. Yet the brilliance of "Street Fighting Man" is in its forethought and restraint, which might not be the most exciting or romantic stuff of political anthems, but which nonetheless should always precede any decisive action. If we demand this of our leaders, the song sagely suggests, we should demand it of ourselves in kind.

1. "Jumpin' Jack Flash" (from *Through the Past, Darkly [Big Hits, Vol. 2]*, 1969)

The greatest song in the history of The Rolling Stones might never have happened were it not for a heavy-footed gardener. His name was Jack Dyer, and he worked for Keith Richards, who, along with his bandmate Mick Jagger, was crashing early one morning after staying up all night at Richards's home in the English countryside. They heard Dyer stomping about outside, and when Jagger asked what the sound was, Richards said something to the effect that it was "Jumpin' Jack." To which one of the pair quickly added the word "Flash." The phrase immediately struck the two men as something that had a little rhythmic pop to it, starting them on their way to the finished song and rock legend.

In a way, you can say that Dyer also woke Jagger and Richards up from the psychedelic haze that had washed over them and stalled their momentum as the closest rivals to The Beatles for the title of the world's greatest rock-and-roll band. The Stones had ended 1967 by releasing *Their Satanic Majesties Request*, an album that traded heavily on trippy sounds and sentiments that weren't at all in the band's wheelhouse. "Jumpin' Jack Flash" was released as a single at the end of spring in 1968 and would kick off a five-year run of albums and singles that might just be the greatest consecutive stretch of music put together by any artist or band in the rock era.

Yet "Jumpin' Jack Flash" isn't just worthwhile as the kick-off of The Stones' golden era; even if the band had stumbled after its release, the song brims with such primal power and so effortlessly maxes out on catharsis that it would still be an all-time great. And, this being The

Stones, it's somehow only fitting that there's been some infighting about its creation.

Bill Wyman has claimed that he was responsible for the menacingly forceful riff that repeats throughout the verses, a kind of backward take on the band's riff from "(I Can't Get No) Satisfaction" that he stumbled on while noodling about on the piano while waiting for a session to start. That might be true, but it's really only one of two instrumental hooks on which the song is built. The other is the attention-grabbing opening guitar salvo, which, as on "Street Fighting Man," was achieved by Richards violently strumming highly tuned acoustic guitars into the microphone of a Philips cassette recorder, leading to a fuzzy, distorted sound that you'd swear was being made by electric guitars. (As a matter of fact, Richards has claimed that there are no electric guitars on the track, which shows just how much magic he was able to work with this relatively primitive recording technique.)

Charlie Watts lays down a hustling beat, aided by Richards manually beating on the floor toms while Keith also takes care of the droning bass. Piano by Ian Stewart and organ by Wyman are also somewhere in the mix, and Jagger adds a little bit of wiggle with the maracas, but this song is all about the guitars and drums, which is apropos for The Stones' masterpiece.

To suit such brash, uncompromising music, Jagger (aided by Richards somewhat) needed to come up with lyrics that were rough and tumble and yet not defeated. In other words, these lyrics had to sing the blues but ultimately triumph over them, which is The Stones in microcosm, really. And so he penned a series of lines that are practically mythological in terms of the extent of suffering that the narrator endures from the very moment he crashes into existence: "I was born in a crossfire hurricane / And I howled at my ma in the driving rain."

In that couplet, you can sense the dueling themes of torment and resilience that the song promotes throughout. The narrator's boyhood is scarred by foul parentage and punishment disguised as education: "I was raised by a toothless, bearded hag / I was schooled with a strap right across my back." There's an instrumental break after the second chorus, Richards's guitars winding around each other while his bass revs up again and again. This section is like the aural equivalent of the narrator girding his loins for the battles ahead.

And what battles they are, leaving him nearly drowned, bleeding, and starving. His reward for the struggles and strife is a macabre coronation: "I was crowned with a spike right through my head." By this time, Jagger is wailing, punctuating his lines with "Yeah" and "Come on," as if daring his oppressors to bring it on, taunting them that his body might be broken but his spirit is intact and itching for a fight.

The refrain takes on a similarly indestructible stance, and it also acts as reassurance for the audience, some of whom could probably relate to the litany of disasters that have befallen this guy. "But it's all right now," he insists, and then ups the ante: "In fact it's a gas." The phrase "Jumpin' Jack Flash," in a sense, becomes a kind of mantra, but not a mantra that you might use to retreat from the world into a meditative bliss. It's a mantra that you chant for courage in the world, one with which you can flip off your oppressors and let them know that even their worst tortures only levitate you higher.

In the book *Up and Down with The Rolling Stones: My Rollercoaster Ride with Keith Richards*, Richards's former associate Tony Sanchez told an anecdote about The Stones' reaction following a screening of the documentary *Gimme Shelter*, which infamously spotlighted the band's tragic Altamont concert. Sanchez wrote, "Mick turned to Keith and said, 'Flower power was a load of crap, wasn't it? There was nothing about love, peace, and flowers in "Jumpin' Jack Flash," was there?'"[38]

If Jagger did indeed say that, he inadvertently summed up not just the dark appeal of "Jumpin' Jack Flash," but also the lure of the band and their music throughout their entire career. The Rolling Stones presented an alternative to a pop music world that, prior to their arrival, pretty much only dealt in love and flowers. The Stones fearlessly tread on harsher ground, speaking of life as it was and is, instead of how it should be. And the subtext of their finest songs is that there is a way to come out the other side of these figurative hurricanes and beatings renewed and ready for the next tribulation, a way that sometimes requires a fight and sometimes requires a stubbornness that halfway resembles faith, but a way nonetheless.

That they were able to deliver these messages, often unforgiving, sometimes impolite, occasionally downright ugly, in the midst of music that took the essential parts of roots music's various genres and distilled them all into something that, when jacked up, could pack a devastating punch and, when slowed down, could convey bottomless depths of emotion, is why they hold such a special place in the history of not just rock and roll but music as a whole.

Their ability to do this so consistently for so, so long is why "Jumpin' Jack Flash," while it may be my choice as the band's greatest song, is just one out of one hundred amazing songs that I've listed here, a list that could have gone much, much deeper before approaching anything resembling run-of-the-mill material. As for the thought that The Rolling Stones are still out there, maybe revving up to do it all again and make me rethink and revise these rankings?

I think I can speak for Stones fans everywhere when I say that I can't wait.

... AND 100 MORE

101. "Love Is Strong" (from *Voodoo Lounge*, 1994)
102. "We Love You" (from *Through the Past, Darkly [Big Hits Vol. 2]*, UK version, 1969)
103. "Dancing in the Light" (from *Exile on Main St.* reissue, 2010)
104. "Sway" (from *Sticky Fingers*, 1971)
105. "Hot Stuff" (from *Black and Blue*, 1976)
106. "Doo Doo Doo Doo Doo (Heartbreaker)" (from *Goats Head Soup*, 1974)
107. "Connection" (from *Between the Buttons*, 1967)
108. "Let Me Go" (from *Emotional Rescue*, 1980)
109. "Child of the Moon" (from *More Hot Rocks [Big Hits & Fazed Cookies]*, 1972)
110. "Neighbours" (from *Tattoo You*, 1981)
111. "It Must Be Hell" (from *Undercover*, 1983)
112. "Streets of Love" (from *A Bigger Bang*, 2005)
113. "I'm Free" (from *Out of Our Heads*, 1965)
114. "Till the Next Goodbye" (from *It's Only Rock 'n Roll*, 1974)
115. "Blue Turns to Grey" (from *December's Children [and Everybody's]*, 1965)
116. "Can't Be Seen" (from *Steel Wheels*, 1989)
117. "Indian Girl" (from *Emotional Rescue*, 1980)
118. "How Can I Stop" (from *Bridges to Babylon*, 1997)
119. "Fingerprint File" (from *It's Only Rock 'n Roll*, 1974)
120. "Miss Amanda Jones" (from *Between the Buttons*, 1967)
121. "No Spare Parts" (from *Some Girls* reissue, 2011)

122. "Ride On Baby" (from *Flowers*, 1967)
123. "She's So Cold" (from *Emotional Rescue*, 1980)
124. "Country Honk" (from *Let It Bleed*, 1969)
125. "The Under Assistant West Coast Promotion Man" (from *Out of Our Heads*, 1965)
126. "Rock and a Hard Place" (from *Steel Wheels*, 1989)
127. "Thief in the Night" (from *Bridges to Babylon*, 1997)
128. "If You Can't Rock Me" (from *It's Only Rock 'n Roll*, 1974)
129. "Long, Long While" (from *More Hot Rocks [Big Hits & Fazed Cookies]*, 1972)
130. "Something Happened to Me Yesterday" (from *Between the Buttons*, 1967)
131. "Summer Romance" (from *Emotional Rescue*, 1980)
132. "This Place Is Empty" (from *A Bigger Bang*, 2005)
133. "So Divine (Aladdin Song)" (from *Exile on Main St.* reissue, 2010)
134. "Good Times, Bad Times" (from *12 × 5*, 1964)
135. "Already Over Me" (from *Bridges to Babylon*, 1997)
136. "All the Way Down" (from *Undercover*, 1983)
137. "The Singer, Not the Song" (from *December's Children [and Everybody's]*, 1965)
138. "New Faces" (from *Voodoo Lounge*, 1994)
139. "Biggest Mistake" (from *A Bigger Bang*, 2005)
140. "Soul Survivor" (from *Exile on Main St.*, 1972)
141. "Take It or Leave It" (from *Aftermath*, 1966)
142. "Do You Think I Really Care" (from *Some Girls* reissue, 2011)
143. "Through the Lonely Nights" (from *Rarities 1971–2003*, 2005)
144. "Jump on Top of Me" (from *Singles 1971–2006*, 2011)
145. "Fancy Man Blues" (from *Rarities 1971–2003*, 2005)
146. "Little T&A" (from *Tattoo You*, 1981)
147. "Jiving Sister Fanny" (from *Metamorphosis*, 1975)
148. "Yesterday's Papers" (from *Aftermath*, 1966)
149. "Heaven" (from *Tattoo You*, 1981)
150. "I Just Want to See His Face" (from *Exile on Main St.*, 1972)
151. "Dance Little Sister" (from *It's Only Rock 'n Roll*, 1974)
152. "Don't Stop" (from *Forty Licks*, 2002)
153. "Dancing With Mr. D." (from *Goats Head Soup*, 1973)
154. "Little by Little" (from the *Rolling Stones*, 1964)

155. "Dance (Pt.1)" (from *Emotional Rescue*, 1980)
156. "Might as Well Get Juiced" (from *Bridges to Babylon*, 1997)
157. "Parachute Woman" (from *Beggars Banquet*, 1968)
158. "Sweet Black Angel" (from *Exile on Main St.*, 1972)
159. "Sleep Tonight" (from *Dirty Work*, 1986)
160. "When the Whip Comes Down" (from *Some Girls*, 1978)
161. "Sing This All Together" (from *Their Satanic Majesties Request*, 1967)
162. "100 Years Ago" (from *Goats Head Soup*, 1973)
163. "Factory Girl" (from *Beggars Banquet*, 1968)
164. "Pass the Wine (Sophia Loren)" (from *Exile on Main St.* reissue, 2010)
165. "Hey Negrita" (from *Black and Blue*, 1976)
166. "Terrifying" (from *Steel Wheels*, 1989)
167. "Luxury" (from *It's Only Rock 'n Roll*, 1974)
168. "The Worst" (from *Voodoo Lounge*, 1994)
169. "Claudine" (from *Some Girls* reissue, 2011)
170. "Down in the Hole" (from *Emotional Rescue*, 1980)
171. "All Down the Line" (from *Exile on Main St.*, 1972)
172. "Rough Justice" (from *A Bigger Bang*, 2005)
173. "I Think I'm Going Mad" (from *Singles 1971–2006*, 2011)
174. "You Got Me Rocking" (from *Voodoo Lounge*, 1994)
175. "Slave" (from *Tattoo You*, 1981)
176. "Casino Boogie" (from *Exile on Main St.*, 1981)
177. "Highwire" (from *Flashpoint*, 1991)
178. "Saint of Me" (from *Bridges to Babylon*, 1997)
179. "Back of My Hand" (from *A Bigger Bang*, 2005)
180. "So Young" (from *Some Girls* reissue, 2011)
181. "Sparks Will Fly" (from *Bridges to Babylon*, 1997)
182. "If You Really Want to Be My Friend" (from *It's Only Rock 'n Roll*, 1974)
183. "No Use in Crying" (from *Tattoo You*, 1981)
184. "I'm Not Signifying" (from *Exile on Main St.* reissue, 2010)
185. "Have You Seen Your Mother, Baby, Standing in the Shadow?" (from *Big Hits [High Tide and Green Grass]*, 1966)
186. "Casino Boogie" (from *Exile on Main St.*, 1972)
187. "You Don't Have to Mean It" (from *Bridges to Babylon*, 1997)
188. "Coming Down Again" (from *Goats Head Soup*, 1973)

189. "So Young" (from *Some Girls*, 2011)
190. "Sweethearts Together" (from *Voodoo Lounge*, 1994)
191. "Break the Spell" (from *Steel Wheels*, 1989)
192. "Silver Train" (from *Goats Head Soup*, 1973)
193. "Citadel" (from *Their Satanic Majesties Request*, 1967)
194. "Congratulations" (from *12 × 5*, 1964)
195. "High and Dry" (from *Aftermath*, 1966)
196. "Let Me Down Slow" (from *A Bigger Bang*, 2005)
197. "Blinded by Rainbows" (from *Voodoo Lounge*, 1994)
198. "We're Wastin' Time" (from *Metamorphosis*, 1975)
199. "Hearts for Sale" (from *Steel Wheels*, 1989)
200. "Gotta Get Away" (from *Out of Our Heads*, 1965)

NOTES

THE COUNTDOWN

1. Mick Jagger, liner notes to *Jump Back: The Best of The Rolling Stones*, The Rolling Stones, Virgin, 1993, compact disc.

2. Jonathan Cott, "Mick Jagger: Jumpin' Jack Flash at 34," *Rolling Stone*, June 29, 1978.

3. Jagger, liner notes to *Jump Back*.

4. Cott, "Mick Jagger."

5. Bill Wyman, *Rolling with The Stones*, 1st ed. (London: DK Adult, 2002).

6. Chet Flippo, "Mick Jagger Breaks Down 'Black and Blue,'" *Rolling Stone*, May 6, 1976.

7. Mick Jagger, Keith Richards, Charlie Watts, and Ronnie Wood, *According to The Rolling Stones* (San Francisco: Chronicle Books, 2003), 116.

8. David Cavanagh, "Exile!," *Uncut*, April 1, 2010.

9. Flippo, "'Black and Blue.'"

10. Jann Wenner, "Mick Jagger Remembers," *Rolling Stone*, December 14, 1995.

11. Ibid.

12. Jagger, Richards, Watts, and Wood, *According to The Rolling Stones*, 113.

13. Ibid.

14. Ibid., 89–90.

15. Keith Richards and James Fox, *Life* (New York: Little, Brown, 2010).

16. Rob Chapman, "The Bittersweet Symphony," *Mojo*, July 1, 1999.

17. Richards and Fox, *Life*.

18. Jagger, Richards, Watts, and Wood, *According to The Rolling Stones*, 190.

19. Sean Egan, ed., *The Mammoth Book of The Rolling Stones* (London: Constable & Robinson, 2013), 293.

20. Richards and Fox, *Life*.

21. Wenner, "Mick Jagger Remembers."

22. Will Gompertz, "Sir Mick Jagger Goes Back to Exile," BBC News, May 14, 2010, http://news.bbc.co.uk/2/hi/entertainment/8681410.stm.

23. Wenner, "Mick Jagger Remembers."

24. Jagger, Richards, Watts, and Wood, *According to The Rolling Stones*, 117.

25. Ibid., 141.

26. Jagger, liner notes to *Jump Back*.

27. Jann Wenner, "The Rolling Stone Interview: John Lennon," *Rolling Stone*, January 21, 1971.

28. Richards and Fox, *Life*.

29. Jagger, Richards, Watts, and Wood, *According to The Rolling Stones*, 241.

30. "Get Off of My Cloud," Time Is on Our Side, accessed February 17, 2015, http://www.timeisonourside.com/SOGetOff.html.

31. Richards and Fox, *Life*.

32. Jagger, liner notes to *Jump Back*.

33. Mikal Gilmore, "Love and War Inside The Rolling Stones," *Rolling Stone*, May 7, 2013.

34. Richards and Fox, *Life*.

35. Jagger, Richards, Watts, and Wood, *According to The Rolling Stones*, 141.

36. Wenner, "Mick Jagger Remembers."

37. Ibid.

38. Tony Sanchez, *Up and Down with The Rolling Stones: My Rollercoaster Ride with The Rolling Stones* (London: John Blake, 2011).

BIBLIOGRAPHY

Egan, Sean, ed. *The Mammoth Book of The Rolling Stones*. London: Constable & Robinson, 2013. For those interested in the history of the band in terms of its musical output, this collection of articles and interviews is highly recommended. What makes it even better are the chapters written by Egan, the editor, who is as knowledgeable as they come and makes an excellent and fair critic of the band's work through the years. Someone just learning about the band should really check this one out.

Jagger, Mick, Keith Richards, Charlie Watts, and Ronnie Wood. *According to The Rolling Stones*. San Francisco: Chronicle Books, 2003. This is the best all-in-one source for the four longest-tenured members of the band to reflect on the creation of songs and albums. You could probably accuse them of following The Beatles yet again, since the living members of The Fab Four had done a similar project called *Anthology*. Nonetheless, Stones fans should have this in their collections if they want to know right from the horses' mouths about the how, what, and why of the group's illustrious recording career.

Richards, Keith, and James Fox. *Life*. New York: Little, Brown, 2010. Who knew that Keith was taking such detailed notes all these years? On top of it being a rollicking read and a revelatory portrait of the man behind the caricature, *Life* thoroughly details the thought process behind some of the band's most memorable musical moments. Yes, it takes some cheap shots at Mick Jagger, which might leave a sour taste in the mouths of anyone who thinks of the band as a brotherhood. But you're not going to find many rock memoirs as humorous, insightful, or—who would have believed it?—moving.

Sandford, Christopher. *The Rolling Stones: Fifty Years*. London: Simon & Schuster UK, 2012. So many of the Stones' great songs are directly related to what was going on in their personal lives: who was sleeping with whom, who was getting arrested, which band members were feuding, and so on. Sandford's detailed, exhaustive book really covers all those bases with wit and candor. Although the book is more about those interpersonal things, he also does a nice job chronicling the band's musical output along the way.

INDEX

ABOUT THE AUTHOR

Jim Beviglia is a featured writer for *American Songwriter* magazine, reviewing new albums and looking back at classic songwriters and songs for both the print and online editions. This is his third book in the *Counting Down* series, following 2013's *Counting Down Bob Dylan: His 100 Finest Songs* and 2014's *Counting Down Bruce Springsteen: His 100 Finest Songs*, and he continues to maintain his blog, *Countdown Kid* (countdownkid.wordpess.com), where he delves deeply into the musical libraries of rock's finest artists. Jim was born and raised in Old Forge, Pennsylvania, where he currently resides with his mom; his daughter, Daniele; and his wife, Marie.